Music and the Southern Belle

Music & and the Southern Belle

FROM ACCOMPLISHED LADY TO CONFEDERATE COMPOSER

CANDACE BAILEY

Southern Illinois University Press
Carbondale and Edwardsville

13 12 11 10   4 3 2 1

Library of Congress Cataloging-in-Publication Data
Bailey, Candace, 1963–
Music and the southern belle : from accomplished lady
to Confederate composer / Candace Bailey.
        p. cm.
Includes bibliographical references and index.
ISBN-13: 978-0-8093-2960-1 (cloth : alk. paper)
ISBN-10: 0-8093-2960-3 (cloth : alk. paper)
ISBN-13: 978-0-8093-8557-7 (ebook)
ISBN-10: 0-8093-8557-0 (ebook)
1. Women musicians—Southern States—History—
19th century. 2. Women composers—Southern
States—History—19th century. 3. Music—Social
aspects—Southern States—History—19th century.
I. Title.
ML82.B25 2010
780.82′0975—dc22   2009027632

Contents

Figures and Tables

Preface

The subtitle for this book derives from a phenomenon that occurred in southern culture during the mid-nineteenth century. In the 1830s, young unmarried women who had been trained in the accomplishments (chief of which was music) were demure, inconspicuous, sweet, gentle creatures. They would develop into accomplished ladies and would rarely be heard in public, and on those exceptional occasions, their precise identities were carefully hidden. During the 1860s, southern women began to explore new conceptions of self and place. In music, such re-examination of traditional codes had a profound effect. With the advent of the Civil War, southern women—even those of elite status— published music with their names on the title pages. They boldly moved into the realm of public music, with the ideal of supporting the Cause being their most obvious motive: they became Confederate composers.

Such actions stemmed from a common expression found in southern women's diaries and other materials: the need to be useful. How music enabled women to be useful changed substantially between 1835 and 1865. During the 1830s, sentimentality as a cultural phenomenon became a mainstay in the United States, and how women participated in this culture, especially in the parlor, demonstrated their appropriateness for various aspects of ladyhood. Part of this legacy of ladyhood was the requirement to please others—not themselves. This expectation remained throughout the midcentury until 1861, when women's self-perceptions were suddenly and dramatically altered during the years of the Civil War. Whether women performed in the parlor or in some other venue afforded them by the war, they saw themselves as beings who should be useful. Music was but one avenue by which they could be useful by pleasing others.

The main title itself, *Music and the Southern Belle*, seems straightforward enough—a study of a particular part of the population (women) from a specific area (the South). Thoughtful studies concerning either half of the title already exist; it would seem that the topic of southern women's music has been covered.[1] Surprisingly, it has not. Books on music in the nineteenth-century American South almost invariably deal with men's music alone, at least as far as composition is concerned and, to a great extent, most other aspects of music. More inclusive studies tend not to recognize aspects of gender. As with general histories of the period, the bulk of modern literature deals with men's music that was used in war: if history books tend to focus on politicians or the battles and strategies of commanders, then music books concentrate on professional male composers or martial music and patriotism. Several of these are enlightening, particularly Ernest Lawrence Abel's *Singing the New Nation: How Music Helped Shape the Confederacy*, a study that examines the role music played in forming the idea of the Confederate nation. Abel does not treat women's music per se, but he does comment that women composers authored pieces, noting that no one has looked into these works.[2]

More recently, Bruce C. Kelley and Mark A. Snell's *Bugle Resounding: Music and Musicians of the Civil War* provides a collection of essays from different authors covering various aspects of Civil War music. Despite the fact that the opening essay begins with a quote from Mary Boykin Chesnut, the only woman discussed under "Musical Personalities" is Clara Louise Kellogg (1842–1916), a professional singer born in Charleston but who studied and debuted (in 1861) in New York and remained there during the war. Even Lenora Cuccia's promising chapter title, "They Weren't All Like Lorena," does not really address women's experiences during the war but rather how women were depicted in lyrics. Similarly, although he includes some interesting anecdotes about women and piano music, David B. Thompson's chapter, "Confederates at the Keyboard: Southern Piano Music during the Civil War," deals more with the piano music itself (mostly by male authors) than with the people who played it.

Jon W. Finson's *Voices That Are Gone: Themes in 19th-Century American Popular Song* examines music performed by and written for both men and women in the North and South but does not situate women's music in women's culture. His unique approach begins with the premise that song lyrics reflect songwriters' views and that the intended audience will share those views. Thus, as a cultural history, Finson offers an alternative to the more traditional study. His concern is not to examine music within a specific group. Likewise, Nicholas Tawa has written several volumes concerning American music of the nineteenth century, but his interest has not been music in the context of women's lives, nor has it been exclusively southern in focus.

Looking from the other direction, the topic of women and music in the nineteenth century is the subject of several sensitive studies written in recent years. Ruth Solie's award-winning *Music in Other Words: Victorian Conversations* illuminates aspects of gender and music in Victorian England, but English culture of the nineteenth century hardly translates to that of the American South. Christine Ammer's *Unsung: A History of Women in American Music* extends well beyond the borders of this study and is therefore broader in context and less specific on the period in question. While her chapters divide along themes similar to the ones here, she does not differentiate between regions. Closer to the point, Judith Tick's pioneering *American Women Composers before 1870* draws attention to aspects peculiar to American women in music, highlighting in particular five mid-nineteenth-century women composers. However, all of these composers were northerners, two of whom were born in England. One might argue that that does not matter—American women's experience in the nineteenth century was homogeneous enough that these five women can represent the general practice. That none was southern, however, can also be a warning against such generalizations.

This book aims to situate music within southern women's culture. During the antebellum period, music played an important part; yet, it also was carefully controlled and moderated. When southern men left their homes for the Civil War, women began to realize new possibilities concerning their abilities and responsibilities. Those who could compose chose to do so. They became Confederate composers—something unimaginable in the preceding decade.

Acknowledgments

This book has been a joy to research. I have had the opportunity to meet people who have interest in this and related topics, and without their inspiration, advice, and support, this project would not have been possible. Space does not allow me to thank each individual who assisted me throughout the past four years; I apologize in advance for not naming each one. In general, I would like to thank Judith Tick, Annegret Fauser, Kitty Preston, and Marcia Citron for their early support in this process. They each gave me confidence in its importance and worth for the scholarly community. Sylvia Frank Rodrigue of the Southern Illinois University Press has also been stalwart in her dedication to the project, and I sincerely appreciate her advice and suggestions. Many e-mails have flown back and forth between us.

Numerous libraries and collections have been made available to me throughout the South—to identify each one is beyond the scope of these acknowledgments. I do wish, however, to specifically thank Henry G. Fulmer, Curator of Manuscripts, of the South Caroliniana Library; Sybil McNeil of the Archives and Special Collections at Wesleyan College; Nicholas Butler, formerly of the South Carolina Historical Society, and the staff there; and various librarians at the Wilson Library (including the Southern Historical Collection and Music Library) at the University of North Carolina at Chapel Hill. Additionally, travel to various locations has been assisted by a faculty grant from the North Carolina Central University Faculty Senate.

Finally, I wish to thank two personal friends for their assistance above and beyond the call of duty. My aunt Jacqueline Starnes gave numerous hours in the editing process, and without her help, this book would not be what it is today. Julian Prosser deserves more recognition than these acknowledgments can relate for his unending support for the project, driving me around various states into all sorts of rural areas in search of cemeteries, plantations, and other long-forgotten remains. Thanks for everything! And last, but not least, my two children also assisted in various ways with the final product. Emma spent several school vacations traipsing around libraries and taking notes for me. Graham maintained an undying interest in the Civil War that made it possible to spend our family vacations camping in battlefields, going to reenactments, and buying books of maps and other Civil War items for holiday gifts. You guys were terrific!

Music and the Southern Belle

Introduction

Historians have repeatedly demonstrated that the society in which south-ern women lived differed substantially from that in other places—scholarly volumes on southern women's culture figure prominently in several university presses. Southern women of the antebellum and Civil War period have been the subject of many studies ranging from early works by Anne Firor Scott and Elizabeth Fox-Genovese to more recent volumes by Nina Silber, Catherine Clinton, Drew Gilpin Faust, and others.[1] These modern histories contextualize women in southern culture—appreciating that southern society of the antebellum period was a phenomenon whose values did not translate automatically to those of the North. Understanding the idea of the southern belle/lady (unmarried and married equivalents) and how she fit into southern antebellum society is essential to appreciating underlying social and cultural distinctions between North and South.

The reasons for considering the differences between North and South in any discussion of women in nineteenth-century America have been made clear in such studies. In *Battle Scars: Gender and Sexuality in the American Civil War*, Nina Silber notes that the South's more profoundly entrenched patriarchal system yielded a worldview that differed substantially from that of the North.[2] Moreover, Karen Halttunen observes that the courtly tradi-tion of the South, in which southern planters modeled themselves on Henry Peacham's *The Compleat Gentleman* or Richard Allestree's *The Whole Duty of Man*, relied heavily upon the ideals of Christian chivalry. She contrasts this tradition with that of northern professionals, merchants, and tradesmen, who found their instruction in English courtesy manuals of the moralistic tradition, such as works by Erasmus and Sir Walter Raleigh.[3] In other words, the two cultures arose under contradictory philosophies. In the first issue of his *Southern Quarterly Review*, Daniel K. Whitaker (who was raised in New England) wrote that the "North . . . has acted *as* the North," and he petitioned southerners to create their own body of literature that reflected their values.

He further comments that "the plantation States, bound together by common pursuits and common ties of interest, must co-operate, and move together in this matter, and must exert all their strength for their own protection."[4]

Whitaker wrote in 1842—not 1861—yet he strongly sensed major dissimilarities between the two regions. While the distinction between North and South naturally dominates all discussion in primary source materials from 1861 to 1865, comments such as Whitaker's clearly demonstrate that Americans from both regions detected differences between the two much earlier. Another early example of this acknowledgment comes from a letter written in 1841 by a member of the Ebenezer Pettigrew family in North Carolina. In November of that year, Mary Pettigrew (1826–87) wrote to her brother William that among the materials she was reading was *Southern Matron*. Written by "a lady of Charleston," Pettigrew asserts that this work is "true to the reality of southern life."[5] She makes this remark in recognition of the fact that while northerners may write about southern life, only southerners truly understand it.

Southern women writers also remarked on differences between northerners and southerners. In *Domestic Novelists in the Old South: Defenders of Southern Culture*, Elizabeth Moss compares aspects of the two cultures and focuses on how southern writers (all women in her study) chose to distance themselves from northerners. She comments that whereas northern writers attempted to change society by integrating feminine values into society in general, southern women worked to sustain a social and political equilibrium that they believed gave their society moral superiority.[6]

The deep gulf between men and women in the South defined all other relationships.[7] As Joan E. Cashin points out, the austere division between men and women in upper-class society was profoundly restrictive for women.[8] White women were barred from universities and could not enter professions. Married women had no control over property, and divorce was not really an option in most southern states (not at all, for example, in South Carolina). Fertility—which was a life-and-death issue for women in the nineteenth century—was under the control of men, and many planters' wives had at least ten children, often before the age of thirty. Cashin notes several important areas where the lives of southern women diverged from those of northern women: miscegenation, demographic profiles (southern women married at younger ages, had significantly more children, and died at higher rates than their northern counterparts), and legal rights.[9] Most southern white women did not allow that northern women might understand their experiences.[10]

It is in this context that this book should be read: it is not that the ideas herein do not apply to northern women, but rather that this work is a specific study of the music in the lives of southern women. It is not a comparison between the two groups; it is a specialized study of music in the South. The tendency of modern authors to take for granted that music in the United

States was the same on both sides of the Mason-Dixon Line results in assumptions that do not necessarily hold true, but any comparisons must wait for individual studies that focus on each region.

PRIMARY SOURCE MATERIALS

After making a case for the need to distinguish southern culture, it may come as a surprise that the following pages will employ northern publications to bolster statements on southern music. The dearth of printed materials in the South necessitated such an intercourse, even through the Civil War. Certainly southerners produced some native journals and magazines throughout the antebellum period, but rarely did these survive more than a few years. Most well-read southerners supplemented their regular (northern) reading material with home-grown tomes when possible, but it was usually as a complement to the standard literature.

As to the popularity of such journals as *Godey's Lady's Book*, *Graham's Magazine*, and *Harper's* in the South, several southern diarists and authors refer to reading these materials. Mary Virginia Hawes Terhune (1830–1922, who published under the pseudonym Marion Harland) comments in her autobiography that her mother was one of the earliest subscribers to *Godey's*, while her cousin Mary (who lived on Erin Hill Plantation, Virginia) took *Graham's Magazine*—"the only rival to *Godey's*."[11] She later notes that "my companions had their magazines. Mea's, as I well recollect, was *Harper's New Monthly*; my brother had the *Southern Literary Messenger*. Ned Rhodes had taken *Harper's* for me from the very first issue. My father subscribed conscientiously to the *Messenger* to encourage Southern literature. All right-minded Virginians acknowledged the duty of extending such encouragement to the extent of the subscription price of 'native productions.'"[12]

Clearly, Terhune's parents taught her to support southern writing, while at the same time they subscribed to a more general reading list. Gertrude Clanton Thomas (1834–1907), daughter of one of the wealthiest planters in Georgia (and who married into a family of roughly equal wealth), represents what literary opportunities a young woman who had every advantage might experience. (Her father's estate was worth $2.5 million in 1864.[13]) Gertrude's diary includes several references to materials read by her and her social circle. Writing from Rochester (the family's Piney Woods place that Gertrude renamed after the character in *Jane Eyre*) in September 1848, she notes that "Sis Anne received several Ladies papers" when her brother returned from Augusta.[14] Later that year (2 October 1848), Gertrude asked Mrs. Berry to loan her all issues from *Graham's Magazine* between September and October.[15] A week later, she reports that she has read seven of these issues and has begun the January 1846 story "Grace Fleming," which she particularly enjoyed. In February 1849, Gertrude made a list of all the books she had read by age fourteen. This inventory includes "any quantity of Magazines Godey's Graham's and &C."[16] In 1855, Gertrude also writes of reading both *Graham's* and *Harper's*, commenting that "both numbers are unusually interesting."[17]

Even Sarah Josepha Hale, the editor of *Godey's Lady's Book*, remarked on the differences between girls' preparation for womanhood in the North and in the South, and she advocated maintaining one's native customs.[18] A northern girl should attend school in the North and a southern in the South, she writes, "the style of living being so entirely dissimilar, the very housekeeping being a separate study by itself, and the household associations more peculiar than that of any country one can name."[19] She then recommended schools in the South that were appropriate for southern girls. Thus, while *Godey's* was a northern publication, the editor acknowledged her southern readers with regional advice when necessary.[20]

Writers in several southern journals also argued for keeping southern girls in southern schools, but these were more for the preservation of southern institutions.[21] Indeed, the education of southern women is but another area where unmistakable distinctions have been noted. Christie Anne Farnham's *Education of the Southern Belle: Higher Education and Student Socialization in the Antebellum South* and Anya Jabour's *Scarlett's Sisters: Young Women in the Old South* provide new ways of considering how young women were brought up in the antebellum South, particularly regarding expectations on how these women would interact with society. Farnham outlines how southern girls, though often educated by northerners, grew up with distinctly southern expectations of how their society worked.[22] Jabour refreshingly contemplates serious undercurrents of resistance that simmered beneath the perfected veneers of southern ladies-in-training.[23] By looking at an elite southern woman's culture divided into stages, Jabour effectively demonstrates that southern girls were raised with a set of expectations that differed distinctly from their northern counterparts.[24]

DATES

This study considers the period usually described as "antebellum" and continues through the Civil War. These years provide the opportunity to establish a norm (antebellum) and examine the results of its disruption (war). As such, the terminal date is relatively simple to ascertain. Where to begin is slightly trickier. Halttunen defines 1836–56 as the sentimental period in terms of fashion, following the romantic period of 1822–36.[25] Ideas associated with the sentimentalists will inform much of what is found in the musical experiences under examination here and therefore provide a logical beginning date.[26]

Other key events occurred in the 1830s. Of particular importance is the publication of *Godey's Lady's Book*, beginning in 1830. Through *Godey's*, many Americans learned how transparency, the goal of the sentimentalists, translated into moral improvement. Moreover, Farnham notes that Georgia Female College, the first women's institution to use the word "college" in its name and to strive for high education levels (equal to those set for males), dates its inception to 1839.[27] After that year, numerous such institutions sprang up throughout the South. Music instruction became an integral part of these centers of learning in the 1830s.

By the 1840s, American musical culture had changed. R. Allen Lott has pointed out that European pianists began touring the United States in the 1840s; their presence had a great influence on the musical culture of both concert hall and parlor. Pianos were increasingly present in the parlor from the 1820s on; by the midcentury, there was one piano for every 2,777 persons (almost double the number in 1829). Between 1839 and 1843, Ludwig (Louis) Rakemann (one of the earliest pianists to tour the United States) introduced a new repertory to the Americans, including Sigismund Thalberg, Franz Liszt, Frédéric Chopin, and others. William Vincent Wallace, whose music figures in chapter 5, first toured from New Orleans to Boston in 1842–44, thereby laying the groundwork for the storm of virtuosos who followed, beginning with Leopold de Meyer in 1845.[28]

In a similar vein, the operatic repertory shifted at about this time, as did the types of pieces played in the parlor (no doubt due to the changes in the preferred operatic literature). In the early years of the nineteenth century, American theatergoers showed a decided preference for English opera as seen in the works of Thomas Arne and later Henry Bishop. By the 1840s, however, American audiences had acquired a taste for foreign-language operas, especially works by Gaetano Donizetti. Moreover, touring companies of this period regularly began to include a star singer among their troupes, including several famous Italian and English singers.[29]

Correspondingly, sheet music collections from the mid-1830s onward contain a sufficiently different repertory to signify a change in the types of pieces played in parlors. While sources from the early years of the century contain numerous Scottish and Irish songs by (or arranged by) composers such as Thomas Bayley, around 1840 typical collections include arrangements of melodies from popular operas (by Gioacchino Rossini and Donizetti) and an increasing frequency of certain dances, particularly the polka.

AGE AND CLASS

This book contextualizes music in the lives of white women, almost all of whom belonged to the upper classes. Several factors justify this limitation. Most obviously, to attempt an inclusive examination of music in the lives of all women who lived in the South during this period is too mammoth a task for a single volume. Attempting to cover all women in one place would demean their individuality and ignore their personal experiences. Various parts of society experienced music in different ways. For example, two areas where middle-class women exercised influence over music in the lives of southerners were as music educators and church musicians. The repercussions of women entering these areas in greater numbers throughout the century have yet to be considered fully. The music of slaves has been examined from varying points of view, although a gender-specific study could possibly provide a better understanding of music in the lives of women of color at this time. Another area that should be investigated fully is the musical experiences of free women of color.[30] These and other topics in women's music certainly deserve their own studies. The ultimate destination for this study, however, is southern women composers who risked their reputations in order to become useful to the Confederate cause. The likelihood that women of color took part in such a venture in the South is slim.

The main focus of this volume is the young woman. While it may be granted that in a few instances some women maintained their musical activities in much the same manner they had established before their marriages, for most young women the opportunity for and expectations of musical pursuits changed dramatically after marriage. Lessons rarely continued after marriage, for few women had the time to concentrate their energies in that direction. Several books on the lives of women on southern plantations make plain the fact that the southern matron was occupied with a plethora of duties necessary to household maintenance that left little time for leisure activities. Nevertheless, the expectation remained that at least young married women might entertain family and friends until such time as their daughters achieved enough musical ability to take over this responsibility. At that point, it was the duty of the daughter to provide the comforting atmosphere of gentle entertainment in the evenings.

BACKGROUND

Despite the large size of the South throughout the period in question, its population remained low, with only a few large cities. In 1860, the population of New Orleans (168,675) was approximately 80 percent of the population of the state of Louisiana; Baltimore's citizens (212,418) accounted for more than 90 percent of Maryland's population; and even Charleston's considerably fewer 40,522 inhabitants equaled 75 percent of the urban population of South Carolina.[31] These numbers must be remembered when considering the opportunities women would have had to hear professional musical performances, as well as the position of the music teacher in various communities spread across large distances. The higher the population density, the more likely one was to hear professional performances.

Even within these parameters, it may seem impossible to generalize about the southern belle's musical experience during the antebellum period. The geography of the region alone is a challenge for any overview, for the "South" covers an extensive geographical area including several diverse terrains. Indeed, how one defines the South varies, although for this study, restrictive definitions (with the exception of Maryland) do not figure substantially. Many of the wealthier landowners in more remote areas (Mississippi or Louisiana, for example) sent their daughters to schools in the east (or New Orleans), thereby exposing them to the same ideas about music and its study/performance that girls living along the eastern seaboard would have encountered.

The variety of social circumstances, even for the elite, is another frustrating aspect of generalizations about the South. This issue—what is truly representative of southern society—is one that many notable scholars have addressed with some degree of consistency. In the prologue and first chapter of her landmark book *Within the Plantation Household: Black and White Women of the Old South*, Fox-Genovese discusses the problems surrounding how one considers the antebellum world with sweeping statements. Using the case of Sarah Ann Haynsworth Gayle as an example, she notes that any one individual cannot represent the region as a whole but rightly observes that "she shared with countless others, whose position entitled them to claim the status of lady, the structural constraints that governed the lives of privileged women in a slave society."[32]

Southern households of all types (large plantations to yeoman farms) functioned under similar structural limitations, even though the size of the household had a major impact on the types of work done by the women therein.[33] The time and money available for music lessons is one area where those differences might be keenly observed; therefore, this study will focus on those women who had the economic means to participate fully in the musical opportunities available in the antebellum South and place them in perspective relative to the structural constraints that Fox-Genovese and others find omnipresent throughout southern culture.

The South consisted largely of an agrarian economy, and its social and cultural structures were built on that foundation. Many of the women described in this study came from the planter class, a group distinguished by several characteristics. A "planter" owned a plantation and a significant number of slaves; studies stipulate ownership of twenty slaves to belong to this uppermost social class.[34] This group accounted for only 6 percent of the population.[35] The most commonly planted crops were cotton and, in the lower coastal areas, rice. A wide array of other products was also produced, as the plantation was, as a rule, self-sufficient.

This does not mean that all planters lived only on plantations, or even that all upper-class southerners were planters. Some families who figure in this work were not planters but people who led a more cosmopolitan existence entirely in cities such as Charleston or New Orleans. Men who were primarily businessmen or career politicians, involved with commerce, litigation, shipping, rail, and so forth, naturally spent more time in town. Their families resided there too. Many men spent time divided between plantation and town, but in these cases, most of the women stayed on the plantation to oversee its day-to-day running. Their husbands could be absent for months at a time. Fox-Genovese notes that while an urban culture did develop in the South, the "ideal of community" remained grounded in an idea of a network of rural-based households—and this ideal differed dramatically from that of the North.[36] When a young woman spent time in an urban community, she was expected to call on her neighbors, a custom that encapsulated much of southern society's rules. These visits formed one of the most substantial parts of a young belle's life. An example from the diary of Gertrude Clanton Thomas demonstrates how such a day of visiting might proceed and how much time and effort was spent on this convention. She writes in her diary on Sunday, 24 December 1848, that she dressed and went out in the carriage to visit several female acquaintances. She first saw Susan Knight and Lizzy Crump, but Indiana Clark was not at home. She continued on to Mrs. Robison's, whose daughter was also out. Leaving her card there, Gertrude proceeded to see Jane McKeen and then Emma Cumming. At the latter's, Ella Davies was there, so Gertrude "of course did not make it a very long visit." She continued to Mary Dawson's home, and finding that she too was away, went to Mrs. Bryson's. No one answered the door at the next house (that of the D'Antignacs), and Gertrude went home. While she was out, Laura Chew had called on her, which of course meant that Gertrude must reciprocate soon. Gertrude and Isabelle Morrison went for a stroll together after dinner, and they stopped in on Mildred and Lizzy Eve, who were not at home. After a trip to a jewelry repairman, Gertrude stopped by Mrs. Hickman's to see Virginia Whatly.[37] Such a social world dizzies the mind and helps to draw an extreme contrast with the isolation that someone like Jane North must have felt at Badwell, her family plantation in the remote woods of western South Carolina.

While calling on one's acquaintances was a ubiquitous part of a southern gentlewoman's lifestyle, the opportunity to do so varied tremendously. Women who lived on plantations were often separated from others of similar social standing, meeting together only rarely. As Mary Kendall, a New Englander who resided in Georgia, noted in 1853, "I seldom see any person aside from our own family. . . . [F]or about three weeks I did not have the pleasure of seeing *one white female face*."[38] For those who lived in the outermost areas, such occasions were possible only when they spent the "season" in town. In areas where disease spread during particular parts of the year, such as southern Louisiana, the time spent in New Orleans and on the plantation was divided accordingly. Frequently, however, the planter's wife was the only adult white woman on a plantation, and going anywhere would have necessitated a white male chaperone. If the nearest women who were her social equals lived ten or twenty miles away, the likelihood that she visited with any regularity is slim indeed.

Even though most women of the planter class lived in outlying areas where the land was worked, many spent some part of the year either in town (Charleston, for example) or traveling on a widespread tour that often extended as far as Niagara Falls, Canada, and sometimes Europe. Those who could afford to do so spent time at spas, such as Hot Springs. If they were able, many women in these circumstances took the opportunity for lengthy visits with family members spread throughout the region and with acquaintances in the North as well. On such trips, women (wives and/or daughters) might be away for several months at a time. Through such interactions, young women were exposed to a wider variety of musical experiences than they would have been otherwise.

Undoubtedly, the places with the most thriving musical activities were New Orleans (which surpassed even New York City at times during the nineteenth century), Baltimore, and Charleston, and to a lesser degree Savannah, Mobile, Richmond, Wilmington, and eventually Columbia and Augusta. The closer to a major rail system, the more likely a town was to host traveling musicians. Such towns were also more likely to include music stores where one could obtain sheet music (almost invariably printed in the North, at least until the 1840s), pianos, and other musical necessities. Places that fall under these descriptions include Raleigh and Charlotte, North Carolina; Danville and Petersburg, Virginia; Nashville and Chattanooga, Tennessee; and Atlanta, Georgia.

SOURCES

The music that serves as the basis for much of this study is located in several different collections in libraries and private collections in the United States. Most of the musical sources survive in bound collections that often include the owners' names and perhaps other information about them. Details about such sources appear throughout the text and notes. Additionally, diaries, letters, novels, and magazines provide useful insights on music in the lives of elite southern women.

Many of the books, scores, photographs, diaries, journals, and other items are now available on the Internet. For some of the more obscure works, the URLs have been provided for ease in locating the sources. Others may be found in major collections, such as the Library of Congress or the Documenting the American South Collection at the University of North Carolina at Chapel Hill Libraries.

1. Why Did Nineteenth-Century Southern Women Study Music?

*Then there are accomplishments, music, which
is almost necessary.*

—SARAH LOIS WADLEY DIARY, 18 OCTOBER 1860

During the 1850s and 1860s, Isabella Hannah Hunt McGehee, known familiarly as "Belle," studied piano and attained an admirable level of proficiency, if her surviving bound volume is indicative of the type of music she played (see appendix, table 1).[1] Growing up at Burleigh, a plantation house just inside the Person County line, east of Semora, North Carolina, Belle seemed far from the bustling activity of towns such as Raleigh or Richmond. Burleigh, overlooking Hyco Lake (formerly Hyco Creek), is situated not far from Milton, which in turn is close to Danville, Virginia, a major rail town in the nineteenth century. Curiously, Milton was one of only three towns named by a piano distributor out of Baltimore in the *Raleigh Register* in January 1850. Of the four references named in this advertisement, two lived in this tiny border location. This rather high proportion of piano references in the vicinity suggests that music lessons were available and indeed desirable, even in an area seemingly far-removed from places where most professional musical activity thrived, for why else would Milton have received such notice?[2]

Belle McGehee belonged to a wealthy planter family whose impact on the region is still felt today. (One of the larger roads in this area is McGhee Mill Road, named for the mill once owned and operated by the family.) The 1850 census listed her grandfather Thomas McGehee Sr. as being worth $32,000 in one of the counties in which he owned property; at the same time, he and his sons owned several hundred slaves, clearly placing their economic status among the top levels of southern society. Almost a century later, an article in the *Greensboro Daily News* (20 May 1948) describes the elder McGehee as an émigré from Scotland and a friend of the politician Henry Clay. He built Burleigh Plantation around 1825, and Belle's parents, Thomas Jeffreys McGehee Jr. and Mary Allen Hunt (who were married in 1846), later occupied the house. Several of the original buildings (including the main house) survive to this day. Belle was born on 1 November 1849, but her father died shortly thereafter (1852) at the age of thirty-two, leaving Belle and her two siblings with her mother. Thomas McGehee Sr. took over management of the plantation property, and the family continued to live at Burleigh.

Several interesting stories surround the plantation, including one that has abolitionist John Brown being hidden temporarily by slaves there.[3] As intriguing as such stories may be, it is its musical tradition that draws this study's attention to Burleigh and its occupants. Belle McGehee's surviving piano book evinces a technically proficient keyboard player—one of the so-called piano girls of this period—but also more than that, if one is to believe proprietary rules on deportment and display. Typical of her class, Belle studied music from a young age, since most of her volume was collected before she was twenty (at the most). Her 1865 report card from the Chester Female Academy (Chesterfield County, Virginia), when she was sixteen, contains a grade of 100 in piano.[4] Presumably there were other piano books that are now lost, for one does not begin lessons with major piano works by Thalberg, Hermann A. Wollenhaupt, Louis Moreau Gottschalk, and William Vincent Wallace. That she had the time to progress through such literature situates her in the leisured class, at the top rung of antebellum society. Her grandfather was one of the wealthiest men in the region, and her musical training exemplifies that of a girl of her station. That her piano still survived in the parlor in 1948 (apparently along with the original horsehair cushions) suggests that the McGehee family may have come through the ravages of the Civil War with more material wealth than many of their compatriots.[5]

There is more to Belle McGehee's story. The unusual part of her narrative is that this elite belle, in the truest sense of the word, married a music professor on 18 March 1874. Before the war, women of Belle McGehee's class did not usually socialize with music professors, yet she married Robert Smith Phifer (spelled variously Phieffer, Phiferr, and other similar ways) when she was twenty-four years old and he was only twenty-one.[6] For professors to marry their students was not so unusual at this time; Phifer's predecessor at Danville, C. C. Nordendorf, married one of his students in 1865. Phifer, however, did not take up his position in Danville until 9 August 1878, according to a report in the *Charlotte Observer*. His prior position had been organist at the Second Presbyterian Church in Charlotte.[7] Thus, Belle must have married him *before* he moved to the area. The union of a wealthy planter's daughter with a music professor suggests mitigating circumstances. The most obvious explanation is that the family's prosperity took a decidedly downward turn as a result of the war, and those economic conditions, in addition to a scarcity of marriageable men, caused women such as Belle McGehee to marry beneath their class.

On the other hand, the McGehee-Phifer union might be more accurately explained by a strong musical connection between the two partners.[8] Phifer's surviving bound volume includes some indications that he taught Belle, perhaps before marriage.[9] (Fingerings in both volumes seem to come from the same hand.) With dealers' stamps from Greensborough, North Carolina, and Augusta as well as from northern cities such as Philadelphia, Phifer clearly benefited from an acquaintance with a variety of sellers. His book includes a more masculine repertory, including Felix Mendelssohn and Beethoven, than does McGehee's. This division of composers by genre exists throughout this period and contributes to an understanding of women's music. He also added duets and several popular variations on operatic themes to his collection, as well as the requisite pieces by composers such as Gottschalk.

The McGehee-Phifers' sincere interest in music also manifests itself in the hospitality that the couple offered to English composer Frederick Delius, who apparently spent up to three years with the family in the late nineteenth century. (Delius taught music in Danville at the Roanoke Female College for nine months in 1885–86; Phifer secured that post for him.) Music obviously held a significant status among the McGehee-Phifer family, one that overcame bounds of social class in the turbulent Reconstruction era.

Even so, although Robert continued to be involved in numerous musical performances and other events, Belle's name does not appear as a performer in any of the programs. Their daughters appeared in public concerts in the 1870s and 1880s, but as a married woman, Belle did not. No record survives to suggest why she refrained from public performance, but very likely she never quite overcame the strict education in ladyhood that most elite southern women received in the mid-nineteenth century.

In several respects, this story typifies the musical experiences of elite white women in the antebellum South in ways that both satisfy currently held ideas about the musical education of southern women and dispel others. First and foremost, it demonstrates the importance of music in the lives of young women. But that "importance" needs extensive clarification. While there can be little doubt that the traditional view that young women learned music either as a way to secure a husband (by demonstrating their taste and suitable education) or as a way to keep this segment of the population appropriately occupied is accurate to a degree. On the other hand, we cannot assume that these expectations apply too broadly, and many of the women discussed in the following pages clearly pursued music for reasons beyond these.

WHY STUDY MUSIC?

One essential question looms large over anyone engaged in the study of women and music in the antebellum South: why did families spend so much money and young women so much time pursuing musical study? And study music they did—frequently. Diarist Eliza Ripley (1832–1912) comments early in her writings that, in her native city of New Orleans, "every girl had music lessons and every mother superintended the study and practice of the one branch deemed absolutely indispensable to the education of a *demoiselle*."[10] In most school settings, the sheer cost of music lessons (and instrument rental) outweighed the total for general tuition. Many diaries and letters mention girls taking lessons, either from a teacher in town whom they visited for lessons, from an instructor who might come to the house, or in rarer cases from tutors who lived with the family for a period of time.

Even during the war, girls maintained their music lessons whenever possible. Henry Graves wrote to his sister Cora in August 1863, urging her to take music lessons in Augusta that winter if the family moved. He commented that "I had rather you were accomplished and poor when you are grown, than you should be worth a half million and be a dunce."[11] Not only did Henry assume that music lessons would keep Cora from being a "dunce," but he proposed that she spend money on lessons at a time when the war had taken a decided turn against the Confederates.

For the girls themselves, it seems that an hour of practice each day was a bare minimum; more often, two or three hours spent alone with the piano is indicated. In Amite, Louisiana, Sarah Lois Wadley (1844–1920) practiced dutifully, if only two hours each day (but she apparently did not progress quite as rapidly as she wished, a sin for which she earnestly repented).[12] In 1860, Wadley made a revealing statement in which she acknowledged the importance of musical training, even if she had no talent for it: "I know nothing of the sciences and no language except my own and a little of the latin, then there are accomplishments, music, which is almost necessary, and drawing and painting, which I dearly love."[13] Wadley singles out music as a prerequisite accomplishment, listing drawing and painting as something she *likes* to do. Music, it seems, she *must* do. All of this time and effort taken to learn music seems even more striking when considering that these young women would almost never *display* an advanced level of musical achievement.

MUSIC TO PLEASE OTHERS

Wadley was a piano girl. Music was seen as a particularly suitable pastime for a girl for a number of reasons.[14] The practical reason often stated was that young women learned music so that they could soothe and entertain their men, be they husbands, brothers, fathers, or guests.[15] The purpose for music (and other accomplishments) was to enable a young woman to please others, a behavior that southerners felt was paramount in women. Society expected her to learn the piano and to play modestly for guests and the family. All of the rules governing behavior, deportment, and dress can be seen in how the piano girl functioned within the limited sphere available to her controlled world. How young women reacted to this world has been the subject of debate among historians of southern women's culture. Joan Cashin labels it a culture of resignation.[16] In her most representative form, the piano girl embodies this culture of resignation. Everything directed at young women taught them that they should be politely conversant in several subjects, gracious hostesses, and obedient daughters *for others*.[17] Music instruction carried similar expectations. No references indicate that girls learned music because they *wanted* to. Rather, it was always to please someone else. They resigned their lot to spending several hours a day in pursuit of accomplishment in music.

An illustrative example of such expectations can be found in a letter from Marcus Cicero Stephens to his granddaughter Mary Anne Primrose (1826–1916) in 1847. He wrote to Mary Anne while she was attending the Burwell School in Hillsborough, North Carolina. He advised her to work assiduously while in school: "You tell me that you are taking lessons in music, drawing, and French besides the usual studies, all this is very well a young woman ought to perfect herself in all the accomplishments she can, that she may *in the first place* render herself interesting and agreeable *to others* and moreover possess internal resources of pleasure and amusement in those moments of listlessness and apathy to which we are all more or less subjected" (italics mine).[18] Stephens spells out precisely *why* Mary Anne should learn to play the piano—to please others. No comment on whether or not she might enjoy it. He also adds a postscript that commands her to "learn to play and sing 'Highland Mary.' It is the sweetest thing I ever heard and should we ever meet, it will be the first tune I call for."[19] That Mary Anne should learn to play a piece for him in case they should ever meet one another unmistakably directs her to do this in order to please someone else. Stephens had moved around 1836 from New Bern, North Carolina, to Quincy, Florida. Mary Anne still called New Bern home at this time, although she spent most of her adult life in Selma, North Carolina. Whether she ever met her grandfather after this letter is unknown.

The "perfect woman," an ideal which was clearly laid out for southerners, made others happy and in so doing found her own happiness.[20] In Greenwood, South Carolina, Brother Lewis M. Ayer proclaimed in an 1858 sermon that sometimes men delude themselves in thinking that women need only to be good and pure. He proposed that "to be amiable, fair and affectionate . . . requires stays of study—of systematic training." Women, with their pureness, "keener instincts," and ability toward quicker "intuitive perceptions of moral truth," "will yield the wand of power over men with charming virtue, grace, and goodness." To achieve these goals, women must be guided by the Muses, specifically Terpsichore (dance), Euterpe (music and lyric poetry), Clio (history), and Calliope (epic and heroic poetry).[21] His comments suggest that the study of these particular items will guide women to their proper position and in so doing will guide men to theirs.

MUSIC EDUCATION AS AN INDICATION OF CLASS STATUS

Beyond these reasons for studying music, musical accomplishment represented more than a young woman's suitability for marriage and child-rearing: it assisted in casting the woman as a lady, not only economically but also culturally. The object of education for each elite southern young woman was to become a lady. Christie Farnham Pope characterizes the lady as "a woman of good family and social position, a person of good breeding and refined manners to whom chivalrous attentions were due," basing her definition on numerous nineteenth-century publications on the education and deportment of ladies.[22]

Contemporary articles in *Godey's Lady's Book* and etiquette manuals clearly expected that young women could sing and/or play an instrument. In an 1848 issue of *Graham's Magazine*, a description of an ideal young woman and her environs includes "books, too, and music—a harp—a piano," as if any suitable parlor held such instruments.[23] Even more precisely, a later story (1852) remarks that "the splendid piano, in all the glory of its rich rosewood case, now occupied its *destined* position in the front of the parlor" (italics mine).[24] In the *Southern Literary Messenger* of 1861, Mrs. Mary Scrimzeour Whitaker paints a picture of a southern parlor with "musical instruments—the gilded harp and massive piano, the romantic guitar, and mellow accordion, waited until their sweet sounds should be called forth by the magic of touch."[25] Numerous such entries may be found throughout mid-nineteenth-century literature of various sorts.[26]

Another example of the assumption of musical accomplishment occurs in Sarah Ida Fowler Morgan's diary. Morgan (1842–1909), the daughter of Judge Thomas Gibbes Morgan of Baton Rouge, began her diary in January 1862 at the age of nineteen. When she writes that she has low self-esteem and always chooses pursuits in which no one else excels (which is why she ended up being a guitarist instead of a pianist—her sister Miriam took up the piano not long after Sarah did and apparently quickly surpassed her), Sarah further declares that she is not *really* talented: "Miriam is by far the best performer in Baton Rouge, and I would rank forty third even in the delectable village of Jackson [at the time home of Centenary College, which taught music among other subjects]. And yet, I must have some ear for music. To 'Know as many songs as Sarah' is a family proverb; not very difficult songs, or very beautiful ones, to be sure, besides being very indifferently sung; but the tunes *will* run in my head, and it must take *some* ear to catch them. People say to me 'Of course you play?' to which I invariably respond 'O no! but Miriam plays *beautifully*!' 'You sing, I believe?' 'Not at all!—except for father . . . and the children. But *Miriam* sings . . .'"[27]

This excerpt tells much about the culture in which Sarah Morgan lived. Throughout her diary, she points away from herself whenever possible; how much of this is cultural and how much is Sarah is difficult to ascertain. While southern belles certainly were not to draw attention to themselves, Sarah seems to have been extraordinarily reticent about being seen or heard in public, as illustrated by other incidents mentioned in her diary. Nevertheless, additional information may also be learned from this passage. People in her acquaintance assumed that she played and sang, but Morgan claimed to sing only for others—her father chiefly—an appropriate answer for a young southern woman. Earlier in her diary, Sarah wrote that she had dabbled in several musical pursuits before committing to the guitar, for she began piano lessons, sang, and played the guitar. The "tunes" she knew were numerous and not difficult or beautiful; in more recent times, the attributes of difficult and beautiful seem desirable, but such was not always the case under the veiled language of southern culture. To be either very difficult or beautiful would be perilously close to being professional, and that must never be.

The story "Ups and Downs" in *Graham's Magazine* (1852) includes a contrasting use of music as a signifier of deeper values. The story concerns Maria and Henry Dawson, a lovely married couple of upper-middle-class standing. Henry's business fails, and they are forced to sell all their fine things, except his two books and her piano. Maria, naturally, has a piano, although that fact had not been revealed earlier. The writer assumed that the readers would know that the Dawsons had a piano because of their social position. These three items are kept because they will bring comfort to *Henry*, by his reading and by her playing, and will eventually be used by the children. No mention is made of any solace or pleasure Maria may have in playing the piano. Southern girls were given instruction in piano because women provide pleasure for others.

The family moves to the country, where Henry becomes a small farmer. The local wives do not understand why Maria brought the piano:

> [Miss Susan Bitterly:] "They say she has a piano. I wonder what she expects to do with it here."
>
> "Well for my part," says Mrs. Hardmoney . . . "I don't see what farmers' wives have to do with them there sort of things. When I was a gal, we were taught another guess matter than to sit at thumping pianys all day."[28]

Clearly, women of this lower station do not know the rewards of being musically accomplished. Miss Bitterly later specifically derides Maria as an accomplished lady, but not in her presence. In fact, the village women who criticize Maria have never even met her. This excerpt vividly shows the lines between those who are socially and culturally adept and those who are inferior. The Dawsons, in keeping their piano under trying economic circumstances, retained their elegance and thereby to a degree their social place. The others unmistakably belong to a different class.

Musical entertainment by accomplished daughters also displayed the family's acceptable social status via the arena of the parlor. In her study of American culture in the mid-nineteenth century, Karen Halttunen finds that the parlor stood as a necessary place in a closely proscribed social world. At a time when American cities were growing quickly, the socially elite used the culture of the parlor as a way to maintain distinctions between themselves and a world that was coming into their space too rapidly. Halttunen identifies the "antebellum crisis of social confidence" as a critical moment in the cultural history of the United States, a time when Americans confronted a new world of strangers. Proper gentlepeople needed a new system of cultural forms in order to deal with the moral and psychological threats with which they were threatened. On the street, proper men and women might meet with undesirable people, without even knowing they were undesirable, because it was relatively simple to masquerade in public as someone worthy of introduction. The parlor, however, mitigated disastrous situations through a series of elaborate rituals, the knowledge of which indicated approval. The dangerous hypocrisy that dwelt in public areas such as the city street had to be neutralized by the sincerity of social intercourse in the parlor—what Halttunen calls the "sentimental ideal."[29]

One of the most familiar solutions to the problem of undesirable acquaintances was the calling card, which could be accepted or declined by the recipient. The complicated systems of calling cards and their specific uses kept disagreeable people away. The parlor, with its hundreds of rules on proper etiquette, served as a means of establishing "us" and "them," or "self" and "other." Contemporary literature identifies objectionable characters as "confidence men" ("con men") and "painted women" (women of somewhat loose morals). Only by adhering to the numerous rules governing behavior could one hopefully avoid a disgraceful relationship with such people. These rules played out most obviously in the parlor, a space that Halttunen identifies as a barrier between the unknown and frightening outside world of the street and the very private, personal area in the rest of the house.[30] She divides the house in terms of the "rules of polite social geography": between the parlor, where performance (of the proper rules of behavior) was given, and the back regions of the house, where the actor was completely removed from the stage (parlor).[31] Most significant, the parlor itself functioned as a stage, but not a public one. It was not a stage for musical and dramatic theatrical performances but rather one on which the play of society unfolded.

The idea of the parlor as a performance venue in a complex, intertwined world in which reality was masked by the appropriate denial of performing clearly has implications for musical experience. Numerous rules enabled genteel performance in two ways. First, these rules provided the necessary staging for the performance, and second, they simultaneously governed how to politely deny the theatricality of the performance.[32] As such, although a young woman may have performed musically for the gathered, socially approved group, she was not a "performer," at least not in the sense of an opera singer or professional pianist, because she was not displaying her accomplishments publicly. The important distinctions between parlor and public performance had to be maintained at all times. The division of women's cultural world into private, parlor, and public will affect this book's examination of music, for different types of music took place in each.

MUSIC'S USE IN COURTSHIP

Music also served as a means of courtship. Several stories in southern magazines make this quite clear. In "It Is Omnipotent," young Ellen mysteriously receives a melody one evening—it simply comes to her. Her potential beau hears her play it and asks on subsequent evenings that she perform it again. She always refuses. After several parlays around the playing of this particular air, the two realize that the melody "came to" each of them on the same night. (He was in Paris, she in the United States, and they did not know each other at the time.) The two become engaged and finally decide to name the tune. He proposes "The Dryad's Requiem" and "The Naiad's Bridal," but she responds that it is "Love! . . . both first and last, the one, the only love." He takes this as the title, but then, after hearing a story from her past, decides that it must be called "Woman's Power," "because . . . it is omnipotent!"[33] This "omnipotent power" of Woman manifests and reveals itself in music.

Other writers noted music's power. In "My First Serenade," an anonymous author in the *Southern Literary Messenger* compares how a blonde beauty's overly affected performance brought displeasure to the writer, while the softer, more intimate performance of Alegna Onerom pleased him immensely. The scene in which the blonde plays and sings vividly demonstrates what *not* to do:

> My attention was soon attracted by the tones of a piano in an adjoining room, where a bevy of attentive admirers was hanging in apparent raptures about a blonde beauty, who, with all the airs and graces of a Tedesco, was just commencing a piece from somebody's opera, which I concluded at the time was written in Seminole, as the only word which I distinctly heard was *en ca*. Her instrumental was as strange to me as her vocal performance; and as I gazed upon her movements in all ignorance of fashionable piano tactics, I came to the conclusion that she was hammering the instrument into some kind of order preparatory to a regular performance. At first her left hand gently rose and fell, with a springback motion of the wrist, resurrecting a low, wailing sound from the very depths of the instrument; while her right, whose flying fingers lightly kissed the keys, was leaping and cavorting like an untamed courser, in perfect freedom, producing sounds

between the rattle of a snake and the scattering fire of retreating infantry. A scream, not unlike the Irish wail of the dead, now broke from her lips and indicated that the *music* was coming; and the admiring connoisseurs bent their listening ears with an air of wonderful interest and mutual intelligence to her screams and whispers, with variations and embellishments, fortissimo and pianissimo. Her hands approached each other in a sort of echelon movement, but suddenly retreated amidst a volley of small notes; her voice then came to the aid of the right hand against the left; and, amidst the convulsive clutchings and spasmodic poundings that the keys received from the left hand, and the erratic hop, skip and jump movement of the right hand, she closed her performances, with such tones of voice, and such die-away appeals, as might have left no doubt in the minds of the uninitiated that she was in great distress of mind or body.[34]

Not to worry, however. The beauty arose from the piano "wreathed in smiles." While her admirers showered her with compliments, the writer observed that she was a "finished specimen of a fashionable young lady, of the real boarding-school, theorem-painting, worsted-working, Italianised and Frenchified stamp, in tone, manner and dress. Her face was full of animation and consciousness of her power." He then comments on her not-quite-concealing bodice, but notes, "I delight to observe the varied powers of woman, and certainly her tactics were admirably adapted to the small set of small wits whose enthusiasm in her praise knew no bounds, and whose fancy seemed to owe its illumination to the grape."[35]

This young woman had learned the accomplishments technically, but she did not acquire taste as she pursued them. Taste, a sense of decorum, and knowing not to display too ostentatiously are themes that run through most of the chapters in this book. They are paramount to understanding the musical culture of the southern woman.

THE BELLE OF THE OPERA

Before proceeding to discussions of how young southern women experienced music, consideration of Joseph Chandler's article "The Belle of the Opera, Essays upon a Woman's Accomplishment, Her Character and Her Mission" will assist to define further the importance of music in the education of a young lady. A lengthy essay on womanly accomplishment and its usefulness, "The Belle of the Opera" takes as its point of reference a beautiful young woman at the opera, whose pictorial likeness precedes the article. Chandler (1792–1880), a Philadelphia politician, ambassador, newspaper editor, and founder of a young ladies' seminary, contributed with some frequency to *Graham's Magazine*. In this particularly lengthy essay, he puts forth many attributes desirable in a young woman. They eloquently explain why it is important to be beautiful and accomplished—ultimately, the woman who possesses these traits (among others) will educate her children and shape their lives with her cultivation and exquisiteness.

> Let us not hear the platitudes about the worthlessness of beauty; it is not worthless—it is of high price—of exceeding worth—of extensive useful-ness; and appropriately displayed, its influence is humanizing, tranquil-izing, and every way beneficial.
>
> To personal charms The Belle of the Opera adds a cultivated taste for music—a taste which she indulges at the fountain-head of such enjoy-ments. But does she less, on that account, or rather *these* accounts, (beauty and musical taste, namely,) fulfill her mission at home? Does the lesson of virtue which the accomplished mother gives to her young child, fall less *impressively* on the heart because the infant pupil, in looking upward, gazes into a face replete with all of earthly beauty? Is there not a certain coincidence between the looks of her beloved teacher and the excellence of her delightful instruction? or rather, does not her beauty tend to make these lessons delightful? And if the charm for the child is the morning or evening hymn, does not the sacred simplicity of the text drop with extraordinary unction on the ear, if conveyed in the rich melody of a cultivated voice?[36]

Clearly, music education provided the young belle with more abilities than being able to entertain in the evenings—it paved the way for the smooth and easy instruction of the young, something held very dear to southerners. Being beautiful and accomplished made one useful in such social circles.

Music was not the only desirable accomplishment, but an important one. Contemporary wisdom held that women should be well-rounded and know something of all the fine arts. If a young woman spent too much time in pursuit of one specialty, she risked being seen as professional. Chandler warns slightly later:

> Music itself, if it be the only or the principal attainment of a woman, must be valuable only as a means of obtaining money or fame. So of dancing— so of painting—so of poetry, that divine gift—each of these, allowed to become predominant, loses its meliorating influence, and devotes the pos-sessor to a solitary enjoyment, or, at most, assists her in acquiring notoriety and a living.
>
> It is our intention to laud the cultivation of tastes only as parts of the meliorating means of woman's character—the acquisition or rather the improvement of ingredients to fit her for that office of delicate influence for which God evidently designed her. Her personal beauty may be part of the means of her wholesome domestic influence—her love of, and attainments in, music, her improvement in drawing, her literary gifts and acquirements

all go, when all are mingled, to give to her consequence and usefulness in the nursery, and to make her beloved and beneficially influential in the domestic circle, and to add attraction to her charms in social life. There is no incompatibility between all these acquisitions with great personal beauty, between a sense of that beauty, indeed, and the entire fulfillment of all domestic and social duties, that are likely to be devolved on one thus highly endowed, thus qualified by extensive attainments.[37]

Thus, any man who sought to establish his family in appropriate social circles needed a wife who could bring musical accomplishment as part of her dowry, thereby ensuring the proper influence on their children. *Graham's Magazine* was one of the most popular journals circulating in the mid-nineteenth century (Mary Terhune attests that it was second only to *Godey's Lady's Book*), and its readers would certainly look to it for advice such as Chandler's.[38]

Another outlet for discussing the values of the southern home and its matron was the plantation novel. As a genre, the plantation novel, cultivated by southern women for southern women, clearly emphasizes the "regenerative powers" of the southern home and family as governed by the aristocratic southern female.[39] These novels, by authors such as Caroline Gilman, Caroline Hentz, Maria MacIntosh, Mary Terhune, and Augusta Evans, introduced Americans both North and South to the virtues of southern values.[40]

Once such accomplishment and cultivation had been attained, those "in the know" could identify others with the right qualifications. Returning to the story "Ups and Downs," the countrywomen question the worth of the accomplished woman from town. Miss Susan Bitterly makes fun of one of the younger girls present who wishes to learn music and go to boarding school:

"Well, I am glad to hear she's not so set up with her piany and such nick-nackeries as to be above being willing to help herself some. When I heard what a heap of help they had down there, I thought sure as how they were going to bring all their city notions as well as their piany down here into the country."

"Why, what harm can there be in a piano," said the oldest of the Holmes girls, before whose eyes visions of a boarding-school, and a piano, and such like things had been for some time dancing; "I can't see what harm there can be in having a piano. For my part I think it must be very nice, and I mean to go over and see that dear, pretty Mrs. Dawson, and perhaps she will play on hers for me."

"No doubt she will, my dear," said Miss Susan Bitterly; "accomplished ladies like her when they're settled down among such barbarians as we, are glad to meet some one as accomplished as yourself with whom to associate."[41]

Although the use of "barbarians" may be ironic, its meaning is obvious in this context. The mere presence of a piano suggested accomplishment—no one has even heard Mrs. Dawson play. The instrument represented class distinction, education, and accomplishment.

MUSIC FOR THE FAMILY

The correspondence of members of the North-Petigru family repeatedly discusses the importance of musical accomplishment. Since several branches of the family are examined in this study, some explanation of their genealogy will be helpful.[42] Of the nine offspring of William Pettigrew and Louise Guy Gibert, four are of concern here. The eldest, James Louis (1789–1863, the famous Unionist), married Jane Amelia Postell in 1816.[43] Their two daughters, Jane Caroline Petigru Carson (1820–92) and Susan DuPont Petigru King Bowen (1824–75), were both keenly involved in the arts: Caroline as a painter and Susan (Sue) as a writer. William and Louise's eldest daughter, Jane Gibert (1800–1863), married John Gough North in 1827. Their three daughters, Jane Caroline (Carey) Pettigrew (1828–87), Mary Charlotte Allston (1832–?, married in 1857), and Louise Gibert Allston (1833–1906), carried on extensive correspondence, much of which survives today in the Southern Historical Collection at the University of North Carolina.

William and Louise's second daughter, Louise Porcher (1806–69), had four daughters, Jane Louise, Mary Anna, Louise, and Marion; only Marion survived her mother. Their third daughter, Adeline (later changed to the more French "Adèle") Theresa, married future governor Robert Francis Withers Allston in 1832. Of their nine children, Adele ("Della") Petigru Vanderhorst (1840–1915) and Elizabeth Waties Pringle (1845–1921) figure most prominently here. Elizabeth Pringle is perhaps best remembered as the author of *A Woman Rice Planter*.[44] Further complications in keeping the correct person in mind result from the fact that many members of the Petigrus married their cousins, so that Petigrus, Porchers, Allstons, and Pettigrews can be found among each generation.

The letters that Caroline ("Carey") North received from her mother, Jane Gibert Pettigrew North, frequently admonished her for her supposed lack of progress in music, which is ironic considering that Carey later taught her cousins in that art. Jane often derides Carey on not meeting her standards, and music is one area of especial emphasis. (The next most frequently heard complaint concerns Carey's handwriting, which was, undeniably, bad.)

The following excerpt typifies the advice Jane wrote to Carey. In a letter dated 25 January 1841, Jane writes about a visit to the village school where Miss Harrison is "again engaged as music teacher." She further remarks that "the girls seem to make a very pleasing progress in that delightful branch of polite education [music]—do you pay much attention to it dear? I fear that you do not—but only think what a disappointment it will be to me if through negligence on your part you let the opportunity pass unimproved—if you love your Mother let not indolence get the better of you in this, or in any other respect. I am sorry to say my daughter, that your letter was very carelessly written . . ."[45] At this time, Carey was spending a particularly long visit with her relatives the R. F. W. Allstons; Mrs. Allston, Adèle, was Jane North's sister. With their plantation on the eastern seaboard, the Allstons lived closer to civilization (essentially Charleston), and not in the decidedly more remote western part of the state, where Jane's town of Badwell is located. Jane even describes Badwell to Carey in one letter as "a dull place in the woods—without neighbors or any other recommendation."[46]

Later in the same year, Jane responded to another letter from Carey, noting that she is making "reasonable progress" in her studies. Jane comments that "it will be up to you, whether you will be an accomplished woman or not." In other words, Jane has provided all the necessary tools; it was up to Carey to use them. Among the reasons Jane gives Carey as to why she should apply herself is the inescapable eventuality that her "little sister will necessarily depend on you." Thus, music lessons not only helped to make Carey accomplished, they allowed her to be able to instruct her sister.[47]

Next, Jane reiterates that all-important reason to study music: to please others. She was happy to hear that Carey could "play some tunes, and that you pleased your uncle Allston in that way—doubtless your Grandfather will be highly gratified to hear you perform—you know how fond of music he is."[48] Her mother never asked if *Carey* enjoys music. She was expected to be able to perform for her family as part of her role as an accomplished young woman.

Later that month, Jane again writes to Carey that "it gives me sincere pleasure my dear child, to hear that you are making some way in music, and that you give satisfaction to your dear aunt, and your kind teacher."[49] Again, Carey pleased others with her music. But perhaps the most telling person to whom Carey was to give satisfaction was her mother. Jane explicitly wrote the previous December that Carey should not neglect her music. She was to continue diligently so that she could "soothe solitary evenings at Badwell with sweet music, which I love dearly."[50]

Southern expectations of why young women, at least of the elite class, should take music clearly derive from their ideas of being accomplished. On rare occasions, their reasoning extended to personal satisfaction. Mary Pettigrew, a cousin of Carey North, professed a deep respect for music. She wrote in 1843, "Oh what a charming thing music is. It is a heavenly passion and given us I think to lead our mind from this world to that of a better."[51]

Her thoughts on music and its uses differ from those of the rest of her family, at least before the war, and cannot be read as representative. For most women, the two more practical reasons why one studied music, as a vocation or to play seriously (on the stage), seldom entered the discussion. When Mary Pettigrew wrote to her brother in 1843 from school in Washington, D.C., that she wished to pursue music in order to "obtain a livelihood—as so many others in the United States have been obliged to do," she could not be reflecting her personal experience.[52] Her father, Ebenezer Pettigrew, owned substantial holdings in the eastern part of the state.[53] Her brothers attended Bingham's School in Hillsborough before they proceeded to the University of North Carolina. Mary herself had been schooled in Washington, in Hillsborough, and then at Saint Mary's College in Raleigh. Letters exchanged from members of this family hail from Washington; Alexandria, Virginia; and North Carolina estates in Cools Springs, New Bern, Belgrade, Greenfield (near Edenton), Enfield, Hillsborough, Chapel Hill, and others. Unfortunately, her brother's response to this proposal does not survive. Undoubtedly, however, he would not have sanctioned such an idea for Mary, at least not in 1843. After the Civil War, ironically, several of the Pettigrew/Petigru women did teach music in order to earn enough money to survive.

In 1856, music critic John Sullivan Dwight commented that "a musical education should produce such results, that when we hand to a friend the compositions of Mozart, of Beethoven, or of Haydn, or of a musician who is perhaps the ornament of his profession, her intellectual culture should tell upon her instrument, and add the inspiration of a living tone to the thoughts of the departed artist, causing Music to fulfil [sic] its true office, in exalting and adorning our daily life."[54] For the southern girl, music was indeed to exalt and adorn the daily life—not hers necessarily, but that of others. The remainder of this statement, however, seems distinctly removed from the experience most southern girls would have encountered. Mozart, Beethoven, and Haydn were not options for their delicate minds or bodies, and almost no extant collections contain music by these composers. Some do include a minor dance by Beethoven, or perhaps a Mozart aria, but such literature was not a part of the southern woman's cultural experience. Southern girls learned to play pretty tunes in order to please others, to display the fact that their parents had the economic and social wherewithal to secure music lessons for them, and to know when and how much to play for whom. "Thoughts of the departed" Haydn, Mozart, or Beethoven were far from their minds.

2. Women's Interaction with Public Music

Learning that I was in the opera-house where the "show" was held, he had invited me into his private stage-box, and there . . . indifferent to the . . . singing going on, on the stage, we talked for an hour.

—[MARY VIRGINIA HAWES TERHUNE],
MARION HARLAND'S AUTOBIOGRAPHY

If the parlor represented the stage on which southern women presented music rather than performed it, the public stage figured as an area where southern women viewed women performers. Upper-class girls were to have some knowledge of concert repertories and etiquette at concerts, but they were also expected to know where to draw the line between professional musicians' performances and their own. Understanding this difference is a prerequisite to appreciating performance in the parlor versus performance on the stage. As he extols the virtues of the "Belle of the Opera," Chandler states that "I knew The Belle of the Opera, and she was as fond of the dance as of the song, and shared in both in the social circle, and enjoyed them in *others* in more public displays" (italics mine).[1] He makes a clear distinction between performing in one's own circle and in public, and the very proper Belle of the Opera was heard only in the parlor.

PUBLIC MUSIC

The line between public and private music could never be transgressed. Mrs. St. Julian [Harriott Horry] Ravenel, a member of an influential Charleston family, described true southern ladies in her 1912 memoirs, noting reserve in all things. Even though Ravenel writes in the positivist nostalgia that typifies southern literature from the turn of the century, the fact that she noted such distinctions is worth examining. In outlining a southern lady's attributes, Ravenel draws a sharp division between the parlor and stage: "In that day and class, ladies shunned all public exercise or display of talent or beauty. Their letters were admirable, but they did not write books. They charmed

drawing-rooms with their voices or music, but never appeared on a stage.
They talked delightfully, but did not make speeches."[2] With these remarks,
Ravenel makes clear the things a genteel lady would not do. She would not
write books (and by logical extension, she would not compose music), and
she would not perform in public.

"Public" did not refer merely to the stage. The following incident described
in Sarah Morgan's diary demonstrates the utter embarrassment she and her
family felt when Union soldiers "accidentally" heard Sarah and her sister
Miriam one evening. Even though the girls sang in a private space (the balcony of their home), passersby could hear them. This situation resulted, in
effect, in a "public" performance. Once discovered, both sisters were deeply
humiliated, and Sarah bemoaned the lack of opportunity to mix in traditional
settings with girls her own age because of the war.

> Poor Miriam! Poor Sarah! they are disgraced again! Last night we were
> sitting on the balcony in the moonlight, singing as usual with our guitar.
> . . . I could not think singing on the balcony was so very dreadful . . . but
> last night changed all my ideas. We noticed Federals, both officers and
> soldiers, pass singly, or by twos and threes at different times, but we were
> not singing for their benefit, and they were evidently attending to their
> own affairs, there was no necessity of noticing them at all. But about half
> past nine, after we had sung two or three dozen others, we commenced
> Mary of Argyle. As the last word died away, while the chords were still
> vibrating, came a sound of—clapping hands, in short!
>
> Down went every string of the guitar; Charlie cried "I told you so!"
> and ordered an immediate retreat. . . . Mother sprang to her feet, and
> closed the front windows in an instant, where upon, dignified or not, we
> all evacuated the gallery, and fell back in the house. . . . Miriam and I flew
> up stairs—I confess I was mortified to death; very, very much ashamed.
> . . . O Yankees! Yankees! why do you do such a thoughtless thing! it will
> prevent us from ever indulging in moonlight singing again. Yet if we sing
> in the parlor, they always stop in front of the house to listen, while if we
> are on the balcony, they always have the delicacy to stop just above or
> below, concealed under the shadows. What's the difference? Must we give
> up music entirely, because some poor people debarred of female society
> by the state of affairs like to listen to old songs they may have heard their
> mothers sing when they were babies?[3]

That Sarah and Miriam were to blame for this indiscretion vividly demonstrates the important distinction between private and public performance. The
girls were not even seen, but that they were heard was enough to bring their
reputations into question. The correct place to have heard the sisters would
have been in the parlor, where the Yankee soldiers would never have been

invited. Mid-nineteenth-century social customs offered no other choices—no alternative interpretation to the girls' transgression existed. They had performed "in public," even though they were within their own home, because people on the street heard them. They might as well have been on-stage.

THE OPERA

Perhaps surprisingly, despite the acute differences between public and private performers and the extreme negative social implications of being a performer, many well-bred women did attend public music performances, especially the opera.[4] In fact, Chandler argues assiduously that it is desirable for young women to attend the opera, for here "The Belle of the Opera adds a cultivated taste for music—a taste which she indulges at the fountain-head of such enjoyments."[5] According to Chandler, if knowledge and understanding of music is suitable, attendance at the opera is the highest expression of suitability. Margaret Anna Burwell, who ran the well-known Burwell School in Hillsborough, sent her daughter, Fannie, to New York to study music, and in one letter she added this advice: "Go to musical concerts, even operas, and improve your musical tastes."[6] She confirms Chandler's opinion of the importance of some knowledge of the operatic repertory.

A young woman's familiarity with opera was expected by southern men. As members of both sexes traveled in the North, they seized on the opportunity to hear opera. The travelogue of James Johnston Pettigrew's European trip of 1850–51 includes numerous references to operas he attended while overseas. These included Carl Maria von Weber's *Der Freischütz* and *Oberon*; Friedrich von Flotow's *Martha*; Mozart's *Die Zauberflöte* and *Don Giovanni*; Rossini's *Il barbiere di Seville*; Vincenzo Bellini's *La sonnambula*; Beethoven's *Fidelio*; and Donizetti's *La fille du régiment*, among others. (He also heard frequent concerts, including the Beethoven symphonies and Haydn oratorios.)[7]

Appropriate behavior at such required musical events could be difficult to maintain because young men did not always act with appropriate decorum—a commonly repeated complaint regarding opera performances in the South.[8] Ellen Call Long commented on her experiences at the opera in New Orleans, noting that Sunday was the night the Creoles reserved for the opera. She did not believe the Creoles were as committed to the musical performance as to the social milieu, in which young men could call on young women in the boxes.[9]

Various opera companies performed with some regularity in cities and towns throughout the South. Perhaps the most extreme case is New Orleans, which at one point claimed more opera performances than New York City. A report in *Dwight's Journal of Music* in 1858 notes that the *New Orleans Daily Picayune* boasts that it "is the only American city in which opera may be called a fixed institution."[10] Within a period of three months, the following operas could be heard in that city: Rossini's *Mosè in Egitto*; Giacomo Meyerbeer's

Le prophéte, Les Huguenots, L'étoile de Nord, and *Robert le diable*; Giuseppe Verdi's *I Lombardi, Ernani*, and *Il Trovatore*; Fromental Halévy's *La Juive, Charles VI*, and *La reine de Chypre*; Adolphe Adam's *Si j'étais roi* and *Le chalet*; Albert Grisar's *Les Amours du diable*; Donizetti's *La favorita, Lucia di Lammermoor*, and *La fille du régiment*; Bellini's *Norma* and *La sonnambula*; Daniel Auber's *Les diamants de la couronne*; and others. Such an array certainly provided ample opportunities for young women to hear the latest American productions of European operas.

Most cities and towns of any size had a space to perform "opera" during the antebellum period—Mobile boasted seven such places before 1855.[11] Macon, Georgia, and Montgomery, Alabama, also hosted operatic troupes in the 1850s. Temperance Hall in Columbus, Georgia, saw several different Italian opera troupes in the 1840s and 1850s, including performances of works such as Verdi's *Ernani*.[12] In Nashville, a local paper could boast that the citizens of that city were loyal patrons of the opera in 1860. This remark followed performances by Teresa Parodi's Italian Opera Company that included *Ernani, Il Trovatore, Norma, La traviata, Lucrezia Borgia, The Barber of Seville*, and *Don Juan*.[13]

With its operatic traditions extending back into the eighteenth century, Charleston's musical life is well documented and provides a valuable example of what some young women might have experienced concerning both operas and concerts. In December 1839, English singer Jane Shirreff (along with the equally famous John Wilson) performed in ten opera performances there.[14] A playbill from one of these reveals that, in addition to Auber's *Fra Diavolo*, a farce ("Dumb Belle!") was also to be presented. The performance, in English, began at 7:00 P.M., with the most expensive seats going for one dollar per seat.[15]

The audiences for opera in New Orleans constituted a wider variety of people; the St. Charles Theatre reportedly included southern aristocracy, slaves and free blacks, foreigners, housewives, prostitutes, and so forth. In light of how protected southern belles and ladies were from the public, this interaction seems puzzling, yet undeniable.[16] Undoubtedly, each city and town had its own personality and customs, and a more urban environment like New Orleans certainly differed from a more isolated town such as Macon.

Most southern records describe either Italian or English troupes. English opera companies toured the South, performing both concerts and operas. Their repertory consisted mostly of operas that had been popular in the eighteenth and early nineteenth centuries, remaining fashionable in some areas until after midcentury. Works by such composers as Stephen Storace, Thomas Arne, and (later) Sir Henry Bishop included many relatively simple pieces that publishers released for performances by amateurs. In the 1840s, Edward and Anne (née Childe) Seguin were the most popular performers of English opera, and they visited Charleston on several occasions. In 1841, they sang in Richmond, Charleston, Augusta, Mobile, and New Orleans; the Seguins returned to the South frequently until their retirement in 1852.

Singers such as the Seguins attracted large crowds in New Orleans and Charleston. A contemporary newspaper account remarks that a performance in Charleston in 1843 included "the fashion and beauty of the city."[17] It is probably safe to assume that such an audience included the elite young belles and ladies with whom this study is concerned. They may even have seen themselves (or wished to be seen) as the "Belle of the Opera" that Chandler described. The Seguins' repeated performances in the relatively small towns of the South attest to the number of people who attended their concerts, since these events had to be financially viable.

Another connection between public music and southern women was in sheet music sales. Publishers were able to popularize songs by associating them with the Seguins. For example, in his Charleston music shop, John Siegling in 1844 sold "Ah! Bear Me to My Own Sweet Native Hamlet" ("Al dolce guidami") with the added inscription "Cavatina sung by Mrs. Seguin in the opera Anna Boleyn, Donizetti."[18] Katherine Preston notes that the persistence of these two singers as real "stars" helps to define the American opera experience of the 1840s—they were theater performers capable of reaching a broad audience while singing in the vernacular.[19] They also shaped the parlor repertory of the same period.

Italian opera troupes also toured the South during the antebellum period, and a genuine interest in opera sung in Italian began in the 1840s.[20] That same decade saw a dramatic increase in the popularity of Italian melody, as evinced in the works of Bellini and Donizetti in particular. English opera companies provided opera in Italian, but a new group of performers, Italian opera companies, came to the fore as well. The Astor Place Opera Company (from New York) presented in Richmond, Charleston, and Savannah in 1850–51, while the Arditi Italian Opera Company ventured as far as Richmond, Charleston, Savannah, Augusta, Mobile, Memphis, and Nashville (in addition to numerous other cities and towns west and north).[21]

The dominant styles of these operas—French grand opera and Italian bel canto—provided young women ample repertory that was suitable for the parlor, with the exception of the coloratura arias.[22] The adoption of bel canto opera as the mainstay of the theaters affected music in other areas, most significantly (for the purposes of this study) in the parlor. Earlier private collections, such as the collections belonging to Sarah Cunningham or Mary Stedman, contained sets of airs by Thomas Baily (Bayly) and Thomas Moore or Scotch-Irish melodies.[23]

The list of contents in Mary Stedman's vocal collection reflects the typical repertory of the earlier decades of this study.[24] Her book also demonstrates the popularity of various singers (see appendix, table 2). Such pieces as the

"Origin of the Harp, Canzonett sung by Mr. Wilson" (Thomas Moore); "The Lament of the Irish Emigrant" (William Dempster); and "The Rose of Cashmere, Sung by Mr. Wilson" (George Baker) were not part of bel canto operas. Only a few compositions, such as those from *Norma*, represent the Italian operatic repertory.

Slightly later, numerous bound collections attest to a new popularity of Italian opera among the young singers of the South. A collection associated with the female school at Barhamville also includes arias from Bellini's *La sonnambula* and *I Puritani* and Donizetti's *Lucrezia Borgia, Anna Bolena, La fille du régiment,* and *Linda di Chamounix.* Such choices are representative of southern repertory. Undoubtedly, the tuneful qualities of bel canto opera (characteristic in the operas of Bellini and Donizetti) made for their popular appeal. That the arias could be simplified and accompanied by an easy piano part also contributed to their attractiveness.

The bound collection of Mary Gibson clearly contrasts with the earlier one that belonged to Stedman. Roughly ten years later, Gibson's vocal book (she also had a piano collection) begins with Italian opera pieces. Gibson lived in Fort Smith, Arkansas—far removed from the busy musical world of New Orleans or Charleston—but she acquired the latest pieces in both of her music books. As in Stedman's collection, many works are connected with famous singers (see appendix, table 3).

Several works by composers whose last name is Glover appear in Mary Gibson's collection. The Glover family was an English one, with several composers among its members. Stephen was born in London in 1812, working there as a teacher and composer until his death in 1870. His older brother, Charles William (C. W.), worked as a composer in London theaters until his death 1863. Moreover, George Linley was a contemporary of the Glovers and worked in the same circles as C. W., as did Edward Lawrence Hime. The music by the English theater composers whose work appears in Gibson's book suggests familiarity with both the Italian and English musical theater.[25]

As the century wore on, tastes shifted more assuredly to Italian opera. The Astor Place Opera Company under the direction of Max Maretzek left an imprint on opera culture in the United States that extends in several directions. Preferring large cities to provincial towns, Maretzek appeared in Charleston because of its well-known musical culture, and his foray into Augusta was a trial run to a town not too far from Charleston.[26] Between 21 March and 9 April 1851, he brought eight different operas to Charleston, performing four of them twice.[27] Among the operas presented was Verdi's *Ernani,* which had premiered in 1847 in New York. This work, which was the composer's most popular opera throughout the 1850s, received performances on both 21 and 25 March in 1851, as well as another performance (on 14 April) in Augusta by the same company. Its popularity diminished in the 1860s, but its presence in Charleston and Augusta demonstrates that southern women had access to some of the most popular operas of the period.

Other operas included in Maretzek's 1851 Charleston tour included Donizetti's *La Favorita*, *Lucia di Lammermoor*, *Lucrezia Borgia*, and *Parisina*, Bellini's *Norma*, and Saverio Mercadante's *Giuramento*. Clearly, the stars of the 1830s and 1840s still reigned at this time, but the growing influence of Verdi is evident from the numerous performances of *Ernani*. Several critics disparaged Verdi's music for its virtuoso acrobatics, but audiences were steadfast in their admiration.

In an article from 1983, Julian Mates intriguingly asserts that the move from English opera to Italian in the United States was a conscious one toward "refinement" and "elegance," comparing such attributes as the farcical nature of English operas and the romantic, emotional, and dramatic character of the Italian ones.[28] Such a deliberate attempt at social improvement corresponds to the rise in the sentimental documented by Karen Halttunen. The type of musical entertainment one attended reflected one's status in society; Chandler notes that opera is the highest form of music: the opera is "a place of refined amusement, where the richest productions of musical science are properly delivered."[29] As such, opera was a necessary part of southern culture.

Contemporary reports of these performances are scant, but at least one visitor, Elizabeth West Nevins of Philadelphia, described opera attendance in Charleston while she traveled there in 1850. She notes that on the final evening of the Havana Company's stint in Charleston, the theater was "crowded from pit to dome"—quite an endorsement for opera in such a small city.[30]

Several southern women wrote about their experiences at the opera. In 1855, Mary Terhune attended her first opera, *Masaniello*, which featured the debut of singer Elise Hennsler.[31] She mentions some of the members of her party (Caroline Cheeseboro, Elizabeth Oakes Smith, and Samuel Griswold Goodrich—"Peter Parley"), and she was seated beside the kindly old gentleman. She comments that "he was social and amusing, and, withal, intelligently appreciative of the music and actors. He rattled away jovially in the *entr'actes* of other operas and personal traits of stage celebrities, theatrical, and operatic."[32] While Terhune does not remark much on the opera itself, the fact that she and her companion apparently talked through much of it may indicate typical behavior at the opera.[33] Indeed, one of the characteristics that Chandler appreciates in his "Belle of the Opera" is her attentiveness to the music—perhaps such attention to the performance was rare at this time.

When star singers were in town, southern women had the opportunity to hear them in concerts as well as in operas. Concerts were popular throughout the nineteenth century, although the repertory fluctuated tremendously depending on the performers (Italian opera singers or English songstresses), decade, and other variables. Early in the period in question, Scotch or Irish ballads were all the rage. The popular duo of Jane Shirreff and John Wilson included a number of such songs in their concerts of the 1830s, programming pieces like "My Boy Tammie," "The Bonnie Briar Bush," and "The Flowers of the Forest." These types of pieces appeared alongside scenes from operas and other popular pieces as well as "The Star-Spangled Banner," "The Marseillaise," and oratorio arias (such as those from Mendelssohn's *Elijah*).[34]

During the period that Maretzek's company was in Charleston in 1851, famous Italian soprano Teresa Parodi also performed in concert. Parodi returned to South Carolina the following year, for Gertrude Clanton Thomas writes that she was invited to "Mamselle Parodi's first concert." Thomas did not go, however, because the rain was falling too hard.[35] This remark contextualizes the professional singer in the southern belle's world—one of the most famous singers in the country at the time was giving a concert in Charleston, but rain prevented one of the wealthiest women in the state from attending.

When girls were away at school, their administrators might take them en masse to a concert. Such was the case of Madame Togno, who took her students to hear concerts in the 1850s. Elizabeth Waties Allston Pringle wrote later in life that Madame Togno took her students to attend concerts or plays, always placing the most beautiful girls at the front of the procession as they entered.

THE PUBLIC SINGER

Southern women also went to hear singers such as Anna Bishop—quite surprising, considering that Bishop abandoned her husband (composer Sir Henry Bishop) and toured Europe and America with her accompanist (famous harpist Nicholas Bochsa), the implication being that they lived together as man and wife, even though she had not divorced her husband. On the other hand, music with Anna Bishop's picture on the front can be found in numerous collections owned by southern women, which suggests that if they knew of her scandalous lifestyle, it did not keep them from purchasing music with her image on the front cover (figure 2.1). Nor apparently did it hinder their attendance at her concerts, which were particularly popular in Charleston.

Anna Rivière Bishop (1810–84) came to the United States in 1847. She arrived with Robert-Nicholas-Charles Bochsa (1789–1856), the man for whom she had left her husband and three children in 1839. He was also a convicted forger. Such presumably negative associations were hidden by Bishop's "fine form," which she covered in beautiful gowns and jewelry, and by a generally pleasing soprano voice. She toured the South, including stops in Charleston, Savannah, New Orleans, Columbus, and Mobile. These concerts drew large crowds. In Mobile, she sang *Norma* in Italian, and then *Linda di Chamounix* and *La sonnambula* in English. She sang the latter two operas in performance in Columbus, too, in 1852.[36] These works suggest that young women who attended such operatic performances would have heard a heavy dose of bel canto opera.

Fig. 2.1. Anna Bishop, portrait from "Anna Bishop's 'Polka Rondino.'"
Permission and image provided by The University of North Carolina Music Library, Chapel Hill.

A stint in Richmond by John Sefton's Grand Operatic Troupe during the early months of 1849 provided several options for musical entertainment. Nightly performances (except for Sundays) included the operas *La sonnambula*, *The Bohemian Girl*, *Elixir of Love*, *Fra Diavolo*, *Norma*, *Child of the Regiment*, *Cinderella*, and *Maritana!* Interspersed among these offerings were two benefits (Mr. Seguin and Mr. W. H. Reeves). Beginning on 5 March, Anna Bishop performed in *La Sfogato!*, *Buried Alive*, and a "grand vocal and instrumental music concert."[37]

The case of the prima donna Anna Hunt Thillon (1812–1903) raises further questions, for Thillon apparently did not sing that well but was able to compete favorably with Bishop in popularity. Auber reportedly wrote his *Crown Diamonds* (*Les diamants de la couronne*, an opera popular in New Orleans) for her. An English soprano who married her French voice teacher, Thillon's attraction was her great beauty; she was particularly admired by men. One contemporary remarked that "of course, nobody with ears sensitive to musical tones listens to Madam [Thillon] for the music that she affords. . . .

[O]ne looks at her as an uncommonly pretty woman, who addresses herself to the eye and taste of the auditor more than to the ear."[38] Such attraction must have sent messages to young women studying voice and reaffirmed the use of music as a way to catch a husband. It also could conversely warn women about the dangers of emulating professional singers on the stage, who obviously displayed themselves for others' viewing.

Not being beautiful was one of the attributes that endeared the enormously popular Jenny Lind to southern audiences. The illegitimate daughter of a Swedish schoolteacher, Lind toured the United States in the 1850s and was one of the most popular singers to appear in the United States at this time.[39] A writer in the *Nashville Daily Gazette* described her as "simple, chaste, and unaffected, with a face not handsome."[40] A number of extant copies of music associated with her demonstrate her popularity. That she was not simply beautiful to gaze upon might have been a particular draw for southern women.

The Barhamville collection mentioned above includes "My Home—Happy Home" as "sung by Jenny Lind" among its contents.[41] Her repertory exemplified the typical choices heard in concerts at that time. For example, among the works with her name included in some way is "Annie Laurie" arranged by Finlay Dun and published in New Orleans and Baltimore. In Philadelphia, Lee & Walker even published a set titled "Lindiana," songs sung by Jenny Lind arranged for piano with "brilliant variations" for the piano by Charles Grobe. These works exist in southern collections and testify to the popularity of Lind, but also to the importance of attaching a singer's name to music in order to sell it.

During the late 1850s, Ella Wren began a successful career as a singer, but she was not an "opera star." She remained in the South during the Civil War, touring with John Hill Hewitt at one point.[42] Hewitt arranged several pieces for Wren, including some from Michael William Balfe's very popular opera *The Bohemian Girl* (premiering in Drury Lane in 1843 and arriving in the United States the following year). Wren herself composed and published one work, "We Have Parted," in Columbia (and Richmond) in 1863. Whether or not this signifies an end to her work with Hewitt is unknown. Southern women apparently liked to own music sung by such women, presumably for their own use in the parlor.

OTHER PROFESSIONAL MUSICIANS

Other musical events provided opportunities for young women to hear a variety of genres. Some cities were large enough to have somewhat regular outdoor concerts during the warmer months. For example, Richmond's Capital Square had a series of outdoor band concerts beginning in June 1850.[43] Presumably, anyone out strolling in the evening would have heard these entertainments. Other examples include a concert of the Baton Rouge Sacred Music Society

at the Presbyterian Church (13 March 1845) and a "Grand concert at the chapel, by Centenary College Brass Band, under the direction of Prof.s: Kroll
& Hebestreet" (1855).[44]

Touring pianists and violinists also provided music for concerts. Almost
all of these performers were males.[45] In Nashville in 1853, violinist Ole Bull
and Adelina Patti (figure 2.2) presented a series of concerts under the direction of Maurice (Moritz) Strakosch. Bull was a well-traveled violinist from
Norway, but Patti was only ten years old at the time.[46] Pianists who visited
the region included Thalberg, who toured with violinist Henri Vieuxtemps.

Fig. 2.2. Adelina Patti at age sixteen. Used with permission of *Documenting the American
South*, The University of North Carolina at Chapel Hill Libraries.

In the late 1840s, Emelie Hammarskold performed in an operatic concert, Mr. Wilson sang "Songs of Scotland," Henri Herz and violinist Franz Coenan gave concerts, Madame Leati's (English) troupe performed *La sonnambula*, and Eliza Brienti sang in concert—all in Columbus, Georgia.[47]

Local professionals also performed in concerts throughout the South. Such public concerts took place in various southern cities and might include quite a variety of musical selections. The Sloman family put on concerts in Charleston, and Joseph Denck and his son advertised a concert for Winnsboro, South Carolina, in the 1860s.[48] Detailed reviews of two concerts in Louisville exist in anonymous reports in *Dwight's Journal of Music* of 1856. These describe several active music clubs in Louisville, including the Mozart Society, Orpheus, and a Liederkranz (German singing society). Of particular note is a new Louisville Musical Fund Society, whose debut program on 10 February 1856 was made up of the following pieces:

PART I

1. Overture—La Famille Suisse—Full Orchestra . . . Weigl
2. Aria—Ecco il Pegno—Gemma di Vergl . . . Donizetti Sung by L. C[orradi] Colliere
3. Sinfonia—Opus 10, in D (first movement, Minuetto & Trio) . . . Mozart
4. Trio—Ferma Crudele, from Ernani . . . Verdi Sung by Miss Scheidler, Messrs. Mason and Dolfinger
5. Sinfonia—Continuation of Opus 10 (Andante and Presto) . . . Mozart[49]
6. Polka—Najaden . . . Gung'l

PART II

1. Overture—Italiana in Algieri . . . Rossini
2. Scena—D'amor sull uli Rosee—from Il Trovatore . . . Verdi Sung by Miss Bertha Colliere and Mr. Dolfinger
3. Waltzes—Almack's . . . Lanner
4. Comic Scene—Two Beggars . . . Vogel Sung by Corradi Colliere
5. Overture—Tancredi . . . Rossini

The Collieres were apparently a local name, for an L. Corradi Colliere published "In Violata. (Popular Sacred Pieces, No. 5). Who Can Compare" in 1855 (printed in Cincinnati by W. C. Peters & Sons; Cleveland by Holbrook & Long; and Louisville by Peters, Webb & Co.). He also published "In Sunshine and in Shade" in Louisville (Tripp & Cragg) in 1859. L. Corradi Colliere also composed "The Dream of Home," published by D. P. Faulds (perhaps the most famous local music seller) in Louisville in 1859.[50] Colliere, a "noted French baritone," is associated with his performances in the Midwest, particularly Cincinnati.[51] His daughter also performed in the concert.

In April, the same society organized another concert with the same singers. It began with Mendelssohn's "Wedding March" from *A Midsummer Night's Dream* and included song selections by Bellini, Verdi (*Rigoletto* and *Il Trovatore*), and Donizetti, as well as a quartet by Beethoven performed by men only (a father and three sons), a set of variations performed on the "Bird Flageolet" by William Ratel, and several orchestral overtures and dances by Friedrich Heinrich Himmel, Joseph Kuffner, Ferdinando Paer, Joseph Lanner, and Josef Gung'l (by request—a repeat from the first concert).[52] While Ratel's performance apparently caused some laughter among the audience, his rendition pleased them so decidedly that he had to repeat it.[53] (Incidentally, Ratel was vice president of the society.) The anonymous reviewer notes that a grand piano would be better suited for the stage than a square one, which suggests that the concert arrangements in Louisville were not quite up to standards provided elsewhere.

The question of minstrel shows arises in any discussion of nineteenth-century music in the South. Little direct evidence survives to suggest whether or not southern women regularly attended such performances, but at least one female writer comments directly on the subject. In 1852, Gertrude Clanton Thomas attended a performance by the "Campbell minstrels," along with several family members. Thomas was adamant in her dislike of the performance, although she does not say why.[54] Other southerners would have had opportunities to hear such concerts. During the war, "Booker's Negro Minstrels," a group from Macon, performed at least two times in Milledgeville, Georgia. A writer in the local paper, the *Milledgeville Daily Federal*, favorably compared this group with "Yankee stragglers" who performed a similar repertory.[55]

Local amateur musicians might belong to various societies, which performed with some frequency, at least in some places. In Columbus, Georgia, the Orphean Amateur Society, a group of male and female amateurs, began presenting musical soirees in 1854. The same town also included a St. Cecelia Society Women's Chorus that was active in the same period.[56] The participants were probably not upper-class women.

Occasionally, elite young ladies themselves provided music for the public, but in guarded circumstances, almost always after 1861. The "Isabella Society" of the Atlanta Female Institute gave a concert to raise money for the "Library of the Society" in 1862.[57] That such a concert took place during the war years but did not occur as part of the war effort is unusual, except that the lack of funds for the library may have been a direct result of the war.

MUSIC AT CHURCH

Women also heard music in church, but what they heard in that particular venue diverged widely according to many variables. Religious preference greatly influenced the music a young woman might encounter in a sacred setting. In antebellum Richmond, Albert Stoutamire describes a "stark contrast" between Baptist church music (very little besides hymns) and that of the Episcopal church (which held concerts and had choirs and organs) and Presbyterians (who supported singing schools and amateur choral organizations).[58] Even in such a cosmopolitan area, records indicate that J. B. Jeter, pastor of the First Baptist Church (1836–49), opposed instruments in church, and some members of that congregation strongly objected to having a choir.[59] Public debate existed in local papers, and the Reverend Elias Lyman Magoon wrote an article entitled "The Religious Uses of Music" in the *Southern Literary Messenger* in support of instrumental music in church.[60] (Interestingly, references suggest that Felix Mendelssohn's uncle, Lewis Mendelssohn, was the organist at Christ Church Cathedral [Episcopal] in Raleigh around 1850.)[61]

Furthermore, service music at a large church in Charleston or New Orleans differed from that played in a small church in largely rural areas—if there were instruments at all. In more remote regions, only occasional services were available to congregants, removing any possibility of organized church music.[62] And the frequency and nature of church attendance among the upper class does not necessarily represent the experience of the general populace. A young woman living in Charleston presumably attended church regularly, whereas someone living in relative seclusion on a plantation did not. The latter's experience with religious music differed significantly, as discussed below. Convents, particularly in Louisiana (New Orleans), provided yet another variant to the "typical" context of church music.

The influence of foreign organists has yet to be measured, but they certainly must have affected what churchgoers heard on a somewhat regular basis. Foreign musicians were in great demand throughout the South as teachers and presumably supplemented their livings with church positions when possible. One such example is F. W. Rosier, who in 1844 became the organist at St. John's Episcopal Church in Richmond.[63] In taking the position at St. John's, Rosier replaced Edme E. Ulmo (organist since 1842, who published several pieces of music during the antebellum period). Born in England in 1808, Rosier was still living in the area (Henrico County) when the 1860 census was taken. At that time, Rosier appears as a "teacher" in the household of C. Griswold, lawyer (whose estimated worth was sixteen thousand dollars; others in the household included a doctor, wives, and several small children who were aged seven and under).

The Annals of Henrico Parish, Diocese of Virginia lists the organist in 1860 at St. John's as Andreas J. Gerhardt, who was married to Katherine F. Gerhardt in that year.[64] The 1860 Henrico County census contains an entry for a William Gebhardt, a "Professor of Music" (age thirty-three) from Bavaria, who was married to "Cath. Gerhardt." These may be the same person, for no one by the organist's name shows up in the census of 1860. If so, by the end of the antebellum period, the organist at St. John's was Bavarian, not English, but still foreign. St. Peter's Catholic Church had as its organist "Mr. Daniell" from the Royal Academy of Music in London.

Women Organists

Not all church musicians were male. In June 1835, Miss Sarah Sully was appointed organist at St. John's Episcopal Church in Richmond, with a salary of $100 a year.[65] Mrs. Gaynor, formerly Miss Picot, was the first organist at St. Peter's Catholic Church when the organ was dedicated in 1834.[66] A photograph of Mrs. Aglia Garraur (Picot) Gaynor, who was born in 1814, survives in the Virginia Historical Society's collection.[67] However, as noted above, Mr. Daniell later served as organist at St. Peter's. In any case, neither Miss Sully nor Mrs. Gaynor was of the elite class.

Indeed, Sarah Sully belonged to a segment of society in which a few women did work for a living, in this case that of the professional musician. She was, in fact, the daughter of a theater performer who sang novelty and comic songs in the New Theatre in Richmond sometime before it burned in 1811.[68] Her mother, "Mrs. Sully," advertised a concert in 1803 in which she would be accompanied by "several Gentleman Amateurs of Richmond"; she had given her first concert in the city in 1792.[69] Mrs. Sully later (in the 1820s) led concerts that included music by Haydn, Rossini, and Mozart as well as popular melodies of the period. In at least one of these, Mrs. Sully played the piano and "Miss Sully" the harp. Additionally, a "Mr. Sully" played the flute. It seems, therefore, that the Sully family was one of musicians, certainly not one of elite status.

Sarah Sully's first public performance was reportedly in a ballad concert in 1819, in which her mother accompanied Mrs. French; Sarah also accompanied on the harp.[70] Miss Sully's name appears on numerous programs for mostly sacred concerts in Richmond in succeeding years. Most of these were organized by the Richmond Sacred Music Society, which produced "oratorios" that consisted of an amalgamation of several works by composers such as Handel, Beethoven, Mozart, Haydn, Rossini, and so forth.[71] The elite women of Richmond may have undoubtedly heard Sarah Sully perform in various capacities, but she would not have been a member of their social circle, nor would they have aspired to follow her footsteps into a musical career.

Eliza ("Lizzie") Adam Jones (1839–1911) was another woman who is remembered primarily as a church musician. The daughter of a local doctor, Lizzie attended the Burwell School in Hillsborough in the early 1850s. She traveled to New York to study music specifically in 1855–56 but returned to Hillsborough in February 1856. She later became the organist at St. Matthew's Episcopal Church, and in a centennial celebration in 1924, her contributions to the music of that church were highlighted.[72] Lizzie Jones, as she was called, never married.

Church Choirs

While choirs in most churches included both male and female singers, it is doubtful that elite women participated. A letter written in 1855 to Mrs. Richard H. "Sallie" Anderson (née Gibson, wife of a Confederate general) suggests that once women reached a certain social status, they did not sing in the church choir. The incident concerns a visit to Charleston, where the author learned that Fannie Waties (d. 1871) "has married extremely well, the family is highly respectable," so Fannie "has quit the choir!" The choir apparently would not fade away as a result of Fannie's departure, since "Mrs. Carson sings and Mr. Roberts' sister, too, plays and sings very well, church music." The author of the letter further relates that Fannie had gone to the Smithsonian Institute for "an education," perhaps another way to help establish her newly acquired social status.[73]

In the experience of Mary Terhune, religious music figured more prominently than appears in other records. Living near Richmond certainly afforded her the opportunity to experience church music more regularly, and her family's religious habits—staunchly Presbyterian—also influenced what Terhune heard. In her autobiography, she comments that her church had "an admirably trained choir" that "rendered sacred music—such grand old anthems as, 'Awake! awake! put on thy strength, O Zion!'"[74]

Terhune also attended church and oratorio society concerts and occasionally had reason to attend rehearsals. In the same year as her first opera (1855), Terhune went to a full rehearsal for a "grand concert" that featured singer George Root.[75] She continues: "Near the close of the rehearsal, Mr. Root came down to the back of the house and dropped into a seat by me, among the auditors and lookers-on. He was tired, he explained, 'and would loaf for the rest of the affair.' The 'affair' wound up with Handel's Hallelujah Chorus. My 'loafing' neighbor pricked up his ears, as the warhorse at sound of the trumpet; sat upright and poured the might of heart and voice into the immortal *opus*. With the precision of a metronome, and the fire of a seraph, he went through it, from the first to the last note, with never a book or score. It was more to us, who had the good fortune to be near him, than all the rest of the performance."[76]

Terhune was not one of the singers, although she sang regularly at home. Her family entertained the professional musician, Root, when he was in town, but as a young southern woman from the upper class, she did not participate in such public performances.

Terhune also describes music at the "African Church," which she apparently heard at funerals and other times. This Richmond establishment was famous for its music, and the first few pews were reserved for white people who came to hear it. Terhune writes that often it was difficult to get a seat at their services. She states that the choir of the "Old African" was one of the shows of the city. Few members of it could read the words of the hymns and anthems. Every one of them could read the notes, and follow them aright. The parts were well balanced and well-sustained. Those who have heard the Fisk University Jubilee singers do not need the assurance that the quality of the negro voice is rarely sweet and rich, and that, as a race, they have a passion for music. Visitors from Northern cities who spent the Sabbath in Richmond seldom failed to hear the famed choir of the Old African. On this afternoon, the then popular and always beautiful *Jerusalem, My Happy Home*, was rendered with exquisite skill and feeling. George F. Root, who heard the choir more than once while he was our guest, could not say enough of the beauty of this anthem-hymn as given by the colored band. He declared that one soloist had "the finest natural tenor he ever heard."[77]

Terhune appreciated the differences between European-based music and the more traditional African singing style. She noted that the choir members of the "African church" "were not the representative singers of the race." Seeing through the style known as "Ethiopian music," she states that "still less should airs, composed by white musicians and sung all over the country as 'negro melodies,' pass as characteristic. They are the white man's conception of what the expatriated tribes should think and feel and sing." Her association with more authentically African music came from a public funeral procession, which she describes:

Our little party of American travellers drew back against the wall of the reputed "house of Simon the Tanner" in Jaffa (the ancient Joppa), to let a funeral procession pass. The dead man, borne without a coffin, upon the shoulders of four gigantic Nubians, was of their race. Two-thirds of the crowd, that trudged, barefooted through the muddy streets behind the bier, were of the same nationality. And as they plodded through the mire, they chanted the identical "wild, wailing measure" familiar to me from my infancy, which was sung that Sunday afternoon to the words "We'll pass over Jordan"—even to the oft-iterated refrain, "Honor, my chillun, honor de Lamb!" . . . The gutterals [*sic*] of the outlandish tongue were all that was unlike. The air was precisely the same, and the time and intonations.[78]

Thus, not only did Terhune hear a variety of music, but she had a more-than-casual opinion on styles and customs. Being a writer herself, she listened critically and evaluated music in its cultural milieu, as well as its aesthetic qualities. What her contemporaries thought about her conclusions is unknown.

Terhune's autobiography also includes a few pages devoted to a "flourishing" Sacred Music Society that was composed "principally" of amateurs. Terhune and her father, sister, and brother were all members. In December

1855, this group had engaged Lowell Mason and George Root to conduct a musical convention in Richmond whose aim was to improve "public taste in the matter of choir and congregational singing."[79] Preparation for a completely amateur "Grand Concert" (at the conclusion of the "Conference") included classes for "the study of methods and for drill in vocalization."[80]

Other towns and cities had concerts of sacred music that were sometimes performed in churches or other venues. Charleston saw a good many such performances throughout the nineteenth century. Among the favorite pieces were Handel's *Messiah* and selections from other oratorios by Handel and Haydn and mass movements by Mozart. Later in the century, Rossini's *Stabat Mater* also formed part of the regular repertory.[81]

Southern elite women usually had the opportunity to hear a variety of music in public performances. For planters' wives, these experiences most often occurred when they traveled or spent time in a more urban environment. For those who lived in urban areas, concerts were a regular part of their experience. A sharply drawn line kept these women from performing for others, and if an upper-class young lady appeared on the stage for some reason, her name was not included in the program. That the term "public women" referred to prostitutes further supports the conclusion that "public" was not a word to be used in connection with "lady."[82] This distinction was maintained throughout the antebellum period, until the Civil War brought into use the phrase "public-*spirited* ladies."

3. Music at Home: Entertainment and Education

... sitting on the balcony singing in the moonlight or dancing in the parlor! That was real pleasure.

—SARAH MORGAN DAWSON, *A CONFEDERATE GIRL'S DIARY*, 9 JULY 1862

Without a doubt, the majority of music that southern girls experienced was in the home. The grander events, such as balls and concerts, are frequently mentioned in diaries, but these did not occur on a daily basis. More common were the casual visits that southerners (especially women) saw as their social duty. As such, instead of dancing to orchestras at balls, upper-class girls played the piano, guitar, or harp or sang most days of their teen years. They may have simply been practicing, or they may have been entertaining company (often unannounced). In these instances, the girls themselves were the performers, whereas when they were in a public venue, such as the opera, they did not perform. That is, they were the performers, but they were not performers. They may have been playing or singing in the parlor of a friend's home, but it was not a public performance. Even school performances were not public; rather, they functioned as a pedagogical tool in instructing young women how to behave in the parlor.

PLAYING FOR COMPANY

Music at home took place in both the parlor and private (bedroom) areas. Parlor performances ranged from impromptu gatherings and social calls to organized musicales and *tableaux vivants*. Numerous references to the former help to establish that such a musical gathering was normal and expected. For example, Mary Terhune mentions musicales and *tableaux* in Virginia during her youth, especially during the holidays.[1] All attendees were expected to be able to take part, but no one was to monopolize the "stage." Southerners also participated in what was called a "Molasses Stew," a pastiche of performances.[2] Since it was not a stage, performers were not intended to be seen as performers. But they all were expected to perform.

When one was asked to perform in the parlor, etiquette manuals and similar volumes unanimously indicate that one should do so, and do so immediately upon the asking. To feign some reason for not playing or singing was considered impolite and coy to the point of bad taste. Apparently, however, it was a constant issue. In an 1852 essay titled "Hints to Young Ladies on Manners," Rev. J. M'D. Mathews noted that "there is one point of good manners which few school-girls seem properly to understand. When they can sing or play on the piano, they almost invariably refuse if requested to do so. This is rude. However indifferent your music, you should comply at least once, to show your disposition to gratify the company; then if you are hoarse or otherwise unprepared to perform, you can beg to be excused. To refuse when you might sing or play is mere affectation. On the other hand, it is impolite to insist strongly on any one's singing or playing. If their sense of good-breeding will not induce them to do so when politely requested, the matter should not be pressed."[3] These guidelines indicate that girls were to play and confirm that the reason to perform was to please others ("to gratify the company"). These young women found their place and usefulness in antebellum southern society in providing pleasant and enjoyable times for their families and associates.

Diarist Sarah Morgan wrote about several different types of situations in which music occurred at home, in both the semipublic space of the parlor and the private spaces in the other parts of the house. The most frequently mentioned way young women performed or heard others perform was in the parlor, where either dancing or singing/playing for those in attendance occurred. Dancing seems to have been an especially common activity. This may have been due to the fact that in the parlor, young women were allowed a bit more flexibility, compared to more public venues, in what they could or could not do. This was an extension of the public/private divide. Young elite women did not sing in public performances, but they were expected to do so in the parlor. Any activity that was at all questionable was not tolerated in public but might be allowed in the home. For example, female members of the Petigru family were not permitted to dance the polka at balls, but they clearly did so at home.[4]

Similarly, the waltz had been viewed suspiciously since its inception, because it was one of the first European dances in which the partners held each other in close proximity. Author Maria MacIntosh, a self-described "daughter of the South," conspicuously makes it clear in her 1846 novel *Two Lives; or To Seem and To Be* that girls who waltz are of a bad sort. She uses it to distinguish between two southern girls. One is Grace, who waltzes, adopts northern values, and has an illegitimate child by a Frenchman—quite disastrous behavior. The other is Isabel, who does not waltz and is the ultimate heroine of the novel.[5]

Even though they were not approved for formal occasions, waltzes were, nonetheless, danced at home. Sarah Morgan learned to waltz in 1860, notably at home. While fleeing Yankees in 1862, she nostalgically paints an idyllic picture of an evening in August 1860 at Linwood Plantation, where her family had lived during part of the year. She notes that everyone was dancing to tunes from the fingers of either Lydia or Helen Carter, and their performances "would have made a puritan dance." At one of these occasions, two male acquaintances (Howell Morgan and Will Carter) taught her to waltz. But once she learned the waltz, she mentions dancing it only at home.

Such dancing would have occurred to piano accompaniment. Without a doubt, elite southerners expected that those who entertained them would have a piano available and that it would be in the parlor. The case of Ebenezer Pettigrew illustrates the extent to which fathers, even widowers, went to make sure that their homes included the proper instrument. He had inherited Bonarva Plantation on Lake Phelps in Tyrrell County, North Carolina, in 1833. His wife, Ann (also called Nancy), had died giving birth to Ann Blount Shepard Pettigrew in 1830, and Ebenezer relied on his in-laws for assistance in raising his family, particularly his daughters. His wife's brother-in-law, James L. Bryan, wrote to Ebenezer in November 1843 that his wife would be happy to assist Ebenezer in the purchase of a "Piano Forte" when he wanted one. Interestingly, this man of the world, who managed a large property and other business interests, could not buy a piano on his own. With the shopping assistance of his sister-in-law, the piano arrived on 27 December of that year via steamer from Washington, D.C.[6] With a piano in the parlor at Bonarva, Ebenezer Pettigrew could be certain that his daughters were properly equipped to entertain their social equals in the expected fashion.

Parlor performances occurred at any time during the day—they were not limited to evenings. In her references to antebellum experiences at Linwood, Sarah Morgan comments that "we danced at all times . . . morning, noon, and night, just as we pleased." They also spent time "sitting on the balcony singing in the moonlight or dancing in the parlor!"[7] Modern television and movie scenes have given the impression that such performances were in the evening after dinner, but the primary evidence suggests otherwise. Young elite southerners played or sang music at various times throughout the day.

The North-Petigrus of South Carolina certainly entertained at all hours of the day. In the following description, Jane Caroline North (familiarly called "Carey," daughter of Jane Gibert Pettigrew North) relates a morning event while visiting at Hot Springs on Friday, 5 September 1851. Her testimony illustrates a typical, if comical, performance situation that occurred early in the day. A married woman (Mrs. Vanderhorst) first provided the music for dancing. She failed to keep a regular pulse, however, which hindered the dancing. As a result, the diarist stepped in to assist the matron. They played in mixed company, and Carey assisted a man (Mr. Elliott) in dancing lessons. That a young lady would teach a married man anything seems remarkable, but the fact that such an occurrence took place in the home assists in excusing this reversal of tradition. Carey then sight-read some music and finally accompanied herself while singing. The hostess joined in the song, much to the humor of those in attendance:

> Emily Elliott asked me to Polka with her, Mrs Vanderhorst played for us & a funny morning we had. Mr Elliott & his daughter Caroline who has been indisposed since their arrival were here at first the only persons present & Mr E took lessons in the schottisch[e] from me as Mrs V. played rather irregularly. I played the tune that she might get the time. Mrs Van went into extacies [sic], pronounced my touch & time perfect. After playing some dances for the Elliotts to practice by I tried at her request some of her music, among others "Sleeping I dreamed of Love," she urged me to sing, refusing was of no avail, the old Piano dreadful, but getting desperate I began (not being much in awe of my judges) what was my consternation when Mrs Van piped up too! Words cannot describe our duet at the end of the first verse Mr Elliott snatched up his hat & rushed from the room. I was suffocating with laughter. [Carey later played polkas and schottisches.] [8]

The piece Carey played is shown in figure 3.1. Numerous versions of the melody, which was arranged for piano and guitar, with variations, attest to its continued popularity throughout the mid-nineteenth century.

These gatherings, whether for dancing or not, could include mixed company, as several other entries from Carey's diary reveal. For example, she writes that on Saturday, 20 September 1851, "I played a good deal tonight. Mr Gordon expressed himself as very much indebted."[9] Rarely was the music limited to a single type of performance; instead, it usually included singing, dancing, and piano solos, as the following excerpt from her diary details: "Mrs Laurence played for us tonight & I danced the Polka & Schottisch[e] with Willie Calhoun & waltzed with Uncle Henry, Mr Gordon & Gourdin. . . . Mr Gordon sang for us extremely well".[10] Again, the two dances she was forbidden to participate in at balls, polkas and waltzes, were danced at home as if it were perfectly acceptable.

That men also performed on musical instruments is clear from contemporary accounts. Sarah Morgan recalls an occasion in 1862 when "Will played so beautifully on the violin."[11] Similarly, Mary Pettigrew intended that her brother should also learn to play the violin and that all of her family should be able to play a musical instrument.[12] These references are not as frequent as those in which women perform musically, but they occur with enough regularity to suggest that many southern men were competent musicians.

MUSIC AND MEN

Some parlor performances were large gatherings, others more intimate. While the problem of performing too well is explored elsewhere in this book, there

Fig. 3.1. "Sleeping I Dream'd, Love," by William Vincent Wallace, page 1. Library of Congress.

were other potential risks. Young people had to be watched carefully when performing together in the parlor for numerous reasons. A warning on the dangers of duets between members of both sexes is found in "Julia Grandon: A Coquet's Story," in an 1851 issue of *Graham's*. The episode is worth reprinting in its entirety, for it describes musical performances at home and how they might occur. Of all the possible combinations, the author singles out the piano duet as the most problematic because the physical nearness of the participants allowed them freedom that would not have been permitted under other conditions.

For many weeks after this, Frank Bellingham was a frequent visitor at the residence of Julia. The musical parties that were frequently occurring, gave the pretext for visits that finally became almost daily. Hour after hour did they spend by the piano, practicing the pieces for the next *soirée*. Vocal duets or those for the piano or harp and flute, absorbed much time. Though the ostensible offerings was [*sic*] Apollo and Euterpe, Cupid, by stealth, obtained the large share of the gift. The numerous intervals, the preparations were too propitious not to be improved.

Of all dangerous situations for any one, far more so for the susceptible, is the place at the piano. There is a communion of sentiment established immediately. The voices are striving for harmony and blending together in unison. The same air is respired by each, and in its passage seems laden with contagion. The accidental and occasional touch of the body, or the intermingling of fingers as they meet upon the keys, are as noticeable in their results as if they were the poles of an electrical battery.[13]

Such prospective treachery in piano playing must have caught the attention of readers and may have provided more reason for chaperoning young women. The flute would have been played by Frank, not Julia, but clearly the most problematical pairing was the piano duet. The physical proximity of the performers transgressed the boundaries of proper behavior and ran the risk of labeling the female participant a "coquette" (as Julia is described in the title of the story).

Another story from *Graham's* yields other clues as to the dangers young women might face when music and men combined. In "Clara Gregory," a man named "Don Whiskerando" (a reference to Don Giovanni, or simply a dangerous foreign man who happens to be a musician?) plays the flute and accompanies the protagonist, Clara Gregory, one evening in song. No one seems to really know who this man is, but Clara is smitten with him. Despite several warnings from various parties to avoid him, Clara elopes with Don Whiskerando. As they arrive at the hotel where they are to spend their first night together, his first wife—from whom he is not divorced—confronts Clara before it is too late. The first wife tells Clara the truth about the amoral Whiskerando, and Clara leaves immediately.[14] The moral is to not trust the mustachioed flutist who is so dashing but about whom one knows nothing. It is unknown if the author intended to shed further light on the man's character by associating him with the flute, but it is not the instrument of choice for most parlor scenes—two references in *Graham's* (Frank and Don Whiskerando) are proof enough of that.[15]

While most diarists refer to music in the parlor as somewhat spontaneous and on occasion almost silly, sometimes the parlor performance milieu was more formal. In her memoirs, Mrs. St. Julien [Harriet Horry] Ravenel describes a typical evening of the socially elite in Charleston before the war as a perfectly natural, easy, and entertaining experience. The group would usually assemble around 8:00 for tea, which was followed by "talk, music, games, perhaps a little dance—ice cream and cake, a glass of wine for the men, lemonade for the ladies, and by twelve every one at home again;—no trouble, no display, no *gêne*!" Ravenel thought it important to note that no one displayed a virtuoso talent, a decided musical genius. Ravenel's work is largely a tribute to "the good old days," however, and she reports only how things *should* have been. To take one issue, antebellum diaries suggest that dancing was commonplace, whereas Ravenel reports "perhaps a little dance." Music, however, is present in most accounts, regardless of the writer's intentions.[16]

Ravenel also paints an interesting description of Mrs. Holland, an English-woman in somewhat reduced financial circumstances but nonetheless upper-class. Ravenel notes that she was in "middle life" and beautiful. Although Mrs. Holland "dressed a little oddly (always in white)," she effectively remained the most popular hostess in Charleston. Mrs. Holland did not own a large house but rather rented two small rooms in the home of a friend. Despite this situation, one of the rooms became "her *salon*." She had a "delightful voice" for singing and speaking and played guitar while singing in Italian, English, or Greek.[17] This widow, whose fortune might not run along the lines of Ravenel's other acquaintances, maintained her position in society through her proper use of the parlor, including her abilities to make music.

RELIGIOUS MUSIC AT HOME

Religious music also falls within the purview of the home, especially on isolated plantations. In her autobiography, Elizabeth Waties Allston Pringle describes how women on plantations might experience religious music in an informal setting that took the place of the organized church. Writing about an event in 1903, her account probably nonetheless reflects an older practice. She notes that the rector came for a service, and in the evening, between 8 and 10 o'clock, all of the neighbors assembled for sacred music. Unfortunately, Pringle does not say whether or not she herself participated in these gather-ings. She does muse that it pleases her to see all of these people enjoying "this very simple way of passing the evening," which suggests that she may have been more of an onlooker than a participant.[18] The social aspect of the music seems to have been more important than its religious meaning.

For some young women, religious music formed a regular part of their repertory, and in her recollections, Mary Terhune provides an extensive ac-count of religious music at home. Even though someone in Terhune's social position did not perform in the church choir, she did sing hymns with her family and close friends at home.[19] Her account of religious musical experi-ences before marriage is quite illuminating and detailed. Her father led the family (and others) in singing lessons, the purpose of which was to better sing religious music: "Once a week we had a singing-class which met around our dining-table. My father led this, giving the key with his tuning-fork, and now and then accompanying with his flute a hymn in which his tenor was not needed."[20]

These events were filled with members from Terhune's social circle, which she boasts included some of the "first families" of the state.[21] Sacred music as a concert event was popular in Richmond at this time, and "a singing-master, the leader of a Richmond choir," had run a school at the Court House during the previous winter. Terhune notes that, as part of their instruction, "*The Boston Academy* was in every house in the village."[22] This was probably *The Boston Academy's Collection of Church Music*, published in 1836 by Lowell Mason. Mason was one of the most popular of the American hymnodists, and his pieces still appear in several Protestant hymnals. Its basic instruction is in singing intervals, and it progresses to the four-part hymns that are typical in other American hymnbooks of the period.

The Terhune "musicales" hosted a group of regular attendees from a variety of backgrounds. She notes in later years that "I could run glibly over the names of the regular attendants on the Tuesday evenings devoted to our *musicale*." Among the singers was George Moody (seventeen years old), her father's ward, who was attracted to another singer, "Effie D., my especial crony." Her father's business partner, Thaddeus Ivey, and a clerk in the employ of Hawes & Ivey, James Ivey (notably unmarried and apparently unattached), rounded out the bass section with George Moody. Occasionally, "Cousin Joe" joined them.[23]

Terhune alludes to five sopranos, whose part was called "treble" rather than soprano, and two "second trebles." Her father and a "weak-voiced neighbor" sang tenor. These musicales took place before the singing teacher became commonplace ("until a year or two before the singing-master invaded the country")—a time when "women sang tenor, and the alto was known as 'counter.'"[24] Voice teachers were definitely available in Virginia long before the middle of the nineteenth century, but Terhune's description alludes to a time when a less-studied amateurism was the sort of music that proper gentle-people participated in, not the more specialized performances bemoaned by James Huneker in 1904.[25] Writing several decades later, Terhune remembers some of the hymn tunes that the group sang, "including familiar ones, such as 'Lanesboro' and 'Cambridge' and 'Hebron' and 'Boyleston' and 'Zion,' and new ones, such as 'Yarmouth,' 'Anvern,' and 'Zerah.'" They sang from *The Boston Academy*, sometimes without enough energy, according to her father. He reminded them to "Sing *at* it!," admonishing those in the group that they would never learn to sing if they did not try more wholeheartedly.[26]

MUSIC IN THE PRIVATE AREAS

While most discussion of music at home describes experiences in the semi-public area of the home—the parlor—music also took place in the private areas. In particular, Sarah Morgan mentions several different instances in which she and her friends or family played music. Of particular note is the fact that she often played the guitar in her room while others were present. Such a space is distinctly different from the parlor, and different rules apply. The performances that Sarah describes are much more impromptu, relaxed, and casual than when young women played or sang in the parlor. No one was obligated to listen, and no one was compelled to play in any particular manner.

Sarah notes, for example, that she played the guitar while Anna and Miriam sat on the bed playing cards.[27] More than likely, this is a case where Sarah was playing for Sarah, not for the others. At a later time, she notes that because Anna gossiped so negatively (and consistently) about her sister Miriam ("downright falsehoods"), she (Sarah) played the guitar loudly simply to keep from hearing Anna.[28]

Such use of music as a diversion is rare in southern diaries—more typical is the use of music to entertain and please others. This is not to say that southern women did not take pleasure in the parlor dances and other musicales in which they participated. Most accounts suggest that they enjoyed them immensely. But their pleasure is almost always tempered by admonitions (usually by a parent) to practice their music more diligently in order to please someone else. Sarah Morgan presents us with the rarely stated possibility of another purpose—personal use.

Sarah also describes a religious musical experience in which the "servants" (most southerners typically did not use the word "slave") in the household participated in her bedroom—a private space.[29] In describing a typical summer day in 1862, Sarah depicts evening religious observances in her quarters. She reports that she usually held a Bible class at 10:00 P.M. in her room for the "servants," and in this environment, she attempted to bring harmony to any discord among them. On this particular occasion, she notes that two women were having a serious dispute about something that happened earlier in the day. Once all of the disagreements were mended, singing commenced. Sarah lists some of the pieces they might sing, saying that "sometimes Lucy sings a wild hymn 'Did you ever hear the heaven bells ring,' 'Come my loving brothers,' 'When I put on my starry crown,'" and such.[30] Clearly, Sarah heard spirituals—"wild hymns"—and it would seem likely that many other women in her position did as well.[31]

Other mentions of music occur frequently during Sarah's account of running from the Yankees as they headed through her native Louisiana. These were necessarily spontaneous and figure as private music, even though they were not performed within the house itself. One illuminating example occurred as the family fled their plantation, leaving (she repeatedly bemoans) their piano. She notes that they "sang 'rough impromptus'" while riding in a cart away from a Yankee advance on Baton Rouge.[32] Indeed, several accounts by other authors mention singing as a means of distracting themselves during the war.

MUSIC LESSONS AT HOME

Music instruction was another way music was heard in southern homes. Early in their lives, many girls undoubtedly heard music performed by their mothers, for the expectation that the wife should provide such entertainment when the husband was home in the evenings surely did not disappear immediately once children arrived. As families grew, though, it seems to be the case that the offspring took over this duty, along with friends and visiting relatives. Similarly, mothers and relatives often were the initial teachers of music to the children, as in the case of Emily Rowena Bell (1846–1913) of Plymouth, North Carolina. Even though the Bell family hired an "academic tutor" to live with them, Emily studied piano with her mother. (She later attended the Burwell School in Hillsborough.)[33]

While most wealthy southerners of the mid-nineteenth century believed that their daughters should eventually be sent to school, the decision of when to begin their education before that time and under whom was far less uniform. While some fathers placed a high value on a thorough education, even to the point of undertaking some of the work themselves, some stood on the other end of the spectrum and hardly paid any attention.[34] Most girls' experience probably lay in between these two extremes.

Because so many of their letters and other documents have survived, the extended members of the Petigru family of South Carolina make for excellent case studies of music education at home. In this family, aunts, sisters, and cousins customarily provided the initial lessons in a variety of subjects, including reading, writing, arithmetic, history, geography, French, and music.[35] Some members of that family approached the early education of their daughters with some informality, while others demanded a strict schedule and high degrees of accomplishment. The North Carolina branch of this family (who kept the spelling "Pettigrew") left valuable correspondence as well, particularly concerning the education of both the girls (in Washington, D.C., and at Saint Mary's, Raleigh) and boys (Bingham School in Hillsborough and the University of North Carolina at Chapel Hill). Their experiences also represent the place of education in the antebellum household—a wide variety may be found throughout extant descriptions, even among members of the same extended family.

The case of Jane Gibert Pettigrew North (1800–1863) and her daughters illustrates how an industrious pursuit of musical education might occur during this period.[36] The plantation where Jane spent most of her time was Badwell, not far from Abbeville, South Carolina. The estate's location, in the southwestern part of a state where most "society" remained in the east, resulted in more impediments for the women there than had they lived nearer the coast.[37] At Badwell, Jane North went so far as to build a small schoolhouse where her children could be schooled, as could the cousins who might be visiting at any given time. She seems to have focused primarily on reading, language, and music. Jane eventually realized that she could not maintain the position of schoolmistress herself and hired Mary Ayme to teach her younger daughters, Mary Charlotte and Louise Gibert, at the Badwell schoolhouse. Ayme was an English governess who had been recently employed by Ann Petigru for the education of her children. She was not popular with the North family, but she lived with them at Badwell while teaching their children.

Apparently, Miss Ayme was effective enough to be subsequently engaged by another branch of the family, the Allstons, in 1851. Jane North had convinced her younger sister Adèle Allston that she should hire Mary Ayme; despite the difficulties she might have had with her socially, Jane felt that the superior quality of Ayme's tutoring outweighed all other issues. Thus, after some initial waffling on the subject, Ayme was engaged to come to the Allston plantation, Chicora Wood, where she remained for two years. Chicora Wood, which still stands, is not far from Pawley's Island but noticeably far from Badwell Plantation. (The English governess may have felt lucky to be moved from such an outlying area as Jane North's house.)

Adèle recognized the positive aspects of Ayme's teaching (her subjects included "all the branches of an English education," among them music, French, Italian, drawing, and rudimentary Latin), but the negative aspects that Jane North saw in Ayme persisted at Chicora Wood.[38] Among her disreputable traits, Ayme insisted on having a place at the family dinner table and in the drawing room. These actions did not sit well with the Allstons, who were not altogether displeased to see Ayme leave after two years. Ayme represented what must have been a conundrum for young women learning how to be ladies. She clearly had attributes that they needed, music among them, but she was not their social equal. That Ayme insisted on breaking the rules of how various classes interacted must have caused some consternation for the elite Allstons.

Before Mary Ayme came to Chicora Wood, the Allstons had engaged another woman, Miss Wells, to tutor their oldest daughter, Della (Adele). Wells arrived in 1850, when Della was ten. She reportedly stiffened the curriculum for Della—which implies that one was already in place—to include French, music, drawing, grammar, geography, and writing. The schedule set for Della provides insight into expectations in the Allston family: piano practice from 9:00 to 10:00 A.M., followed by two hours in the schoolroom before dinner, then dinner, another hour in the schoolroom, drawing lessons, and a final session in the schoolroom before her instructional day ended at 5:30 P.M.

Clearly, outside women were brought in to teach the young members of the extended Petigru family. But when Miss Wells left Della Allston abruptly in 1850, a family member stepped in to assist. While the Allstons spent that summer and early fall on Pawley's Island, their cousin Carey North (Jane's oldest daughter, twenty-two at this time) arrived to instruct the young Allstons in music and French. When this sojourn ended, Della accompanied Carey back to Badwell for further training. Carey's program, however, proved too taxing for Della, who rebelled, and Carey writes that both women learned lessons about moderation from this experience.[39]

The case of the extended Petigru family demonstrates that young girls received music lessons at home from various types of teachers. Mothers were often the first instructors, but governesses were also brought in to take over such duties. When necessary, relatives performed as music teachers. In all of the Petigru cases, the home music teacher was female. Such was not always the case, as examples presented below clearly involve male teachers.

The daughters of Ebenezer Pettigrew, a cousin of the aforementioned Petigrus, also studied music. The eldest, Mary, seems to have been particularly gifted musically. Their mother, Ann Blount Shepard, died in 1830, and Ebenezer later sent the girls to schools in New Bern, Hillsborough, and Raleigh, as well as in Washington, D.C., when he served as a member of Congress. As a result of this somewhat nomadic lifestyle, the girls studied piano with various instructors. Ann's brother-in-law John Bryan oversaw much of their activities in Raleigh and Hillsborough.[40] In a letter that he wrote to Ebenezer in December 1835, the only mention of Mary is that she "learns her music very well."[41]

When Mary and her sister, Ann, moved to Washington to study, they encountered a new series of teachers. Mary wrote to her brother William S. Pettigrew in 1843 that she was studying piano with John Hill Hewitt, further noting that she was his "best scolar [sic]."[42] Under his tutelage, she reported learning "the Parisienne" and also commented that Ann was taking piano as well.[43] After being passed from one teacher to another, Mary began to detect differences in teaching styles and experiences. She describes one of her music teachers in a letter to her uncle: "I found I knew nothing at all about music when I began to take lessons with this teacher, and I think that Betsy and Nancy had better not take at all than take from Mrs Lucas or Mrs LaMersura[ier] for I dont believe they know much more about teaching than the children themselves; they dont even begin right, and Mrs. Badger seems to think the same."[44]

Almost a year later, Mary wrote to her brother James Johnston Pettigrew that she intended all of her family to be musically adept, even the males: "It would be very good employment for you, during the holidays to learn on some musical instrument, but I suppose this is impossible; so you will have to sing, as much as you can, and read the remainder of the time. I am very anxious for all my brothers and my sister to cultivate their musical talents; and devote, on an average, three hours a day to the study of music myself."[45]

Mary Pettigrew was an independent-minded young woman who thought nothing of directing how the rest of the family should spend their time. Perhaps the absence of a mother permitted such bold comment from the eldest daughter. "Finished" at Saint Mary's School, Mary was now considered sufficiently prepared to step into the role of matron.

MUSIC TEACHERS

Male and female music teachers instructed young girls, and some actually became a part of the household of the students. In southwestern Virginia, Letitia Burwell (1830–1905) had the opportunity to learn technique and a new repertory from a German music professor who remained in their home for an extended period. Thus, she not only had direct lessons but also indirectly learned an alternative style of music. In *A Girl's Life in Virginia before the War*, Burwell makes a few comments about music educators in her life: "In due time we were provided—my sister and myself—with the best instructors—a lady all the way from Bordeaux to teach French, and a German professor for German and music. The latter opened to us a new world of music. He was a fine linguist, a thorough musician, and a gentleman. He lived with us for five years and remained our sincere and truly valued friend through life."[46] This is probably the same German music teacher Burwell later describes: "Besides these teachers we had a German gentleman, a finished pianist and linguist; and the recollections of those days are like the delicious music that floated around us then from those master-musicians."[47]

Many music professors in the South were immigrants from Europe. The case of Arnaud Eduard Préot is also instructive regarding the position and experiences of the foreign-born music professor, which were probably more common than has been recognized. Born in Lille, France, and educated in Paris, Préot came to America in 1837, spending a few years in New York and Pennsylvania. He taught at Walkhill Academy in Pennsylvania before moving to Petersburg, Virginia, where he taught music and languages at Southworth College. Préot married one of his music students, Elizabeth Anne Hammatt of Chesterfield County, in 1848. His teaching duties continued in Buckingham County in the 1850s, where he served as music professor at the Female Collegiate Institute, and he remained there with his family until the school faltered at the beginning of the Civil War. In 1861, they moved to Farmville, where he served as professor of music and languages for one year, and Mrs. Préot taught music and French there. In 1862, he became the president of Farmville Female College (now Longwood College), an office he held until 1869.[48] Similarly, Charles Chaky de Nordendorf (born Karl Sauer Csaky, edler von Nordendorf) emigrated from Vienna to the Confederate States of America in 1862, teaching as a music professor at the Danville Female College in Virginia. He also published more songs (over eighty) than any other composer of the Confederacy.[49]

How much influence foreign teachers' choice of repertory had on southern taste has yet to be explored fully, but Letitia Burwell's German music professor clearly brought new music with him.[50] Two of the piano teachers at the Nashville Female Academy had studied at the Conservatoire Impérial under Henri (Heinrich) Herz: Camille Brunet and Athalie Casche.[51] Presumably they taught a technique and repertory similar to that they had experienced in France. One of the favorite local music teachers in Charleston during the 1850s was Louis Hambruch, originally from Hanover but recently at the University of Göttingen.[52] He came to Charleston because several Charlestonians (all men) had been studying with him in Göttingen. He, too, presumably brought German music with him.

Katherine Hines Mahan notes that German musicians dominated musical life in Columbus, Georgia, in the 1840s and 1850s. Their influence could be felt in dance, choices of music literature, and various music groups. Richard Wagner and Verdi were particular favorites of the local population.[53] Dr. Robert M. A. Koch, reportedly a pupil of Carl Maria von Weber, arrived from Dresden in 1844 and offered to teach brass, strings, woodwinds, theory, church music, and piano tuning.[54] Hermann Bernreuter (Bernrender) arrived two years later to teach music on all instruments.[55] Other German teachers in Columbus included Mr. A. Joerson at the Columbus Female Academy (arriving in 1839) and Mr. Edward Brenan at the Muscogee Seminary (also in 1839).[56]

Exactly which pieces of German music these teachers brought with them remains unknown. One likely composer is Mendelssohn. In 1849, J. Bayard Taylor wrote "A Recollection of Mendelssohn" in *Graham's Magazine*. He comments that the loss of Mendelssohn was the greatest musical loss since the death of Weber and laments that the composer will never be replaced. Among Mendelssohn's attributes, according to the author, his music "is of a more purely intellectual character than that of any modern composer." Taylor met Mendelssohn at his residence, and, after noting what he considered the composer's Jewish facial characteristics, Taylor mentioned Mendelssohn's interest in "the native negro melodies—which, after all, form the only peculiarly national music we possess—and that he considered some of them exceedingly beautiful and original."[57]

That Taylor chose to revere Mendelssohn in such a journal raises interesting questions concerning his choice of subject with regard to his audience. In 1849, the complete title of the magazine was *Graham's American Monthly Magazine of Literature and Art*, but its original title had been *Graham's Lady's and Gentleman's Magazine* (in 1841–42 and later in July 1843–June 1844). Clearly, George Rex Graham was attempting to reach the broadest audience possible. In doing so, however, such an article as the Mendelssohn recollection must have been intended to draw upon the ladies' knowledge of concert repertory, for few German songs and almost none of that composer's music is encountered in sheet music collections compiled before the Civil War.

If the sheet music evidence does not indicate that German musicians brought much German music for their female students to learn, they certainly may have performed it themselves. The "Erlkönig" also appears in a concert in Charleston in 1861; it may have been one of those pieces that everyone knew—an isolated work, not representative. On the other hand, concert programs from Charleston indicate that German art songs were indeed performed there.[58]

George Putnam Upton comments on the popularity of foreign musicians in the South during the antebellum period in his *Musical Memories* (1908). He relates a story told to him by violinist Julius Dyhrenfurth of the times when Dyhrenfurth and pianist Joseph Hermanns toured together in the United States in the 1830s. After playing in various northern locales, the two musicians traveled south to New Orleans and other southern cities. Upton noted that "it is curious how many foreign musicians, as soon as they landed, went to the South in those early days," confirming the popularity of foreign music teachers in the region.[59]

The 1860 census for Richland, South Carolina, provides a sample of how ubiquitous foreign-born musicians were in the more urban areas of the South.[60] Richland County includes the state capital (Columbia) and, in 1860, the prestigious South Carolina Female Collegiate Institute at Barhamville. Among the musicians listed in the census, several Germans appear, including Charles Zimmerman (aged sixty and worth $6,500), Henry Schaller (thirty-six), August Keopfrer (thirty-eight), and Nathan Peterson (twenty-six). Furthermore, the South Carolina Female Collegiate Institute included English, Italian, Spanish, and Polish musicians among its faculty. Such a diverse group of musicians must have had some affect on music instruction in that area, but little evidence of a shift toward any national style is evident in music collections.

Musical life in antebellum Savannah includes a similarly wide array of influences. Two of three female music teachers were local, according to the 1860 census; only one, Maria Chastanet (aged twenty-eight), was not a native of the United States. A "teacher of music," she was born in Levignon, France, and was the wife of Frederick Chastanet. The other two women were southerners. Born in Charleston, Isabella Evans (aged fifty), "music teacher," held the place "head of household" in 1860. Her son John (twenty-four, a blacksmith) had been born in Montgomery, Alabama. How and when she arrived in Savannah is unknown. Finally, young Harriet Richardson (aged sixteen), daughter of county constable John A. Richardson and seamstress Eliza, was a "music teacher" from Savannah.

Additionally, four men are included in the 1860 Savannah census as music teachers or "professors." As is typical for southern music professors of this period, several are listed as foreign-born. These include Frederick Dietz (aged thirty-one) and Siegmound Berg of Bavaria, as well as Frederick Chastanet of Bordeaux. Samuel L. Speissegger, aged sixty-eight, was a "professor of music" from Charleston who worked in Savannah at this time.[61] Henry Richards, of New York City, rounds out the list of music teachers in Savannah in 1860, as per the census.

This distribution of foreign- and native-born music teachers seems to mirror similar cities and towns in the area. In the same census, Macon had two music teachers: Oscar Brisow (or Bristow) of Prussia and Henrietta Swift (aged forty) of Georgia. Milledgeville, the capital of Georgia at that time, had no music teachers in its list (although one fencing master was included). Augusta, the other more metropolitan city in the state, had one music teacher listed in the census: Cecelia Boyle, aged thirty-five, head of household (with three children), from South Carolina.

The Sloman sisters of Charleston also taught music, and they apparently instructed young men as well as women. Evidence for this exists on the cover of compositions by William Henry Capers. At age twelve, this young composer published the "Buchanan Polka," which is dedicated to Governor Robert Allston of South Carolina. Allston held that position from 1856 to 1858; he was the husband of Adèle Petigru Allston, mentioned in chapter 1.[62] (James Buchanan, presumably the namesake of the polka, was president from 1857 to 1861.) The cover sheet proclaims that Capers, of Charleston, South Carolina, was a student of Miss Sloman's. The South Carolina census of 1860 includes a William H. Capers, aged fifteen, living at home with Thomas Farr Capers and Mrs. A. B. Capers, both aged fifty.[63] Thomas's occupation is listed as auctioneer, and his net worth was $25,000. Thus, this upper-class young man, living in one of the most culturally distinguished southern cities, studied music with a female teacher.

Capers also composed the "Rifle Regiment Quickstep," which was reported to have been James Johnston Pettigrew's favorite musical work (it was dedicated to him) and one played frequently for his troops.[64] Since it was published before Pettigrew was named a general (he is styled "colonel" on the dedication), the work must have been composed before late February 1862. The cover sheet also notes that Capers was a former pupil of "Miss A. Sloman."[65] This is almost certainly Ann Sloman, sister of the composer Elizabeth Sloman.[66] While Elizabeth was noted as a singer and harpist (having studied with Nicholas Bochsa), Ann was a pianist of some renown.[67] It appears that Capers may have studied with Ann rather than with Elizabeth (or Ellen). That a young man of some means would credit his musical education to a woman both before and during the war suggests that she was a significant figure in Charleston's musical world.

Music teachers habitually traveled from place to place, rarely remaining in one town for any length of time. This nomadic lifestyle affected the pupils as well as the teachers themselves. Even when employed by a seminary, teachers usually remained for only a couple of years. The case of Sarah Lois Wadley demonstrates inconsistency in lessons at home in Amite, Louisiana, and she writes several times in her diary about her experiences. In 1860, she temporarily studied music in her home with Mr. Eaton, with whom she had her second lesson on 29 May.[68] Later that year, she began lessons with Mr. Nocepelius (G. A. Gnospelius), a German musician, for Eaton moved to New Orleans. He reportedly told an acquaintance of Sarah's that "the reason he went was because he wanted to attend the opera in the evening, he had no amusement here except to go and see the young ladies and as he could not do that without its being reported he was going to marry them, he had nothing for amusement. Though not a speech for a gentleman to make it is characteristic of Mr. Eaton, who is both conceited and indolent."[69] Eaton's move to New Orleans was a natural one for a musician, since New Orleans rivaled New York City at this time as a place to hear entertainments such as opera. "Mr. Eaton" is probably the composer Edward O. Eaton. His earliest publications appear to have been in 1856, and an 1859 publication describes Eaton as being from Natchez.[70] Several pieces dating from the 1860s are his handiwork, published in various cities throughout the South. He composed several popular patriotic works during the Civil War.

Sarah's new music teacher, Mr. Nocepelius, also worked as the organist at Wadley's church, but she writes several times that he missed church because he was presumably ill.[71] Unfortunately, Mr. Nocepelius did not work out either—he drank too much, had binges, and missed lessons. At one point, Sarah notes that "Mr. Nocepelius has been on a 'spree' the reason why he did not give us our music lessons. He came Thursday and excused himself by saying that he had sprained his ankle and could not walk, poor man! I feel very sorry for him, he is an educated man, is a perfect gentleman when sober, but he is too weak to resist the love of liquor, he was pale and haggard Thursday and his ankle was so lame that he walked with difficulty."[72] When Nocepelius did appear for Sarah's lessons, she was chaperoned during the tutorial, as was typical at this time.[73] Later in December 1860, Sarah began spelling her teacher's name "Gnocepelius," and she also commented that he would come over to Monroe to give "them" lessons once the road was repaired.[74] (Several entries give the impression that more than one pupil was present, and they may have indeed been group lessons.) This is Sarah's final reference to the German teacher. Nocepelius made his way to Savannah apparently, for in 1863, he is mentioned in the diary of Josephine Clay Habersham as being employed at Christ Church, Savannah.[75]

Exasperated by the various inconsistencies with men teachers, Wadley's mother answered an ad for a woman music teacher in March 1861. The arrangement differed from the previous two in that this woman lived with the family. Her salary of $600 per year was more than what tuition cost at a private school, although the fact that she was a Virginian (as opposed to a northerner) and an Episcopalian evidently carried weight with Wadley's parents.[76] Clearly, music was considered a significant part of Wadley's education, for her parents spent significant time and money seeing that she had qualified teachers.

Wadley went to school in 1862, studying French and music with Mrs. Dwight, whom she calls a "scholar." The encroaching war brought this relatively stable period in Wadley's education to a close in early 1863, and the school closed. Mrs. Dwight, "with tears in her eyes," asked Wadley's mother if she could stay with their family for a month, teaching French and music for her board.[77]

The case of the music teachers for Susan Branch Bradford sheds some light on how music lessons required a specialist, perhaps because there were so many unqualified teachers available. Born in 1846, Susan lived on Pine Hill Plantation, north of Tallahassee, Florida. Her parents hired various governesses to educate Susan and her siblings, including one Letitia Hannah Damer, who arrived when Susan was eleven years old. Damer, an English lady, lived with the Bradfords as a governess, but she did not teach music as part of her duties. Even though Damer had reportedly trained to perform on the stage, her family had not permitted it. The Bradfords hired a music master to come into the home from Tallahassee. According to Susan, Damer sang "gloriously" and had time to do so when the music teacher was there.[78]

Within a year, Damer received news that she had inherited a great fortune in London and left Pine Hill with the barrister who brought the news.[79] The Bradfords hired a northern governess in November 1859, Cornelia Platt of Rhinebeck, New York. Her only qualifications for the position were that she was a gifted musician and competent mathematician. Platt proved to be an ardent abolitionist whose main object in coming to Pine Hill was to disrupt the slaves. She was soon sent back to New York.[80]

Such different governesses appear to have been the norm for young women. Notably, both Damer and Platt were talented musicians—something that enabled them to obtain employment in a southern plantation household. A writer in the *Southern Literary Messenger* listed the primary requirements for a governess: "I should wish her to be very accomplished, of course; to be a perfect musician, and a good French scholar; also a graceful dancer."[81] Of all the qualifications, being a "perfect musician" was paramount. Other capabilities, such as French, dancing, and the "minor branches" (grammar and philosophy!) were valuable, but musical accomplishment was first.

Sometimes young women traveled to their teachers for lessons, as was the case with Sarah Lois Wadley's friends Mary and Eva. Mary ventured into "town" (New Orleans) twice a week for lessons with Mrs. Delary, beginning in September 1863.[82] Two months later, Eva began lessons with Mrs. Delary as well.[83] The war also disrupted these, and in January 1864, both girls received lessons from Wadley herself.[84] Eventually, in 1865, a letter from these two girls tells Wadley that they have once again resumed their music lessons.[85]

Many young women took music lessons at the local female academy, even if they were not regular boarders. Labeled "parlor boarders," these students were not entirely popular with the regular boarders. At the Nashville Female Academy in 1853, the number of parlor boarders had risen so high that a separate building was constructed for the music students, leaving more peace and quiet for the regulars.[86] In Columbus, Georgia, young women could take music and painting lessons at the Columbus Hotel in 1832, under the direction of Mrs. E. J. Smith.[87] Local girls could also take lessons at the South Carolina Female Collegiate Institute in Barhamville and other similar institutions. Adele Logan Alexander proposed that the mulatto daughters of Nathan Sayre and Susan Hunt (a free woman of color who apparently lived with Sayre at Pomegranate Hall) study music at the Sparta Female Model School in Georgia as day students.[88]

Some music teachers operated something similar to the modern studio. Eliza Ripley, a young belle who wrote an engaging social history of New Orleans before the war, took lessons in the home of Madame Boyer in that city (figure 3.2). According to Ripley, young girls would arrive with their music and proceed to the lessons room. In this place, she sarcastically notes how the girl, teacher ("immense in bulk"), and piano coexisted during the lessons. According to Ripley, Boyer was *par excellence* the most popular teacher" of many in New Orleans.[89]

Little information survives about the personalities and circumstances of these teachers. They certainly did not belong to the planter class if they were teaching—at least not before the war—but they must have been of high enough station to be allowed such close interaction with planters' daughters. In a fictional account in *Graham's Magazine*, "Eleonore Eboli," author Winifred Barrington suggests that music teachers had to be of a certain economic position. In this story, the mother of the heroine is capable of teaching music but is not presentable enough in her present state of poverty to do so. Her friend Madame Persaune remarks, "You are a good musician, can you not teach the piano or guitar?" Madame Eboli responds, "Ah, Madame Persaune! I have tried that, but no one would take lessons of a stranger. My garb was an evidence of my poverty, and in their eyes of my inefficiency."[90] All ends well for her daughter, though, who, after marrying the Duke of Lazun, becomes an intimate of Princess Marie of Orleans.[91]

Another story in *Graham's Magazine* further illuminates qualities of the music teacher. In her diary, Gertrude Clanton Thomas writes in 1846 that she has particularly enjoyed the story "Grace Fleming."[92] In this work, Grace is a dutiful daughter of a wealthy planter, much like Thomas herself. However,

Fig. 3.2. Eliza Ripley at age twenty-two. Used with permission of *Documenting the American South,* The University of North Carolina at Chapel Hill Libraries.

when Grace's father's fortunes fail and he faces bankruptcy, Grace refuses to marry a wealthy suitor who promises to pay the father's debts. Naturally, Mr. Fleming is furious, but Grace holds her ground. Moreover, she secretly becomes a music teacher, degrading herself before former acquaintances by earning a living. When her father learns that she has been making money to support the family (she has two sisters), he has a stroke. Ever the devoted daughter, Grace remains at home supporting her invalid father, shunning a proposal of marriage from her cousin (whom her sister eventually marries) and all other options except that of music teacher and caretaker.

Grace Fleming faces several obstacles when she begins teaching. One prospective employer, Mrs. Howard, comments that she thinks Grace is charging too much ("I believe *ladies* who give music lessons, seldom ask more than

fifteen dollars a quarter"), but she does not want to let a German music professor teach her daughter, for she questions his morals. Mrs. Howard continues:
"'In many respects, Miss Fleming,' said Mrs. Howard . . . 'I must say I prefer
a gentleman teacher. I think them more scientific. But one does not like to
trust a pretty girl with those German professors, and one of our own people
is not worth having, so, as Mrs. Lawrence recommended you highly, and you
think twenty dollars the least you can take, why I suppose we may as well
conclude upon the terms.'"[93]

Other writers expressed similar hesitation in letting foreign men teach
their daughters—and with good cause, as several piano teachers (for example,
Nordendorf and Préot) married their students. At the South Carolina Female
Collegiate Institute, a Mr. Vass (who may or may not have been foreign but
was certainly male) received the cryptic description "Fine performer. Bad
man."[94] The delicate balance between attainment of the proper accomplishments and association with the correct people seems to have been difficult
for many southerners when it came to music instruction.

The foregoing discussion has demonstrated that throughout the period in
question, much music education took place in the homes of the elite. Music
instruction occurred in several different ways. Mothers, older sisters, and
cousins were often the first teachers of the young. Lessons generally began
around the age of ten and could be arranged by numerous methods. Occasionally, music teachers lived in the home of the family and sometimes worked
as governesses (teaching several topics and looking after the children), as did
Miss Ayme. At other times, musicians in the homes of the wealthy did not
perform as governesses but taught only music or music and languages, as in the
case of the Burwells' German music teacher. Less commonly, young women
went to the teacher's "studio" for lessons, as did Eliza Ripley. Lessons could
be taken as a solo lesson or as a class for several pupils, especially voice lessons.

Music lessons might continue after a woman was married, but most married southern elite women had too many responsibilities to carry on. Once
they had learned to play in order to please others, the task quickly altered to
preparing others to do so. Thus, their usefulness increased: not only could they
provide soothing entertainment, but these young women could also provide
elementary instruction to their younger siblings, cousins, and, soon, children.

The broad range of performance situations at home represents the experiences
of many young southern women. Most often, these were times when young
women sang or played the piano (or both, or perhaps played the guitar) in
front of assembled guests, who may or may not have been listening. This sort
of exhibition was a way in which young women displayed their accomplishments. It demonstrated that they not only had some musical talent (or education at least) but also knew what was appropriate to play or sing and how

much actually to "display." Too much technical display or lengthy pieces, as discussed in later chapters, was a marker of poor taste. Whether or not others in attendance paid much attention is noticeably less relevant. Merely being able to entertain at home with some level of accomplishment indicated that a young woman was suitable for marriage. Her parents cultivated her into a refined representative of their social and economic status, and they displayed her fittingly in their parlor.

4. Music Education in Schools

"Woman Nobly Planned—How to Educate Our Girls"

—WILLIAM PORCHER MILES, SERMON TITLE

By the mid-nineteenth century, daughters of upper-class families in the South could expect to be sent to school during part of their teen years. While finishing schools had been popular during the early years of the century, after 1840, a college education functioned as one signifier that a young woman was part of the elite classes. In the introduction to *The Education of the Southern Belle*, Christie Anne Farnham makes the case that although many southern women's schools imported northern teachers, the philosophy behind educating young women differed profoundly between the two regions. Opposition to the higher education of women in the industrialized North derived in part from a fear that education would open various professions to them. Southerners (at least those who could afford to educate their daughters), on the other hand, had no intention or expectation that their women would work outside the home.[1]

Moreover, some enlightened southerners realized that a well-educated woman would be much more interesting to spend time with than someone who could talk only of fashions and the latest gossip. When Marcus Cicero Stephens wrote his granddaughter Mary Anne Primrose that he was pleased she was learning French and music at school, he added a sort of apology for the way women had been educated in the past. After noting that it is useful to know something of the "higher branches of education . . . History, Geography, and some of the best ethical writers," Stephens acknowledges that "generally speaking, the women have not been treated with Justice by the male sex. . . . That fact appears to be this, the men have entered into a kind of conspiracy to keep the women in the background—a prejudice has been excited against their improvement beyond a certain limit—the women have been cowed if I may so term it—for should she in her remarks on any subject of conversation show any superiority of intellect, she is instantly denounced. . . . How ungenerous!"[2] Stephens's remarks touch on the heart of the reasons to educate southern girls: they were to be fit for conversation with men, just as their musical education was to prepare them to entertain men.

IMPORTANCE OF SOUTHERN SCHOOLS

Southern schools blended the expectation that women's curricula equal that of men with instruction intended to develop young women into proper ladies. Thus, geometry and needlework coexist in school catalogs. The idea of being "finished" at an institution that specialized in cultural education—the accomplishments—was commonly expected. At such schools, girls were further instructed in the code of conduct that was supposed to govern them their entire life.

So crucial was the inculcation of southern cultural values in these young women that most writers advocated a southern institution rather than a northern one. Sarah J. Hale, editor of *Godey's Lady's Book*, recommended that southern girls go to southern schools, so different were the expectations of their roles in society. Some independent-minded fathers felt otherwise, though, and sent their daughters to school in the North. James Petigru, for example, sent his daughters to school in Philadelphia—but he also voted against secession when the time came.

Confirmation of the need to stay in the South for an education can be gleaned from an 1836 notice in the *Southern Literary Messenger*. Commenting on "The Song" as a "burlesque somewhat over done, but upon the whole a good caricature of Italian bravura singing," the writer implies that the musical education that Miss Aurelia Emma Theodosia Augusta Crump received in Philadelphia was not appropriate for the genteel parlor. Her mannerisms in performance certainly did not reflect southern standards, and credit for this problem seemed to lie with the northern school and its foreign teachers. The anonymous writer explains:

> Miss Crump was educated at Philadelphia; she had been taught to sing by Madam Piggisqueaki, who was a pupil of Ma'm'selle Crokifroggietta, who had sung with Madam Catalani and she had taken lessons on the piano, from Signor Buzzifuzzi, who had played with Paganini.
>
> She seated herself at the piano, rocked to the right, then to the left,— leaned forward, then backward, and began. She placed her right hand about midway the keys, and her left about two octaves below it. She now put off the right in a brisk canter up the treble notes, and the left after it. The left then led the way back, and the right pursued it in like manner. The right turned, and repeated its first movement; but the left outran it this time, hopt over it, and flung it entirely off the track. It came in again, however, behind the left on its return, and passed it in the same style. They now became highly incensed at each other, and met furiously on the

middle ground. Here a most awful conflict ensued, for about the space of ten seconds, when the right whipped off, all of a sudden, as I thought, fairly vanquished. But I was in error, against which Jack Randolph cautions us—"It had only fallen back to a stronger position." It mounted upon two black keys, and commenced the note of a rattle-snake. This had a wonderful effect upon the left, and placed the doctrine of snake charming beyond dispute. The left rushed furiously towards it repeatedly, but seemed invariably panic struck, when it came within six keys of it, and as invariably related with it tremendous roaring down the bass keys. It continued its assaults, sometimes by the way of the naturals, sometimes by way of the sharps, and sometimes by a zigzag, through both; but all its attempts to dislodge the right from its stronghold providing ineffectual, it came close up to its adversary and expired.[3]

Miss Crump received some sort of musical education while in Philadelphia, but it was not what upper-class southerners desired of their understated, elegant girls.

MUSIC AS PART OF THE CURRICULUM

Most southern schools had an impressive number of students from a wide geographic area. The girls who attended LaGrange Female College in LaGrange, Georgia, hailed from southern states, as was typical of most southern institutions. Here, thirteen faculty members worked with 160 students in 1850.[4] Enrollment increased over the next few years, and in 1851 there were 210 pupils, 217 in 1852, and a total of 200 in 1853. Astoundingly, of the 210 students in 1851, 110 paid essentially double the regular costs in order to take music.[5]

The curricula at such schools varied. Some bulletins appear to have offered a limited number of options for girls, but, as in the case of the Greensborough Female College in North Carolina, the catalog of texts to be covered indicates a much broader spectrum. In 1843, the Sharon Female College, in Madison County, Mississippi, advertised the following options. In the Preparatory Department, girls could take orthography, reading, writing, English grammar, geography, arithmetic, mythology, progressive exercises in composition, Bible and its natural history, Latin and Greek grammars, Latin tutors and readers, and vocal music. The Collegiate Department offered ancient and modern languages, algebra, geometry, trigonometry, mensuration, syntax and English composition, analysis, rhetoric, natural philosophy, chemistry, geology, mineralogy, botany, astronomy, logic, elements of criticism, ancient and modern history, ancient geography, philosophy of natural history, physiology, mental and moral sciences, introduction to the study of the Bible, evidences of Christianity, daily use of sacred Scriptures, music, drawing, painting, wax, coral, and ornamental needlework.[6] The perceived need to study all of these subjects confirms William Porcher Miles's dictates from an undated sermon delivered to the Yorkville Female College in South Carolina: "Women 'Nobly Planned'—How to Educate Our Girls."[7]

Chief among the accomplishments taught in women's academies was music, but it did not become an expected part of the curriculum until the 1830s. Before that time, music instruction was usually a later addition to the curriculum, presumably after repeated requests made it financially feasible. For example, the Athens Female Academy in Alabama opened its doors in 1822 but did not include music as part of its offerings. A few years after the incorporation of the academy, provision was made for a course in music with a teacher and one piano.[8] Similarly, an early school in Mississippi, the Elizabeth Academy at Washington (Adams County, established 1817), added the study of piano music in 1833, whereupon it became part of the courses regularly taught. Interestingly, the faculty members in 1839 deemed worthy of note in later years were Miss Lucy A. Stillman, principal governess, and, less expected, Miss Mary B. Currie, music teacher.[9]

By 1835, almost all schools included some sort of music instruction—all of the institutions examined in this study included it. Even with small faculties, music professors and teachers seem always to have been present. The several versions of a female college in Port Gibson, Mississippi (1843–1908), provide for a case in point. The school began in 1826 as the Clinton Academy and changed its name in 1829 to the Port Gibson Academy, which was more or less successful until about 1843. In that year, a group of prominent gentlemen established the Port Gibson Collegiate Academy, which took in students in 1844. Its faculty then included Mr. L. G. Hartge, professor of music.[10] Music was also a part of the Nazareth Academy in Kentucky when it first opened. Authorized by the Kentucky legislature in 1829 under the title of "Nazareth Literary and Benevolent Institution," Sister Ellen O'Connell was the first directress of studies, and Sister Scolastica O'Connell was the first music teacher.[11]

Similarly, from the first session (6 September 1830) of the Tuscaloosa Female Academy (Alabama), Mr. A. Pfister and Mrs. Patrick had "charge of the music department." An A. S. Pfister is listed in the 1860 Alabama census as a musician, and his place of birth was apparently Nassau, the Bahamas.[12] Evidently, one of the selling points for this particular school was music: "a great attraction, as every one was anxious for his daughter to have a musical education."[13] Mr. Pfister had a favorable reputation as a music teacher, and he also taught French. Rarely did a male teacher *only* instruct in a modern foreign language, and Pfister's double duties of music and language represent a normal load for someone in his position.

Under Caroline Lee Hentz, who operated a large and flourishing school for young ladies in Florence, South Carolina, music was considered part of the "usual" curriculum.[14] Among her teachers was a German professor of music. After Hentz's departure in 1842, the Florence Female Academy was organized but not chartered until 1848. It, too, offered instruction in music.

Undoubtedly, the quality of music teachers varied throughout the South during this period, but that music instruction was a prerequisite to lady-hood remained consistent. With the blossoming of female institutions, new standards in curricula awarded this particular accomplishment the place of highest esteem. Proof of music's place in most schools' curricula is found in the high proportion of music faculty in women's schools: more people taught music than any other subject. Clearly, parents expected that their daughters would receive lessons in music while at school, most often in piano and voice.

The types of entertainments allowed at schools varied tremendously. Some schools were rather restrictive in what they permitted the students to do for entertainment. Parlor performances were common; public performances (except graduation recitals) were rare. The bulletin of the Elizabeth Academy states emphatically that "no pupil shall be allowed to receive ceremonious visits. All boarders in commons shall wear a plain dress and uniform bonnets. No pupil shall be permitted to wear beads, jewelry, artificial flowers, curls, feathers, or any superfluous decoration. No pupil shall be allowed to attend balls, dancing parties, theatrical performances, or festive entertainments."[15]

Schools that sought to prepare young women for the upper echelons of society made certain that the pupils were exposed to different types of per-formances. Some matrons allowed students to attend public performances as a group, such as the outings organized by Madame Togno. Other places, such as the South Carolina Female Collegiate Institute, brought performers on campus for the benefit of their young women.

FINISHING SCHOOLS

Most women of the Petigru family (both the South Carolina branch and those from North Carolina, the Pettigrews) attended schools.[16] For the generation concerned in this study, the first of the Petigru girls to attend school away from home was Caroline Petigru, daughter of James Louis Petigru and Jane Amelia Postell.[17] Her first experience away from home was during the early 1830s, when she moved to Charleston to attend Miss Susan Robertson's school. Although known for its teaching of English and history, James Petigru felt this establishment lacked what Caroline needed, particularly the mastery of French that was deemed obligatory among a southern belle's traditional accomplishments. Consequently, he eventually sent Caroline to Madame Binsse's school in New York, which was popular with other prestigious South Carolinians. At these schools, Caroline developed and nurtured a lifelong interest in music and art.

Caroline's education did not end as happily as it might have. She evidently was capable of quite a number of intellectual pursuits, performed well at the

New York academy (despising every minute of her time, apparently), and satisfied her father's expectations. But her mother, Jane Amelia, had long suffered from a state of semi-invalidism (whether real or imagined can only be speculated), and Jane Amelia eventually persuaded James to bring Caroline back home to assist her mother in running the household. James regretted his decision and confessed that he indeed had done "wrong" in bringing Caroline back at age fifteen, and that he had done it "knowingly." Caroline continued her education at home, but James never overcame the guilt he felt in having stopped her formal education at such a young age.[18]

The education of Caroline's younger sister, Susan (Sue), also sheds light on how upper-class parents educated their daughters. Like Caroline, Susan DuPont Petigru King Bowen attended school in Charleston.[19] She enrolled in the best available schools, including Madame Talvande's École pour Demoiselles in Charleston. The high regard given to French was evident at Madame Talvande's, for French was the language both of instruction and conversation—a fact that made it especially distasteful to Sue. While her parents and Caroline traveled extensively in the North in 1837, Sue was forced to remain at school in Charleston. In 1838 at age fourteen, Sue went to Philadelphia to study at Madame Guillon's boarding school. Again, like Caroline, she hated being in the North, but unlike Caroline she did not thrive against the odds. The two daughters were of different natures, and whereas Caroline was obedient, Sue longed for excitement. Sue became an author, and in one of her texts (*Lily: A Novel*), she decried the habit of spending money on educating young women only to marry them off where they would not have the opportunity to practice what they had learned. Among the wasted pursuits Sue lists is music. Thus, although both Sue and Caroline attended school and participated in music lessons, only for Caroline did it ensure an interest in music that lasted her entire life.

Their cousin Carey North also attended Madame Talvande's when her parents considered her old enough to do so. Seemingly always short of money, Carey's mother Jane North nevertheless spent as much as she could on Carey's schooling. By borrowing money and economizing where she could, Jane sent Carey to Charleston in 1840 at the age of twelve. She reprimanded her daughter for not practicing the piano enough and thus wasting the extra money spent on lessons. She reminded Carey that her tutelage in music was to "soothe solitary evenings at Badwell with sweet music, which I love dearly."[20] Jane's sister Adèle learned by example, and when her daughter Della was old enough, she sent her to school in Charleston.[21]

A number of girls attended school in Charleston, and many families considered the institutions there to be the best the South had to offer. Madame Talvande's school was one of its most reputable, including among its attendees Mary Boykin Chesnut. Housed in a "grand old mansion" at 33 Legare Street, many daughters of wealthy South Carolina cotton and rice planters were sent there to be educated, or at least finished.[22] Ann Marson Talvande, a French Haitian emigrant, stressed "the social skills needed in southern society."[23] Among its outstanding qualities were her instruction in French and music.[24]

The living arrangements at Madame Talvande's typified those in most schools. Usually, the girls slept in large rooms that accommodated between eight and twenty boarders. Chesnut describes the living space at Talvande's as a large room that overlooked the river and Charleston Battery. Twelve girls slept in this one space. In addition to washstands and dressing tables, it also held a piano.[25] This was one area where students could practice their music, apparently oblivious to other activities around them. Chesnut comments that "while we dressed, some early bird of a conscientious turn of mind was always practicing; with wide stretched mouth singing her solfeggios. We heeded her not, the roar of our chatter would have drowned the ocean."[26]

Whether or not the diarist was accurate in her physical description of the singer or was merely painting a caricature, that singers practiced solfège, a system for learning to sight-sing using the syllables of the diatonic scale (do, re, mi, and so on), is undeniable. At least one other woman offered solfège in Charleston during this period: Marie Petit, a professional musician from Belgium, who ran a "School for Young Ladies" in Charleston in the 1850s.[27] Her husband, Victor Petit, advertised a solfège class in Charleston in 1853. When he died in 1856, his daughter Herminie carried on teaching piano and solfège.

Most of the Charleston institutions, such as Madame Talvande's, were essentially finishing schools. Madame Talvande's, also known by its French title, École pour Demoiselles, was not considered an institution of higher learning, which would later be known as a "college." Schools were given several different titles during the antebellum period, and little credence can be placed on most. Christie Farnham Pope notes an indiscriminate use of most titles (academy, institute, seminary, school, and so on) but finds that purpose distinguishes two groups. One of these is more academic and might include the words "college" or "collegiate" in its name. At these schools, a systematic course of study through languages (including Latin and Greek), sciences, literature, and the like formed the basis of the curriculum. These types of institutions grew in popularity through the mid-nineteenth century. By 1860, at least fourteen schools for girls in North Carolina alone contained the word "college" in their titles.[28]

The other type of school that was an option for southern girls operated more along the lines of a finishing school, like Madame Talvande's. The academic rigor was relaxed in favor of a focus on refined manners, deportment, and character. Two schools attended by the daughters of Ebenezer Pettigrew also fit this description: the Select Boarding and Day School of the Misses Nash and Kollock in Hillsborough, and Saint Mary's School in Raleigh (both North

Carolina). These institutions did not confer degrees; Saint Mary's did not offer graduation. Most of these institutions, such as the Burwell School in Hillsborough, were run by a husband and wife team, although the Nash and Kollock school was controlled by two young women, Maria Jane Nash (1819–1907) and Sally Kollock Nash (1811–93; figure 4.1). Like their rival educator Aldert Smedes (discussed below), these two women acquired their music teachers through an agency in New York and then brought them to North Carolina.[29]

PARLOR PERFORMANCES: SAINT MARY'S SCHOOL

One of the most prestigious finishing schools in the South was Saint Mary's School in Raleigh, founded by Rev. Aldert Smedes in May 1842. An Episcopalian clergyman, Smedes established the "pre-eminent example of the finishing school."[30] Ideally, students pursued a course of study that was designed for five years, but if a pupil desired to add "accomplishments" such as music and art, Smedes preferred a longer period of residency. He believed a pupil could not adequately pursue more than four subjects of an advanced grade at one time.[31]

Music was apparently a favorite pastime at Saint Mary's. Ann Blount Shepard Pettigrew wrote to her brother William in 1843 that she enjoyed

Fig. 4.1. Maria Jane Nash and Sally Kollock Nash, principals of the Select Boarding and Day School of the Misses Nash and Kollock in Hillsborough, North Carolina. Published with permission of The Archival Collection of the Historic Hillsborough Commission.

studying both French and music at Saint Mary's. Her letter refers several times to Smedes and is a reflection of the high esteem his pupils had for him.[32] The school owned several burnished pianos, and attendees frequently performed in the parlors there. When professional singers happened to be in the area, they often stopped by Saint Mary's to perform. Twice a month the seminary held soirees. At these events, notables such as the governor were invited to hear some of the students sing or play the piano or harp. While such evenings garnered much excitement, they were not seen as public performances. They were staged to teach the students how to behave in such situations, how to conform to the ideal of the *lady*.

A few of the pieces heard at Saint Mary's have been documented. Specifically, "Then You'll Remember Me" is named as a composition performed in the parlor soirees at the school.[33] An extremely popular work from Balfe's opera *The Bohemian Girl*, it typifies arrangements from the stage that made it into parlors throughout the South. The publication shown in figure 4.2 might well be the version used at Saint Mary's, as it was published in the South (by Benteen in Baltimore). Other pieces mentioned are "Yankee Doodle" and "The Old North State" (the North Carolina state song) at a Fourth of July celebration.[34]

Music at school often served as a surrogate or evening training ground for home parlor performance. While some institutions held "concerts," these were not usually public performances, because most of the time they were for invited guests only. For example, as mentioned, the North Carolina governor was regularly invited to Saint Mary's to provide part of the "audience" for whom young ladies could perform. They were not playing for the governor in a concert but rather entertaining him as they might have done in their parents' homes. School administrators used such performances to teach their wards how to behave in polite company. In this sense, such a school setting was a substitute for home.

Similarly, dancing in the school's parlor also substituted for analogous situations at home. Margaret Anna Burwell noted that in her school at Hillsborough, parlor dancing was used as an "exercise." She wrote to her daughter, Fannie, on 8 February 1856 that one of the students, Bettie Carrington, had been playing the piano while the other students danced. She reported that "the girls are 'kicking up a dust' literally in the other room. They have been so confined that I told them tonight to dance for exercise. Bettie Carrington is playing, & I went to the door just now & could hardly see across the dust."[35] Indeed, since the parlor "at school" was often the parlor of the school's owners, the parallels become even more obvious.

The Nash and Kollock school, also in Hillsborough, where Mary Pettigrew attended, had a type of performance that they called a "Soirée Musicale" at various points in the school's history. For example, in 1860, Professor Henri

Fig. 4.2. "Then You'll Remember Me," from Michael Balfe's *Bohemian Girl*. From the Historic American Sheet Music Collection in the Rare Book, Manuscript, and Special Collections Library, Duke University.

Baseler directed a soirée musicale whose repertory included the famous "Oft in the Stilly Night," "Kathleen Mavoureen," and "The Last Rose of Summer," as well as various polkas and a "Potpourri from *Norma*."[36]

The significance of the parlor and being able to perform one's role properly in that venue was one of the most important parts of a young woman's training. Without a doubt, young women performed in the parlor for approved guests, and most references to music in primary sources involve such venues. When they performed in the parlor of a school like Saint Mary's, it was meant to serve as a parlor performance and not as a public one.

GRADUATION RECITALS

Graduation recitals performed similar functions while simultaneously giving parents an opportunity to hear their daughters. Most of these performances were not truly public, either, and guests were invited to attend. The repertory performed was essentially the same as that heard in the parlor at Saint Mary's. In the following excerpt from a Columbia newspaper, the niceness of the atmosphere is clearly of utmost importance. Even though it was a graduation recital, it in no way resembled a public performance of difficult music. The author reported that he (or she; the writer is listed only as a "visitor") had the honor of hearing the commencement at the South Carolina Female Collegiate Institute at Barhamville in 1849. On this occasion, to which he was happily invited, the "earlier part of the evening was devoted to music, in which most of the fair pupils participated; and without any desire to repeat the hackneyed technicalities of criticism, we can at least express the deep felt satisfaction we enjoyed, not only in the music itself, but in the satisfactory evidence thus afforded that the advantages of the institution had been so fully and correctly appreciated. Hard must have been the heart that could have remained unmoved, while gazing on that 'troop of shining ones,' and listening to the notes of soft, and witching harmony that came sweetly blended as from hearts that throbbed and beat in common."[37]

That the writer was equally enamored of the visual as well as of the aural typifies how society perceived young southern women. In this case, they were ornamental, not true musicians. The vision of "shining ones" comes first. Notably, "soft" notes mark the performance—not brilliant display. Moreover, this view of the commencement recital as a performance by pretty young women who perform softly and sweetly justifies the interpretation of such performances as mimicking those at home.

At the exercise in Barhamville, a printed program may have provided part of the names of the participants as well as their selections.[38] Surviving programs from other graduation exercises indicate that the type of literature performed at such gatherings mirrored the repertory of young women throughout the South, regardless of where they played or sang. The fact that the program contained their names also suggests that it was not a public performance, for public performances listed elite young women only as either "ladies" or "amateur ladies."

Programs from two commencements and a concert at the Georgia Female College in Macon (now called Wesleyan) reveal the type of literature one might hear at such gatherings. These are transcribed below as they appear in the programs. The arrangements remain unknown but were probably those found in contemporary bound volumes of sheet music.[39] The first, marking graduation in 1851, includes only religious music:

Georgia Female College, Commencement Day, Thursday, 11 July 1851

"Before Jehovah's Awful Throne"
"Lift Up Your Stately Heads"
"Peace Troubled Soul"
"The Lord Descended From Above"
"How Beauteous Are Their Feet"
"Our Lord Is Risen From The Dead"
Farewell Ode

The other two belong to the commencement celebration of 1852. In this example, religious music once again forms the graduation exercises performance, but the concert consists of a popular repertory, and it is a secular one. Such concerts typically formed part of the graduation event, as several letters reveal. In the case of Georgia Female College (which Farnham notes was the first women's institution in the United States to use that label), the concert consists of a mixture of opera arias, popular songs, and a few instrumental works.

Georgia Female College, Concert, 14 July 1852

PART I

1. Overture, From "John of Paris" [Boieldieu, 1812]
2. "Oh! Haste Crimson Morning" Song From "Lucia Di Lammermour"
3. "Le Diademe, Brilliant Variations" [possibly based on a waltz by Richard B. Taylor]
4. "It Was Here In Accents Sweetest," Song From "I. Puritani"
5. "O Dolce Concento" [from Mozart's *Die Zauberflöte*]
6. "Scenes That Are Brightest," Ballad, From "Maritani" [William Vincent Wallace]
7. Variations To "Nel Cor Piu" [aria by Paisiello]
8. "A Governess Wanted," Song
9. The Celebrated "Medley Overture" of Aldridge
10. "While My Thoughts Still Turn To Thee," Song, from "Giovanni di Napoli" ["Tornera nel mis core," described as a brilliant cavatina on sheet music that includes an image of Teresa Parodi, from the opera *Giovanna di Napoli* by Maurice Strakosch, 1851]

PART 2

1. "L'elegante fantaisie, pour la Harpe," by Bochsa
2. "Salut a l'amerique," song [Louis Ernst, 1852]

3. "National Schottishe" [piano duet by Charles Grobe]
4. "The Wildflowers Soon Will Shed Their Bloom, Song from "Lucia di Lammermour"
5. Friendship Polka, by Miss F. R. Guttenberger [several piano works have this name, but none are attributed to Guttenberger]
6. "I'll Be No Submissive Wife," Song [George Alexander Lee]
7. Emerald Waltz [several waltzes by this name exist]
8. "For Our Queen And Liberty" Brilliante Aria and Chorus from "Giovanni di Napoli" ["Combattiam per nostra regina," from *Giovanna di Napoli*]
9. "Battle of Resaca de la Palma" [celebrating an American victory in the Mexican-American War, composed by John Schell, 1848]
10. "Fare-Thee-Well," Song

The commencement music is similar to that of the previous year:

Georgia Female College, Commencement Exercises, 15 July 1852

"Sanctus and Hosanna"
"Our Father Who Art In Heaven"
"Be Kind To The Loved Ones At Home"
"How Lovely Is Zion"
"When The Bosom Heaves A Sigh"
Farewell Ode

At these events, the girls performed secular music for the commencement concert and sacred for the commencement itself. The repertory mirrors that sung by the girls in lessons and parlors throughout their music studies at school. Many of these pieces remained in vogue for years, at least until the Civil War.

The Burwell School's graduation exercises also included music interspersed in the examinations as well as a "Soiree Musicale." In 1849, the graduation exercises included performances of arias from *Lucia di Lammermoor* as well as popular songs. A tragedy in which most of the main characters die, *Lucia* may seem like an odd choice for such a celebration, but its popularity was sustained through its connection to Sir Walter Scott's novel (*The Bride of Lammermoor*) as well as its bel canto style. The recital that occurred on Friday night during the graduation weekend included several more opera arias and choruses, piano duets, and piano solos. While generally positive in his review, the "Auditor," writing in the *Hillsborough Recorder*, was displeased that a young performer wore her "hair with dandelions as set her to playing such vulgarities as negro melodies." He much preferred her later performance of Bochsa's "Rondino" (the same from which the image in figure 2.1 is taken).[40]

EQUAL EDUCATION: SALEM FEMALE ACADEMY,
SALEM, NORTH CAROLINA

Salem Female Academy, in what is now Winston-Salem, North Carolina, occu-
pies a distinct place in female education in the South because of its connections
with the Moravians. Manuscripts of piano music in archives in Salem demonstrate a high degree of composition skills among several Moravian women in
the mid-nineteenth century. From the academy's earliest days, piano lessons
and class voice were available; by the end of the nineteenth century, the school
offered an extensive array of music courses.[41] Pope posits that the importance
of music in Moravian worship flowed into an emphasis on music in education.
It certainly brought a number of talented musicians to the community and
with them excellent opportunities for instruction on instruments, including
the organ.[42] As a result of Salem's excellent reputation, a number of southern
dignitaries sent their daughters there; its alumnae boasted Sarah Childress,
wife of President James Polk; Mary Morrison, wife of Thomas "Stonewall"
Jackson; and Martha Martin, wife of Stephen Douglas.[43] Another consequence
of Salem's excellent music reputation is the significant number of music teachers who worked in schools in the surrounding area, which is explored below.

Contradicting the norm throughout the South, Salem did not hire a full-
time male professor of music until 1857.[44] Until that time, the Single Sisters'
Choir had provided music instructors for the young women at the academy.[45]
(The "Choir" was not a musical group but rather a term that embraced all
single Moravian women within the community.) Salem Female Academy's
history of female music teachers extends back into the eighteenth century,
when one Johanna Elizabeth Praezel gave music lessons at the tender age of
twelve.[46] The women who taught music at Salem Female Academy apparently
were paid well. A letter of 1837 mentions that if a qualified woman could teach
both music and painting, she might earn up to $800 per year.[47] This is an
astounding figure considering that most male teachers earned $400–$600 per
year during the midcentury, and women usually earned approximately three-
fifths the amount men received.[48] Clearly, Salem Female Academy valued its
music teachers.

FACULTY: GREENSBOROUGH FEMALE COLLEGE

With a high percentages of girls taking music lessons, it should come as no
surprise that music professors/teachers accounted for the largest percentage
of many faculties. When the Georgia Female College opened in 1839, the following people made up the faculty: Rev. G. F. Pierce, president and professor
of English literature; Rev. W. H. Ellison, professor of mathematics; Rev. T.
B. Slade, professor of natural science; B. B. Hopkins, tutor; John Euhink,
professor of music; Miss Lord, first assistant in music; and Miss Massey,

second assistant in music.[49] Of the seven teachers, three were hired for music.

Correspondingly, the growth of the music faculty at Greensborough Female College is indicative in several ways and deserves examination. A Methodist Episcopal school, the 1846–47 bulletin lists Dr. Solomon Lea as president and professor of ancient languages and his wife, Mrs. Sophie Lea, as principal of the music department. The school also employed an unnamed assistant in music. In its first year, tuition was $70, while music instruction cost $20 (apparently including both vocal and instrumental, although vocal may have been different). In comparison, Spanish, French, and painting were an additional $5. All of the students were from southern states.[50]

Beginning in 1847, the music faculty at Greensborough Female College saw unprecedented growth. In that year, after listing three men professors (in other subjects), the bulletin names two music teachers: Miss Augusta [M.] Hagen, principal of music, and her sister Miss Janette Hagen, assistant.[51] The Hagens were members of the Moravian church; their father, Francis Florentine Hagen, moved to North Carolina from Bethlehem, Pennsylvania.[52] Before coming to Greensborough Female College, Augusta Hagen served on the music faculty at Salem Female Academy (1845–47). She remained at Greensborough Female College for a number of years, although she relinquished her title (and position) when a male "professor" came onto campus.[53] In 1849, Hagen was still principal, but her assistants were Miss Francisca L. Benzien and Francis Cocheu.[54] Like Augusta Hagen, Benzien was also previously a faculty member at Salem Female Academy (1846–48 and 1854–56).[55] The 1850 Greensborough Female College catalog (printed in New York City) included Andrew G. Kern, Esq., as "Professor of Music"; Hagen remained but was no longer styled "principal." Miss Rocinda Dougherty also participated as a member of the music faculty. Interestingly, in 1850 the cost of tuition fell to $60, but piano instruction continued at $20. Guitar lessons were cheaper ($10), while painting was $15 and French and drawing cost $5.

In 1851, the catalog (printed in Greensborough) still listed Kerns, Hagen, and Dougherty as members of the music faculty and added another teacher, Miss Anne M. Lyman. The cost for the use of an instrument was $2.50. Guitar lessons had increased since the previous year to the point that they equaled piano lessons ($20). Voice instruction was the cheapest of the music options at $3. The next year, the catalog included the same teachers (female) and professor (male). Of note is the first (and only) mention of a "concert" the day before graduation. Such an event was typical for school girls, but propriety ordained that only a limited repertory was available for public display—if this was considered "public," for it was only for invited guests.[56] This was also the first year in which a student who was not from the South was included in the list of attendees (a girl from Massachusetts).

The next available bulletin, for the academic year 1854–55, shows significant alterations in the music faculty at the Greensborough Female College. Of particular interest is Theo[dore] F. Wolle, Esq., professor of music. Wolle was a product of the Moravian school in Bethlehem, Pennsylvania, and in 1860 he took charge of music affairs there.[57] No doubt, close connections with (and proximity to) Salem brought Wolle to Greensborough. Augusta Hagen and Miss Caroline A. Blake appeared as "assistants in the music department," and Miss Sallie Duty was the "Teacher on Guitar." For 1856–57, all of the music teachers remained under the same titles except Miss Mary A. Howlett, who replaced Caroline Blake. In 1857–58, the "Spirit of the Age Office" in Raleigh printed the catalog for the Greensborough Female College. Among the changes therein is that guitar use fell to $1 and piano use fell to $2. (They had each been $2.50.)

In 1858–59, the entire previous music faculty remained, plus two new teachers: Miss Pattie J. Cole and Miss Louisa Van Vleck, both teachers of the guitar. Van Vleck, a Moravian musician from Salem, was also a composer. By this time, the Greensborough Female College had attained a matriculation of 155 students. Of these, those participating in "Extras" were noted: 25 in Latin, 32 in French, 22 in painting, 15 in guitar, and an astounding 102 in piano. The charges remained the same as previously, and there was no extra cost for voice instruction.

The next year saw yet another increase in the music faculty, with Miss Fannie M. Ogburn, Miss Addie Sussdorff, and Miss Sallie H. Perry added to the previous group as "assistants." Thus, of the twelve people teaching at the Greensborough Female College, nine were employed only to instruct in music.[58] This year, the institution had 199 students, and the proportions in music remained high: 135 in piano, 26 in guitar, 55 in Latin, 51 in French, and 43 in painting and drawing. Clearly, piano instruction was particularly important to parents. In 1860–61, the bulletin lists a blank for the professor of music, with Hagen, Howlett, Ogburn, Sussdorff, Miss Sue [Sallie from 1854?] Duty, and Miss Geneva E. O'Brien as assistants; Miss Mittie J. Bethel taught guitar. (Hagen eventually moved to Williamston Female College in South Carolina.) The 202 students included girls from as far away as Texas (no northerners). Of the 202, no less than 158 were involved in piano study.

The faculty at Greensborough Female College included a number of teachers who had been either students or teachers at the Salem Female Academy. Undoubtedly, the emphasis on music in the Moravian community, where women frequently participated as church musicians, helped supply nearby seminaries with music teachers. Nearby Edgeworth Seminary (also in Greensborough) may have benefited as well.[59] Not all areas were so fortunately placed, however, and music teachers and professors changed positions frequently.

A WELL-DOCUMENTED SCHOOL: THE SOUTH CAROLINA
FEMALE COLLEGIATE INSTITUTE AT BARHAMVILLE

One of the best documented schools where music figured prominently is the South Carolina Female Collegiate Institute at Barhamville, near Columbia.[60] Several of the professors can be identified, as can some of the students and the instruction books used for music study. Few southern institutions received as much recognition as the South Carolina Female Collegiate Institute; the name appears in almost every discussion of women's education in the antebellum South. The history of the school as retold in Mrs. I. M. E. Blandin's *History of Higher Education of Women in the South Prior to 1860* (1909) provides a fitting background for examining music there because its origins and clientele help to define the type of young women whose musical experiences are examined here.[61] As to its reputation, "this was a school where work was done, good work, thorough work, for education at Barhamville was equivalent to practical sense with all the *accomplishments* acquired by young ladies of that era of time. From those dear and consecrated walls, hundreds of women went forth, types of the *ladies* of those days of the long ago" (italics mine).[62]

The school's history began with the arrival of the Humphrey Marks family in South Carolina in 1785. Wealthy planters along the seaboard asked Marks to move to the state to invest money in mortgages on rice and indigo plantations in the region. One of Humphrey's sons, Elias Marks, a medical doctor trained in New York City, returned to the South after his education to open a female academy. Marks frequently commented on the importance of female education, noting that "the torch of intellect is to be kindled on the altar of domestic affection."[63]

At this, his first foray into female education, Marks was briefly principal (along with his first wife, Jane Barham) of the Columbia Academy (basically a day school) from 1817 to 1820. Around 1819, Marks decided that a move away from the Congaree flats (and the diseases associated with such areas in late summer), as well as farther from the young men who went to school in Columbia, would provide a healthier environment for young women. Construction in the sandhills outside of Columbia began in 1821 with a single building, which was subsequently replaced with three new ones in 1840. New buildings were erected in 1841, after the physical plan of Edgeworth School in Maryland, and Marks named the school in honor of his wife.

Jane Barham Marks died in 1829, and in 1832, he brought Mrs. Julia Warne (née Pierpont) to Barhamville. Warne previously had been the head of a large and flourishing ladies' school in Sparta, Georgia. Born in Connecticut in 1793, she had been one of the first students of the celebrated Emma Willard, both in Middlebury, Vermont, and later (when Willard moved) at the Troy Seminary, New York. Her family had all the correct connections, and Warne was able to use her social skills to mingle with the most prominent citizens in Columbia.[64] As to her pedigree, Warne met all expectations—even those of skeptical parents: "All of her associations at the North were of the highest distinction. We are told she was an enthusiastic educationist, a woman endowed with remarkable powers of quiet, unconscious government, of deep religious feeling, dignified—what we call at the South, and mean much when we use the term, a lady."[65] Marks and Warne married in 1833. The Marks family ran the school until 1861.

The social connections established by the Markses enabled them to attract the daughters of some of the wealthiest families in the South, as well as some from other parts of the country. Included among their students were Martha Bulloch (of New York), the mother of Theodore Roosevelt, and Elizabeth Waties Allston Pringle, daughter of Adèle and Robert Francis Withers Allston, a planter, worth about half a million dollars in 1860, who also served as governor of South Carolina.[66] One writer refers to the students at Barhamville as "thoroughbreds," another acknowledgment of the social status of the young women who attended the school.[67]

In June 1861, the seventy-year-old Marks leased the school to Madame Aliza Togno of Charleston. According to the 1880 census, R. A[célie] Togno, a widow living in Henrico County, Virginia, was noted as having been born in France. She most likely is the same woman. In 1858, she wrote to Robert Allston (Elizabeth and Della's father) for assistance in selling some property.[68] She was succeeded as lessee by Madame Sophie Sosnowski, from Baden, who was herself followed by Madame Torriani, a refugee from Charleston. From 1865 to 1867, Dr. Marks and his family lived on the grounds. In the latter part of 1867 they went north, leaving the buildings in charge of a former slave who now worked there as a janitor. On 18 February 1869, fire destroyed the school buildings, resulting in a complete loss.

During the 1840s and 1850s, Mrs. Marks personally organized each student's daily schedule. She also supervised the teachers, a duty that apparently caused her some difficulty. The day was divided into forty-five-minute periods, beginning at 8:00 A.M. and ending at 4:00 or 5:00 P.M. Students were required to attend prayers every morning at 7:45, ate breakfast at 8:15, and had some free time (an hour or so) until classes were called. The girls had lunch ("soft gingerbread") at 11:30, then classes continued until 2 o'clock, when dinner was served. Classes resumed after dinner and ran until 4 or 5 o'clock. Prayers were held again at night, and the roll was called as in the morning.

Socially, the students at the South Carolina Female Collegiate Institute entertained in the parlor and sometimes in the library, but rules forbade any male visitors except brothers or cousins. According to former students, however, it seemed that every male student from the college in Columbia had a cousin or sister (real or imagined) at Barhamville, so there was never a lack for social company. The girls participated in activities typical for their age and station, such as regular May Day parties. At these they elected their queen, danced around the maypole, and enjoyed themselves quite as much as college girls of the present time.

In 1850, eight teachers were responsible for the education of 120 students. Professors taught music, painting, modern languages, chemistry, philosophy, mathematics, and English. One aspect of the South Carolina Female Collegiate Institute that undoubtedly contributed to its success was the relatively high salaries paid to its instructors. Between 1850 and 1861, the annual outlay for teachers (most of whom came from the North) was from $12,000 to $14,000.[69] (Marks listed his tax value as $65,000 in the 1860 census.) The faculty included a chaplain, who taught Christian evidences, Paley's moral philosophy, ethics, and Butler's analogy, besides preaching every Sunday. (In a remarkably tolerant gesture, Marks engaged a chaplain from a different Christian denomination each year.) He also employed "a gentleman, a graduate of a first-class college," to teach the classic languages, the sciences, and higher mathematics. Additionally, two "lady teachers" taught mathematics, geography, and history, among other subjects. Marks himself lectured on history for an hour every day. As was the practice in most places, "foreign" music teachers (two) provided music instruction. Other faculty included teachers of drawing and painting and a dancing master.[70]

A list of some of the faculty between 1857 and 1861 demonstrates the distribution of classes, as well as the distinctly European slant of the teachers themselves. Elias Marks, although a medical doctor by training, served as principal and was in charge of the department of history and belles lettres. His wife, Julia Warne Marks, taught writing and held a reputation for establishing the "famous" Barhamville hand. The other faculty included M. Douvilliers—French, drawing, modern languages; Rev. Mr. Donnelly, Prof. Reynolds, Mr. Alexander, and Mr. Ward—chaplains at different times; Mr. Orchard (an Englishman)—music master; Madame Sosnowski (German)—painting and drawing; Madame Feugas and M. Strawinski (Polish)—dancing; and M. Manget—French.[71] In the academic year 1857–58, the school faculty included "a Hungarian pianist—expert—the best we ever had." Unfortunately, this pianist remains anonymous.[72]

Luckily, accounts exist that provide detailed information about music at the South Carolina Female Collegiate Institute. Because of the proximity to the state capital and the Markses' social connections, musical solo performers and companies visited Barhamville whenever they were in Columbia. These included the famous Norwegian violinist Ole Bull, who had performed with Liszt and whom Robert Schumann compared favorably to Niccolò Paganini, and Blind Tom, the black pianist Thomas (Greene or Wiggins) Bethune, whose engagements included a command performance for President James Buchanan in 1860.[73]

During the mid-nineteenth century, the cost of lessons on the piano was $50; on the harp or guitar, $60. In other institutions, guitar and voice did not cost as much as piano and/or harp. Henry Campbell Davis lists an "introduction to the music department" that cost $5; what exactly this fee was for remains unknown. In comparison, the cost to board at the school was $67.50, while tuition in the "regular" courses (Latin, drawing, and so on) combined for a total of $32. Dancing lessons were $10 per quarter. The use of a piano for practicing purposes was $6—three times the cost for the same at the Greensborough Female Academy.[74] Perhaps this charge was to cover the purchase of the new pianos with which the school was furnished in the 1850s.[75]

The instruction books in music mirror those used in other schools. For piano lessons, standard tutors by Henri Bertini, Franz Hünten, and Carl Czerny were required. Bertini was a French pianist who had studied with Muzio Clementi. He composed many popular works for the piano during the nineteenth century, and his two methods (*Le Rudiment du pianiste* and *Methode de piano elementaire et facile*) may be found in many publishers' catalogs from that period. Hünten also composed numerous works, including several transcriptions/arrangements of famous arias from operas such as Bellini's *I Puritani* and *Norma*. A student of Anton Reicha's (as was his more famous contemporary and touring pianist, Henri Herz) and Luigi Cherubini's, Hünten's works rarely require a high degree of technical proficiency. His *Scales and Exercises for the Piano Forte* were still in demand during the war years: a announcement in the *Southern Literary Messenger* notes that the Randolph publication of this work is "a much needed publication, since we have been cut off by the blockade from foreign publications of a similar character."[76] The music of Czerny has remained in circulation to the present day and is frequently used for technical studies.

Guitar students practiced music by Ferdinando Carulli and Matteo Carcassi, two of the most famous guitarists of the nineteenth century. Carcassi's method book (Op. 59) and studies (Op. 60) influenced generations of guitarists, and the composer was a favorite performer in fashionable European salons. Carulli's penchant for simple, direct melodies assisted in making his music popular with young students. Voice students apparently learned in a class situation, using either *Nason's Vocal Class Book* or *Kingsley's Juvenile Choir for Classes* (part of the National Series of Standard School Books, published by A. S. Barnes, New York).[77] In 1857, the curriculum at the South Carolina Female Collegiate Institute included a course on the "theory and practice of instrumental music and vocal music"—whether or not this is close to what today is considered music theory is unknown, but it is unusual to find a course on the "theory" of music among institutions in the United States at this time.[78]

An article in the 1847 Barhamville Register claimed that the "department of music [at the South Carolina Female Collegiate Institute] is filled with the most accomplished performers," noting especially the quality of the vocalists. In 1849–50, the school employed two full-time music teachers: William Henry Orchard and Miss Serena Bluxome, who instructed on guitar, piano, and organ. Orchard was born in Bath, England, and in 1835 advertised to teach music (harp, piano, guitar, and flute) in Tallahassee, Florida.[79] He married Helen Zubly Williams on 3 January 1836 at Beech Island, South Carolina. At least one of his daughters, Lizzie (Elizabeth), attended the South Carolina Female Collegiate Institute, beginning at age seven. (Eight children were in the home when the 1860 census was taken, but Lizzie was not; she graduated from the institute in 1857 and presumably moved out of the family home. She composed a patriotic work, "Major General Hampton's Quickstep," during the war.) William Orchard died in 1880 in Columbia, South Carolina, and Lizzie in 1909. William also received recognition for a heroic demonstration before Sherman's troops, in which he stood at the top of the stairs leading into the school daring the Union troops to enter.[80]

Little is known about Serena Bluxome. Bluxome is an English surname, and Serena may have also come from England.[81] Several women with the surname Bluxome are associated with music in this period. In New York City, one writer reported that "Miss Bluxome has much improved as an accompanist" in 1857.[82] A Georgiana Bluxome taught piano in Wilmington, North Carolina, and her students were said to have had "a good degree of proficiency in piano—showing the skill of their talented instructress."[83] No connection with Serena has been found, however.

Orchard exemplifies the preference southerners had for foreign music professors. Several other foreigners taught music at the South Carolina Female Collegiate Institute, including one J. La Taste who taught at the Columbia Female Academy and also at Barhamville.[84] According to the 1852–53 annual report, Manuel M. Párraga was responsible for teaching piano and Spanish during that academic year. The report of 1856, the next year for which the data is available, lists Carlos Mera providing instruction in piano and Spanish; Miss M. M. Sherwood Dawes (of England) also taught piano, in addition to French and German, during that academic year. According to the 1860 Virginia (Richmond) census, Mera was born in Chile and was thirty years old. He is not listed as owning property, but his wife, Cornelia (born in New York), is credited with having $800 in personal property. His occupation in that census is "music teacher."

Two years later, Madame Sophia Sosnowski (a "German") was teaching German, vocal and instrumental music, and painting. Sosnowski's biography is better documented than that of most of the other instructors. Born Sophie Wentz (in Baden, 1809), she married Joseph Stanislaus Sosnowski, a Lithuanian of Polish extraction, in 1833. That year they sailed for the United States. They eventually settled in Pennsylvania with their four children. Upon

Joseph's death, Sophie took a position teaching music, French, and German at the Emma Willard School. She moved south to teach at Madame Dupree's School in Charleston, and later (1853) Sosnowski joined the faculty at the Montpellier Seminary in Macon, Georgia, and also Bishop Elliot's Seminary. After the fall of Columbia, Madame Sosnowski went to Athens, Georgia, where in 1861 she took charge of the Lucy Cobb Institute (which had opened its doors in 1858). She subsequently established the Home School in Athens in 1865, employing her daughters and a granddaughter, Ida Schaller. Schaller had studied music at the Boston Conservatory and hence took over music instruction at the Home School. An 1889 author praises Sosnowski for her "high character, fine culture, and ability as a teacher."[85] She died in Athens on 18 July 1899 at the age of ninety.

Some personal details on the music teachers at Barhamville help establish the types of relationships students had with them. One particularly illuminating example is a letter from Párraga to Mary H. McAliley, dated 6 July 1854.[86] He sends Mary a copy of his composition the "Barhamville Valse" (entitled "Barhamville Valse Brilliante pour le Piano" on the front cover, figure 4.3), along with a warm recognition of her piano abilities. (See the transcription below.) Párraga notes that Mary has played music that requires more technical proficiency than this "valse brilliante" but hopes that memories of Barhamville will compensate for any simplicity.

My dear pupil:

I have received "Barhamville valse," and as you always seemed interested in the beautiful art in which I had the pleasure of instructing you, and also liked to hear me play that poor composition, not at all worthy of the popularity which it has met, I send you a copy of it.

The name of the piece will always bring to your recollections the place where you spent your days of study and received your education, as also your friends and companions. The obscure name of the composer will perhaps remind you of your teacher, who will never forget one of his best pupils, and with whose application and success was always pleased.

If you return to Barhamville the next session, as I hope you will; you will find your teacher always the same and always trying to instruct you with all his power.

You will not find *Barhamville* difficult, as you play much more complicated pieces, and my first desire would be to have you learn it, and when you play it remember your friends, companions, and your teacher and
humble servant

Manuel M. Parraga[87]

The "Barhamville Valse" typifies the music most young women played at school. The work is not difficult and falls easily under the fingers. Mary apparently was indeed at least a moderately successful piano student. In 1855, she performed in a recital with Sarah E. Thompson of Liberty Hill and Mary D. Ancrum of Camden.[88]

Fig. 4.3. "Barhamville Valse Brilliante pour le Piano," by Manuel M. Párraga, page 1.
Library of Congress.

Letters home offer other information on the type of music heard at the South Carolina Female Collegiate Institute. Cornelia Boyd wrote to her father in December 1857 asking him to tell her mother that she had completed learning the piano piece "Musidora Mazurka" (by Ja's. Bellak). Her most recent vocal study included "I Wish Somebody'd Come" (there are several settings of this text).[89]

Fig. 4.4. "Chicora: The Original Name of Carolina," front cover showing the South Carolina Female Institute at Barhamville. From the Historic American Sheet Music Collection in the Rare Book, Manuscript, and Special Collections Library, Duke University.

In 1861, Prof. A. Hatchsek, a member of the faculty at the South Caro-lina Female Collegiate Institute, set to music lyrics by Elias Marks entitled "Chicora: The Original Name of Carolina," which was dedicated to "Patriotic Ladies of the Southern Confederated States of North America." Published by C. B. Estvan in Barhamville, the ornate cover page includes a drawing of the school by F. Roeth and an acanthus, a palmetto tree (symbol of South Caro-lina), under which sits a winged female figure on some hills (see figure 4.4.)

The South Carolina Female Collegiate Institute at Barhamville provided its students with a wide array of musical opportunities. They also employed a number of foreign musicians to teach the young women and afforded numer-ous occasions for them to hear professionals. Other schools, such as Salem Female Academy and the Greensborough Female College, also made music a major focus of their curricula. The repertory taught did not vary much, as far as can be discerned, and most of the venues for performance also seemed to be similar from place to place. This consistent approach to music education in southern schools underscores the importance of being moderately musical and knowing how to perform properly in company.

5. The Piano Girl

Practice in private music far more difficult than that you play in general society.

—"MEMS FOR MUSICAL MISSES," HARPER'S, 1851

"Passed away is the girl who played the piano in the stiff Victorian drawing rooms of our mothers. It has always seemed to me that the slippery hair-cloth sofas and the 'Battle of Prague' dwelt in mutual harmony. . . . There really was a piano girl—and more music was never made before in the land!" Thus wrote renowned critic James Huneker in 1904.[1] He continues the above passage with, "The piano girl was forced to practice at the keyboard, even if without talent. Every girl played the piano; not to play was a stigma of poverty." Music lessons, especially piano lessons, were ubiquitous throughout the upper classes in the antebellum South. The piano's universality in and domination of parlor culture during this period is undeniable and warrants individual consideration.

Huneker's comments correspond to a repertory surviving in extant volumes of piano music that can be positively identified with young American women of the nineteenth century. They also suggest a consistently amateur level of piano playing, one that fits nicely with what is known about the deportment of young women, the constraining design of their costume (at least in midcentury), and the technical requirements of much of the extant sheet music published for piano solo. Huneker's statements were made at the turn of the twentieth century (even though the "Battle of Prague" first appeared in print in 1757) and do not point to any specific time period other than the nineteenth century. The heyday of the piano girl, at least in the American South, coincides within the chronological boundaries of this study, and how aspects of piano study and performance represent key facets of southern women's culture deserves special attention.

The social context for young women pianists, "piano girls," has been described in several modern works, particularly since Arthur Loesser's seminal *Men, Women and Pianos: A Social History.* In the 1980s, Judith Tick made the term "piano girl" a familiar one in musicological studies, and since that time the idea of the piano girl and her role in society has been explored by others.[2] Most of these studies describe the social phenomenon of the piano girl, but how she played, whether the repertory differed based on occasion, and the extent of application have yet to be fully considered.

How and what young women played can be discerned from various sources. Sheet music collections provide many titles; those with markings confirm that the works were indeed played, at least in some context. Diaries often provide a better sense of the context in which young women performed. Domestic novelists help complete the picture by demonstrating how society understood musical performance by young women.

Descriptions in Susan Petigru King's *Lily: A Novel* (1855) provide some insight into attitudes toward piano playing and young women pianists in general. King was an interesting paradox among southern plantation women, and her questionable actions—from publishing novels to flirting excessively—clearly place her somewhat outside the normative behavior of someone of her age and class. Literary historian Karen Manners Smith notes that King was one of a few southern women novelists who waged "a literary war on the belle and the lady. . . . [She] insisted that their section could not afford to cultivate feminine ideals that included vanity, weakness, venality, or self-indulgence."[3] Nonetheless, King grew up in the antebellum South and was brought up to be a belle, and her descriptions of young women and the piano concur with statements found in etiquette books, commentaries, and the like throughout the mid-nineteenth century.

As described in *Lily*, King's heroine Lily Vere might be typical of the piano girl: "Three hours a day her fresh, young voice, or her pretty, graceful touch was heard at the piano. She was no great musician, but she had taste, if not execution; sang with sweetness and correctness, though her notes were few, and was, in short, one of those unpretending performers to whom one can listen without an hour's praying and prelude." Lily's cousin Alicia, with whom she is attending school in New York, continues:

> "I know why you plod over your music in that untiring way," Alicia said . . . Lily patiently deciphering a difficult passage in Thalberg, and Alicia lolling back in the easiest chair she could find. . . .
>
> "Why?" asked Lily, pausing, and turning round for a second, with her finger raised over the next note.
>
> "Because Clarence Tracy has chosen to go mad at Heidelberg over the trombone, or ophicleide, or Jew's-harp, or Heaven knows what, and you intend to perfect yourself so as to perform duets with him."[4]

In this passage, King records society's definition of admirable qualities of the young female pianist. She practices three hours a day, which implies a certain economic background since she does not have to spend her time in chores. She is "no great musician," which would be the right words to describe someone from the upper class, for it suggests a profession. She has taste, which signifies culture, presumably attained after some financial support has prepared her. She lacks "execution," somewhat surprisingly, since she practices three hours a day, but too much execution seems to connote an undesirable level of testosterone. She sings with "sweetness and correctness," with only a "few" notes, which distinguishes her from the lower-class of stage performer who might have a wide vocal range but is no "lady." She is "unpretending," not touting herself. In other words, she is an ideal young woman. That such a young lady would spend three hours a day, and her parents (or guardians, in this case) a considerable sum of money, learning to play the piano *not very well* begs the question of why.

THE PIANO GIRL IN THE SOUTH

As early as 1810, a correspondent of the *Raleigh Star* noted that women thought it was necessary to know how to play the piano only in order to get a husband, and the excerpt from *Lily* verifies that many indeed thought that to be the case.[5] Such a pursuit did seem to be on the minds of fathers seeking to find the most suitable matches for their daughters, and the proportionately large amount of money spent on piano lessons, especially when compared to other aspects of education, clearly placed a priority on piano abilities. (Only harp lessons approached those for the piano in cost; voice lessons were usually considerably less expensive.) Pianos were available in a variety of styles and sizes, which naturally affected the price. A January advertisement in the *Raleigh Register* in 1850 lists pianos in rosewood or mahogany available with metallic plate and six octaves for $180–$250; with metallic frame and 6.5–6.75 octaves for $250–$300; and with a metallic frame and seven octaves for $300–$400. By June, the same firm, Kuhn, Anthony & Co. of Baltimore, offered "grand" pianos for $500–$1,000.[6] Other pianos were also available.[7] Writing during the war years, Malvina Waring could report happily that her Steinway managed to remain unscathed by the Yankees' assault on her home.[8]

One of the most surprising aspects of southern women pianists is how dedicated they seem to have been in pursuing music lessons even during the war. Writing on 29 October 1863, Sarah Lois Wadley's friend Miss Mary entertained her with a description of her music lesson and teacher.[9] During the early part of her husband's tenure in Richmond, Anita Dwyer Withers continued to practice and took regular lessons with composer C. T. DeCoëniél at least once a week. Mollie Ford kept up her lessons even while the Confederacy breathed its last, writing to her brother in April 1865 that "I like Miss Ellen very much as a music teacher."[10] And at least one young student wrote to her mother on 4 April 1865 that she had piano lessons daily at that time—which seems incredible considering the state of the South in April 1865. This young pupil, Emma, wrote that she had "learnt 'Lorena' with variations, and I know you will like it." She assured her mother that she practiced an hour before breakfast and after dinner.[11] Surely such devotion to practicing and lessons demonstrates a stronger tie to music than merely obtaining a husband. It is at odds with what we know women endured in the South during the Civil War, yet there can be no denial that playing the piano was integral to many women's lives. It certainly suggests that piano lessons meant more to some than simply part of the arsenal for obtaining a husband.

An excellent visual representation of the piano girl and how she was supposed to perform can be seen on the front cover of the "Happy Family Polka" (figure 5.1) The young woman sits politely, with excellent posture, performing some piece almost solely for her own enjoyment—certainly no one appears to be listening to her. Her performance does not draw attention to her nor distracts the others within hearing but continues on as pleasant background music.

Indeed, the idea of performance demands explanation if one is to understand the piano girl and why she played what she did. The parlor provided the necessary staging for the performance, but the piano girl was not a performer. The "Happy Family Polka" illustrates this point: hardly anyone is listening to her, and she appears to be providing background music. She is not the center of attention. Moreover, she would not display with a virtuoso talent.

REPERTORY

A variety of sources assist in determining what music young women played in the parlor. Most surviving antebellum piano music exists as printed sheet music, often bound in collections. These volumes, whose contents usually span a couple of decades, reveal much about what was considered fashionable among southern women. Vocal music often appears alongside piano solos, although some albums are restricted to piano music alone. The few manuscripts that have survived, such as the Cunningham Manuscript found in the Georgia Historical Society, mirror the repertory found in contemporary bound collections.[12]

Women learned to play from a standard list of piano tutors, not unlike how the piano students of the 1950s-1970s learned from the John Thompson series. Among the inventory advertised for his Augusta store in 1861, A. E. Blackmar includes "Piano Instruction Books" by the following authors: Henri Bertini, Charles Grobe, Ferdinand Beyer, Franz Hünten, Friedrich Burgmüller, Johann Baptist Cramer, Nathan Richardson, Jean-François Latour, and H. C. Baker. Records from the South Carolina Female Collegiate Institute confirm that Bertini and Hünten were used as instruction books there.[13] Bound collections also include these names, as the collection belonging to "B. Allston" currently housed in the Charleston Museum reveals; its contents include Cramer and Hünten.[14]

Fig. 5.1. "Happy Family Polka," front cover. Permission and image kindly provided by The University of North Carolina Music Library, Chapel Hill.

The bound volume that once belonged to Mary E. Hunt of Jonesville, North Carolina, includes exercises in scales and cadences (up to three flats or sharps).[15] After several showy compositions, the entire *Pupils Daily Exercise, for the Piano Forte. Consisting of Cadences & Scales of Major & Minor Keys. Ascending and Descending. Properly Finger'd* appears. The fingering used is the English style, with the thumb marked "x" and the index finger "1."[16] While no publication year is printed on these exercises, they date from earlier than most of the other music bound in the volume (1840s–1850s).[17]

Occasionally, a single volume contains music by only a few composers. For example, a volume that belonged to Louisa Cheves (McCord) of South Carolina contains works by Muzio Clementi and Friedrich Kuhlau.[18] Four different books are bound into this single volume: *Sonatines par M. Clementi* (Op. 36, 37, 38. Revues et doigtées par Louis Köhler, pp. 1–67); *Sonatinen von Fr. Kuhlau* (Revidirt und mit Fingersatz versehen von Louis Köhler und F. A. Roitzsch. Band I, pp. 69–135); *Sonatinen von Fr. Kuhlau* (Revidirt und mit Fingersatz versehen von Louis Köhler und F. A. Roitzsch. Band II, pp. 137–87); and *Beliebte Rondos für Pianoforte von Fr. Kuhlau* (mit fingersatz versehen und herausgegeben von F. A. Roitzsch, pp. 189–240).[19]

The Cheves collection does not represent the norm. More typical, however, are collections that include a variety of music for both solo piano and solo voice (with piano accompaniment) and occasional choruses. These volumes abound in collections throughout the South, and the piano works in them include variations on favorite melodies (including the operatic repertory), dances, sentimental pieces, and an occasional work by a "classical" composer (such as Handel). Publisher A. E. Blackmar's Augusta store advertised the following exemplary collections in 1861: Louis Jullien's *Music for the Millions*, Oliver Ditson & Co.'s *Parlor Companion*, and Elias Howe's *Drawing Room Dances*.

In bound collections, the most common types of solo pieces are polkas and schottisches, an interesting combination since polkas were not considered quite appropriate music for southern belles at public dances. In contrast, at balls, quadrilles were the most acceptable dances, then the schottisches, followed by round dances. According to Jane H. Pease and William H. Pease, "nice girls might perhaps dance the schottische; more daring ones were permitted to waltz; but only the most liberal of chaperones smiled on the polka."[20] Jane North, discussed in previous chapters, would not allow her daughter Carey (Jane Caroline North) to either waltz or polka.[21] Despite her youthful protestations, later in life Carey continued her mother's customs for her own daughters, noting it was not the dance but those who "polked" who were the problem. Yet numerous polkas were purchased and played, even for dancing, in private homes. Mary Gibson's bound collection (see appendix, table 4) contains a typical representation of repertory, including polkas and schottisches.

Pianists provided music for most gatherings in the home, and such enter-tainment could occur at any time and in various types of company. Similarly, how music was used varied; young women not only performed piano solos but also accompanied others or themselves while singing or provided music for dancing. The company in which young women played could be all female or mixed genders. The description by Carey North of her visit with the El-liotts and Vanderhorsts in chapter 3 is one example of how the duties of piano girls could vary in one setting. In this instance, and numerous others, young women sang and played music for dancing. As such, many surviving collec-tions include a number of dances, usually polkas, schottisches, and waltzes.

Adaptations of popular songs and opera arias also ranked high in south-erners' esteem, as can be seen in the latter pieces in Gibson's piano book. These reflect a general trend throughout the entire United States, and many are of the sort described as "brilliant but not difficult." These types of works usually include a number of variations on a popular theme, such as "Auld Langsyne," or melodies from operas, as made fashionable by touring pianists. In particular, Henri Herz's works appear regularly in collections owned by young women and in other references.[22]

What is generally missing from most collections of piano music from the mid-nineteenth century owned by young women is what would be considered "classical" literature today. Only rarely did abstract music composed for the piano make its way into a young woman's book. The culture was essentially a popular music culture, not an overly sophisticated one.[23] Christie Anne Farnham mentions that "by mid-century it was possible to find young women learning to play Beethoven and Schumann," but this comment needs clarifica-tion.[24] For example, while a few popular waltzes by Beethoven made their way into collections owned by young southern women, the sonata movements did not. As Katharine Ellis finds in her work on French female pianists, Beethoven sonatas were not considered appropriate for women, being entirely too mascu-line in conception and indeed in the physicality required to perform them.[25]

This opinion seems to have been the case on both sides of the Atlantic.[26] That women were not to perform masculine music is confirmed by a state-ment in an 1859 etiquette book: "Do not sing songs descriptive of masculine passion or sentiment."[27] How far this extended to piano music has yet to be determined, but it surely must have had some influence, and the lack of Beethoven and other "masculine" composers in women's books evinces gender distinctions within the piano repertory.

Pieces by Stephen Heller, Cramer, Kuhlau, and Clementi are more typically found than those by Beethoven or Schumann in southern women's volumes. Of the major composers for piano now considered part of the canon, only Chopin appears in any source I have examined. In this particular source, in the Moravian Archives at the Archie K. Davis Center in Winston-Salem,

North Carolina, Chopin's D-flat prelude from Op. 28, entitled "Etude" in the manuscript, is included; this is hardly one of the composer's most demanding pieces.[28] The source itself is exceptional for numerous reasons but chiefly because it represents the musical education and expectations of women in Moravian seminaries (including the Salem Female Academy where at least two of the owners of this book, Amelia Adelaide Van Vleck and her sister Lisetta Maria, attended).[29]

The case of Belle Hannah McGehee, discussed in chapter 1, illuminates many aspects of southern pianists. She lived on Burleigh Plantation, near Milton, North Carolina, and her piano book was compiled in the 1850s and 1860s. McGehee's volume includes only piano music, but most of it requires a high level of technical proficiency.[30] She apparently played music more difficult than the simple polka, yet she did not include compositions by Beethoven or Franz Schubert among her repertory.[31] (See table 1 in the appendix.)

Burleigh Plantation was in Caswell County, on the North Carolina–Virginia border; nearby Milton was on the railroad route in Danville, Virginia— a major rail center during the mid-nineteenth century. While its relative obscurity today places Burleigh far from the musical life of Charleston or even Richmond, its significance as a place of commerce can be demonstrated by the advertisement in the *Raleigh Register* mentioned above (5 January 1850). The list of North Carolina references for the piano dealers of Kuhn, Anthony & Co. of Baltimore includes both Mr. Holden and Dr. Thornton of Milton.[32] Even though removed from any major town, piano girls in and around Milton obviously had opportunities to acquire the most up-to-date music and instruments available, a fact that suggests an avid interest in piano music for young women.

PIANO LESSONS

In schools, piano instruction often cost almost as much as full tuition in other subjects, and sometimes it even equaled tuition. The list of expenses from the Danville Female College in Kentucky, 1862–64, exemplifies the various costs a young woman could incur while at school. Music lessons cost $30, plus $5 for the use of an instrument for one hour each day.[33] In 1855, $25 covered tuition, but piano or guitar added another $25 for instruction and a $5 fee for rental of the instrument at Mansfield Female College in Louisiana.[34] These numbers typify the rate for music lessons at seminary.

Lessons could be arranged in a number of ways when young women were not in school. In smaller towns, a school's teachers were often members of the family of the owner. Writing retrospectively in the latter years of the nineteenth century, Letitia Burwell comments that "Mrs. Lomax had several accomplished daughters who assisted in her school, and the harp, piano, and guitar were household instruments."[35] Independent music teachers often inhabited larger towns. When James Aykroyd moved from New Bern to Hillsborough in 1823, he advertised lessons on the piano ($12 a quarter with lessons every other week) and voice ($3 for the same amount and frequency of lessons).[36] In Savannah, Mlle. Angela de Busserole "from Paris" advertised in 1861 that she would teach French, singing, and piano "at Mrs. Jacob Miller's, 108 S. Broad St. or at the residence of the ladies who may favor her with their patronage."[37] Not surprisingly, in the most proper homes, men tutors were not left alone with women pupils, as the case of Anita Dwyer Withers shows: "I commenced taking Music lessons from Mr. DeConoel [C. T. DeCoëniél]. Miss Susan sits in the room."[38] At this time, Withers was married, not single, but her diary supports the code of conduct in the South that restricted women from being alone with men not of their own household, whether or not they were married. Still other music teachers actually became a part of the household of the students. Letitia Burwell records two thoughts concerning a German professor who lived with the family in *A Girl's Life in Virginia before the War*. How much influence foreign teachers' choice of repertory had on southern taste has yet to be explored, but clearly, from Burwell's recollections quoted in chapter 3 of this book, her German music professor brought new music with him. Burwell wrote from Bedford County, in the western region of Virginia (just below the Shenandoah Valley), which shows how far such foreign-born musicians were willing to travel for work. Similarly, Withers began her diary in San Antonio, Texas, a fact that validates the significance musical accomplishment held in the lives of young women all over the South. This phenomenon is even more striking when one considers that most women of the plantation class were not given the opportunity to meet with other women of similar social standing but led rather isolated lives on remote plantations miles from anyone of similar stature.[39]

PLAYING LIKE A "LADY"

The evidence presented above demonstrates devotion to a degree of musical accomplishment, but they do not indicate the level of playing these women achieved. Judging from the available sheet music that falls under the titles "polka" or "schottische," one might conclude that for the most part, very few technical demands were made on these young women.[40] Evidence suggests, however, that a substantial percentage of these women rose above that level, and, on further examination, clues surface revealing a much more advanced repertory that begs still further questions of deportment and audience. Carey North casually included a reference to sight-reading for the Vanderhorsts—as if doing so was nothing extraordinary. The piece in question is given in part in figure 3.1. It is not particularly challenging, but if she was playing and singing simultaneously and apparently with no trepidation, her abilities can be judged somewhat. She probably represents the piano girl. But a host of references in other diaries and in sheet music collections themselves reveals a significant undercurrent of serious accomplishment, far beyond the basic expectations of the piano girl—one in which talent was allowed to flourish. More important, it appears that this accomplishment was a personal one, rarely vetted before the public, as surviving recital programs of the period do not include the same repertory.

That some young women aspired to a more difficult repertory is certain. When she had the opportunity to hear Louis Moreau Gottschalk ("the young Créole") play at a "grand concert" in Washington, D.C., Virginia Clay-Clopton noted that "the concert was a memorable one. . . . At that time Gottschalk's popularity was at its height. Every concert programme contained, and every ambitious amateur included in her repertory, the young composer's 'Last Hope'" (figure 5.2).[41] Most of the repertory for young women falls easily under the fingers, even the more technically demanding pieces. While many

Fig. 5.2. Virginia Clay-Clopton. Used with permission of *Documenting the American South*, The University of North Carolina at Chapel Hill Libraries.

of the simpler arrangements are in C, many of the moderately difficult works are in a flat key, such as A-flat or possibly D-flat. Such keys lend themselves comfortably to certain types of passagework and figuration, such as extended arpeggios on tonic and dominant, and contain an equally convenient closely related key for the trio or B section.

Hand-crossing is surprisingly common, which begs the question of how one accomplished such a physical move in a low-cut evening dress, presumably with a potential beau standing nearby if not over the shoulder (figure 5.3). Circumstances suggest that this type of passage was either not played in mixed company or that more conservative attire, such as a walking costume, was the norm for performance of solo piano music in the parlor. (Such dressing for piano performances seems reasonable, considering that many of the spontaneous performances in the venue were the results of the ubiquitous calling on acquaintances that was necessary in southern cities and towns.) Many

Fig. 5.3. Wood engraving from February 1851 edition of *Godey's Lady's Book*. From the copy in the Rare Book Collection, The University of North Carolina at Chapel Hill.

contemporary portraits exhibit young women in high-necked bodices (often of a dark color), frequently with a lace or white collar around the throat. While this sort of dress would not expose the performer too much, the fact that the armscye (where the sleeve joins the bodice) was cut so low that arms could not be lifted too high further complicates the physical gesture and suggests that playing lengthy figurative passages that extended the entire keyboard, weighty octave playing (as might include the use of the upper arms and even back), and cross-hand sections would not have been played in mixed company.

Another aspect to consider concerning dresses of this period is that women of the upper class had their clothes fitted as tightly as possible. Such close molding to their particular figures indicated that they did not intend to share the dresses and that the clothes were made expressly for them; both factors signified wealth. When coupled with the preference for a constricted fit (over a tightly-drawn corset), the bodice and sleeves do not suggest much physical movement.

Other aspects of antebellum piano literature demand further questions. A number of the more difficult pieces require large leaps from the lower bass to at least the middle of the keyboard in a fast tempo, which is hardly ladylike. Additionally, many compositions include dynamic levels of *ff* (*fortissimo*) or greater, which further strains the idealized picture of the graceful, quiet, subdued southern belle. The raucous Verdi-like accompaniment of "Fantaisie pour le piano sur le 'Bonnie Blue Flag'" provides an example of how difficult it is to reconcile the inherited vision of the piano girl with the music she played. A. Cardona received the credit for this piece, but he dedicated it to Mary Céleste Dimitry. Dimitry, curiously, held the copyright. This circumstance is unusual and suggests a close relationship between the two. Granted, there is no evidence that Dimitry actually played this work, but the fact that she owned the copyright implies that she had some direct connection with it.[42]

A composition that challenges the propriety and docile nature of the southern belle's behavior is "Freedom's Tear Reverie" by the famous Confederate (by way of Europe) composer Theodore von La Hache. La Hache dedicated this work to his pupil Miss Bettie Mahan, and it is tempting, if not provable, to believe that she would have tried to play it. On the other hand, why would La Hache dedicate such a gymnastic composition to a young female student—would not a polka or waltz be more appropriate? Simple parlor gems, as many pieces were labeled, would seem more suitable for a young lady, not this grandiose "reverie." The technical feats include very fast scalar passages, repeated notes in octaves, large chordal leaps, chromatic octave figures marked *fortissimo*, *sforzando,* and *stretto*, and two places where the right hand trills (fingers 4 and 5) while simultaneously playing a melodic line.

Furthermore, the sentiments required to make this work believable are assiduously marked in the score. Among the markings are *Con tristezza, agi-*

tato, con molto sentimento, strepitoso, martellato, con fuoco, and a peculiar *dolce marcato.* These indications challenge ideas about southern women pianists. How can one remain ladylike while playing *martellato* and *con fuoco?* Such physical display seems beyond the demure southern belle, and as seen above, her clothing did not permit it. Moreover, an anonymous etiquette manual of 1839 advises young women not to raise their arms above the waist, not to let their hands appear stiff, and to avoid excessive bodily activity. In contrast, they were urged to use their hands only in expressive ways and not to use them too often.[43] As such, the markings in "Freedom's Tear Reverie" seem to go beyond the reserved nature that society demanded of belles. Such a work could not be accomplished if the performer adopted a stance such as that demonstrated in the February 1863 edition of *Godey's Lady's Book* (figure 5.4).[44]

A QUESTION OF BRILLIANCE

Clay-Clopton further comments that among the attendees at a command performance at the White House by Blind Tom, the famous black pianist, were Miss Phillips of Alabama and her cousin Miss Cohen of South Carolina, "who were brilliant amateur players with a local reputation."[45] These two "pianists" performed a "brilliant and intricate duet" (unnamed).[46] Such works

Fig. 5.4. Wood engraving from February 1863 edition of *Godey's Lady's Book.* From the copy in the Rare Book Collection, The University of North Carolina at Chapel Hill.

incorporate some of the devices noted earlier, such as beneficial key choices, or others, such as staccato melodic lines when trilling in the same hand.

The use of the label "brilliant" twice in one entry brings to mind descriptions of piano music made by various writers throughout the nineteenth century. As early as 1823, the editor of the *Monthly Magazine of Music*, a London publication, appealed to music professors not to be persuaded by "importunate mothers" who demand that "the *showy* thing of three minutes must be procured."[47] Indeed, in *Men, Women and Pianos*, Loesser includes a section entitled "Brilliant but Not Difficult," as he examines music and music pedagogy in England.[48] He traces the phrase "brilliant but not difficult" to Ignaz Moscheles, who complained that mothers of students asked for "something with a pretty tune in it, brilliant but not difficult."[49] Ellis also describes such pieces in vogue in Paris at this time. She draws attention to the marketing of variations on popular operatic themes to women as "brilliant but not difficult" pieces in relationship to Herz and others, noting that in these pieces, "the female pianist gives the impression of displaying more technique than she really has."[50] Advertisements by American publishers and critiques by American reviewers attest that these works were equally popular in the United States.

An 1861 advertisement from Blackmar's firm illustrates how publishers marketed such works. When listing "Her Bright Smile Haunts Me Still; Improvisation," a composition by the most prolific composer in New Orleans at the time, La Hache, Blackmar describes it as "Brilliant, Showy and moderately difficult." Another representative example of the "brilliant but not difficult" piece is "La Louisianaise" by composer William Vincent Wallace.[51] Composed for and dedicated to "Mme. G. Johns" of New Orleans, its subtitle is "Valse Brilliante"—which appears in larger letters than "La Louisianaise." Despite the indication that the work is "brilliant," it in fact does not require much more than basic piano ability. The first page, an introduction, contains the most challenging aspects of the composition, while the remainder is a simple waltz in F major.

A different marketing ploy, but one intimately tied to the present subject, is the use of the names of locally known amateur women pianists. An illuminating example of this practice exists in two piano solos dedicated to Rose Kennedy of New Orleans by two different composers. Kennedy's pieces include William Vincent Wallace's "Grande Polka de Concert" (dedicated to "Madlle. Rose Kennedy de la Nouvelle Orleans" in 1850; see figure 5.5) and Maurice Strakosch's "Sea Serpent Polka" (dedicated to Miss Rose Kennedy of New Orleans in 1850).[52] That two works by two different composers were dedicated to the same woman in New Orleans in the 1850s suggests that she may have been quite a skilled performer. Eliza Ripley mentions Rose Kennedy in some detail in *Social Life in Old New Orleans*, calling her piano playing "incomparable."[53]

Fig. 5.5. Two pages from William Vincent Wallace's "Grande Polka de Concert," dedicated to Rose Kennedy of New Orleans. Library of Congress.

Ripley also notes that Rose did indeed play the "Sea Serpent Polka" for her friends, adding that "it was not an inspiring bit of music, but her wonderfully deft touch would make melody out of anything that had crotchets and quavers in it."[54] She also refers to Kennedy playing the "Grande Polka de Concert" by Wallace.[55]

Ripley further comments on piano instruction in New Orleans at this time. She notes that one teacher insisted on marking up the students' music to the point that some sheets "are so spotted with black pencil marks they are a sight!" Even more intriguingly, Ripley says that, in addition to being required to learn Strakosch's "Mazourka Sentimentale" and Émile Johns's "La Valse Autrichenne," all Madame Boyer's students learned "other bits a thousand times more difficult and intricate, like Gottschalk's 'Bamboula.'"[56]

This remark again demonstrates the paradox between how southern belles were supposed to behave and how they may have appeared when playing the piano. How brilliant should they be? If Ripley and her acquaintances did indeed learn Gottschalk's famous "Bamboula," they must have challenged southern attitudes toward ladylike behavior. An account of the composer and his music in *Graham's Magazine* acknowledges that "La Bamboula" is Gottschalk's "most original" and "most national" composition.[57] In order to appreciate it, the author of the article, H. Didimus (Edward Henry Durell), recommends that one watch the *bamboula* being danced, in order to fully appreciate its wildness.[58] He continues:

> Let a stranger to New Orleans visit, on an afternoon of one of its holydays, the public squares in the lower portions of the city, and he will find them filled with its African population, tricked out with every variety of a showy costume, joyous, wild, and in the full exercise of a real saturnalia. As he approaches the scene of an infinite mirth, his ear first catches a quick, low, continuous, dead sound, which dominates over the laughter, hallo, and roar of a thousand voices, while the listener marvels at what it can be doing there. This is the music of the *Bamboula*, of the dance *Bamboula*; a dance which takes possession of the negro's whole life, transforms him into a savage of the banks of the Congo, and reinvests him with all the instincts, the sentiments, the feelings which nature gave to his race, to sleep for awhile, to be partially obliterated by the touch of civilization, but to remain forever its especial mark. Upon entering the square, the visitor finds the multitude packed in groups of close, narrow circles, of a central area of only a few feet; and there, in the centre of each circle, sits the musician, astride a barrel, strong-headed, which he beats with two sticks, to a strange measure incessantly, like mad, for hours together, while the perspiration literally rolls in streams and wets the ground; and there, too, labor the dancers, male and female, under an inspiration or a possession, which

takes from their limbs all sense of weariness, and gives to them a rapidity and a durability of motion that will hardly be found elsewhere outside of mere machinery. The head rests upon the breast, or is thrown back upon the shoulders, the eyes closed, or glaring, while the arms, amid cries, and shouts, and sharp ejaculations, float upon the air, or keep time, with the hands palling upon the thighs, to a music which is seemingly eternal. The feet scarce tread a wider space than their own length; but rise and fall, turn in and out, touch first the heel and then the toe, rapidly and more rapidly, till they twinkle to the eye, which finds its sight too slow a follower of their movements. Ah! the abandon of the *Bamboula*; the transformations of the *Bamboula*; no wilder scene, no more exciting exhibition of the dominancy of sheer passion, uncultivated, savage, is to be found in the tales of travelera. It is the morale of this; the poetry of this, with all its associations, that Gottschalk strove to embody in his composition.[59]

Later in the same article, "La Bamboula" is said to be capable of exciting young men's emotions beyond control, with its suggestion of dancing girls with tambour and cymbal.

An 1886 magazine article by E. W. Kemble included a drawing of the *bamboula* being danced.[60] Such associations with wild dances that emanated from Africa seem inappropriate for the guarded world of the southern belle, yet Ripley mentions the work's frequent performance by young women of elite status. Authors of etiquette manuals recommended that young ladies not move quickly nor with broad gestures; they were not even to lift their arms above the level of their waists. This dance personifies a completely opposite representation. Were the young women who played "La Bamboula" exerting some sort of resistance to tradition? For whom did they play such a composition?[61] Eliza Ripley comments earlier in her diary that she once performed the "Battle of Prague," a work composed in the mid-eighteenth century, and ended it with a "loud bang." The assembled listeners responded with an extended silence that embarrassed Ripley.[62] If the "Battle of Prague," a warhorse over a century old that requires relatively little physicality, had to be handled properly, how, then, did she manage "La Bamboula"?

RESIGNATION OR RESISTANCE?

All of the rules governing behavior, deportment, and dress can be seen in how the piano girl functioned within the limited sphere available to her controlled world. How young women reacted to this world has been the subject of debate among historians of southern women's culture. Joan Cashin labels it a culture of resignation. In her most representative form, the piano girl embodies this culture of resignation. Here the ideals of southern womanhood may be observed as a microcosm that reflects larger cultural values. Everything directed at young women—belles—taught them that they should be entertaining hostesses, pleasant conversationalists, and attractive companions *for others*. Music instruction carried similar expectations. Practically no references indicate that girls learned to play the piano because they *wanted* to.[63] Rather, it was always to please someone else. They resigned their lot to spending several hours a day in pursuit of accomplishment on the piano.

Many young women performed to expectation within the circumscribed world of southern society. Others did not. In fact, many appear to have accomplished more than they *should* have. In *Scarlett's Sisters*, Anya Jabour interprets southern girls' opposition to engagement and marriage as representative of a culture of resistance rather than as resignation.[64] The freedom to choose male partners was the only personal choice southern women had. Jabour finds that in prolonging this period of freedom, girls resisted their parents' wishes and were as independent as they would ever be. This is the same period in their lives that many of them studied piano.

Resistance—in the form of not marrying—might be desirable for a young woman of seventeen, but by the mid-twenties, resignation to marriage seemed the best option for most. Jabour draws attention to the dilemma many young women faced when they seriously considered a man's offer of marriage. Her reading of a lithograph illustrates a resistance to, or at least serious consideration of, matrimony. In this example, entitled "Popping the Question," the young woman has control of the relationship, and the man is waiting for her to direct that relationship. The young woman knows all too well that she will completely reverse the situation by accepting his offer. Once she accepts the proposal, she simultaneously accepts an inferior status.[65] In this example, Jabour suggests that the wedding day becomes the "threshold" between cultures of resistance and resignation while also serving as a transition from the relative freedom of girlhood to that of adult responsibilities.[66]

Women who pursued piano beyond the expected simple parlor polka personify a similar resistance. That young girls had to learn to play the piano (or perhaps guitar or voice) was a given. But the repertory they were to play was highly proscribed and simple. A woman who played too well ran the risk of being considered something of a hermaphrodite, as discussed below. Examples presented earlier in this book also reveal that being too good, technically, was almost always ill-received. One woman who practiced and studied piano more than was required by contemporary standards was Anita Dwyer Withers. She differs from most of the women described thus far in this study in that at the time she began her diary, she was married. On 4 May 1860, her first entry, Withers wrote: "May the 1st was the first time that I went down to breakfast with my Husband since the birth of our baby. That morning I practised [*sic*] on the Piano, and took a ride in the afternoon."[67] Such an entry is typical of her entire diary, for practicing and lessons appear numerous times therein. At the time she began writing, Withers was living in San Antonio, and the fact that such an accomplished pianist bloomed in the far reaches of the country is yet another fascinating detail yielded by this study. She played for guests, both men and women, and often accompanied her brother Joe, a violinist.[68]

After a short stay in Washington, D.C., the Withers family moved to Richmond after the war broke out. While in Richmond, Withers began piano studies with the composer DeCoëniél, beginning in October 1861, after he had come to her suggesting that she study with him.[69] Tellingly, despite many days of not feeling well for various reasons, Withers rarely missed her piano lessons: "I had a bad head ache all day Friday, but took my Music lesson, and was particularly stupid about it. I went to bed about 5 O'clock."[70] She again had lessons the following Tuesday and Friday. After having a tooth pulled out on 13 November, she "remained in bed for two days, missed one Music lesson"; however, by Tuesday the 19th, Withers was well enough for the next lesson.[71]

Later in that month (29 November 1861), Withers wrote that she began learning "Le Reve" (see figure 5.6).[72] Published in New York in 1843 and composed by William Vincent Wallace (his Op. 21), the work is dedicated to Madame Coralie Frey of New Orleans.[73] It far exceeds the demands of the piano music described up to this point in this study, with chromatic octaves simultaneously in both hands, multiple occurrences of twelfths to be reached in one hand (quickly), tremolos at *fortissimo*, intricate workings for fingers 3, 4, and 5 in the left hand, tremolos spanning a twelfth, a cadenza of alternating chords (both hands), and markings of *pesante*—hardly what one would expect of a demure southern gentlewoman.

Not only is this grandiose work part of Withers's repertory, but also noteworthy is the fact that it is dedicated to a woman (in New Orleans). This does not mean, of course, that the dedicatee played it. But several other similar dedications suggest that composers might have acknowledged accomplished women pianists who were not allowed to perform as professionals but who had reached a high level of technical ability.

Withers had a lesson on 28 December 1861 and subsequently had more on 2, 3, and 4 January 1862. On the 11th, she began a new session of lessons. These continued regularly. On Friday, 17 January, she comments that "I practiced soon after breakfast as usual."[74] On the 25th, Withers began working on "The Whispering Wind," published as a "Mazurka Caprice pour le piano par Hermann A. Wollenhaupt" in New York in 1856. Dedicated to Gottschalk, Wollenhaupt accomplished the "wind" effect with delicate right-hand figures reminiscent of Chopin that continue almost uninterrupted throughout the entire composition. Granted, the keys in which the piece moves (D-flat and A-flat) enable an easier glide over such figures, but they are far from the polkas and schottisches mentioned above.

Fig. 5.6. "Le Réve," by William Vincent Wallace, page 6. Permission and image kindly provided by The University of North Carolina Music Library, Chapel Hill.

Quite unexpectedly, Withers notes on Saturday, 29 March 1862 that "I determined to visit Salisbury—I took my last Music lesson." There is no mention of why the lessons ceased. Perhaps the difficulties expressed by other young women in trying to maintain music (and other skills) while keeping house finally caught up with Anita Withers. She had suffered the loss of her firstborn with great sadness, and a subsequent miscarriage (or two) must have weighed on her as well. Indeed, only one more mention of her playing and singing appears in the diary, and that is on Wednesday, 17 September 1862.[75] Increasingly, the war and its consequences take space in the journal, as does the birth and death of children in the vicinity.[76]

Withers is an example of a female pianist with more than adequate abilities and interest, if her choice of repertory and frequency of mention in her diary may be used to judge. Hannah McGehee's book also contains an admirably challenging repertory, including large-scale works by Gottschalk and Wollenhaupt. To these names, Herz and Thalberg may be added as part of the typical repertory. The quote about the fictional Lily Vere practicing Thalberg also hints at an accomplished player. On the other hand, King presents her as at least technically inferior to her cousin Alicia, who, incidentally, is morally inferior to Lily. How much weight we should attach to the name "Thalberg" associated with pianists is questionable, for George Upton wrote (retrospectively) in 1908: "The Thalberg fantasies were all the rage for a time. . . . Every little piano thumper tackled them."[77]

That Thalberg's music was known in Charleston (where King's characters spend most of their lives) is confirmed both by the fictional Lily Vere's practicing and by two actual letters from Thalberg to Madame Marie Petit that survive in the collection of the South Carolina Historical Society. Petit, a professional musician from Belgium, ran a "School for Young Ladies" in Charleston in the 1850s.[78] Her husband, Victor Petit, was a musician as well, and her daughter Herminie was considered a child prodigy. Victor advertised a solfège class in Charleston in 1853, and he also accompanied Adelina Patti for a concert there.[79] Herminie played for European royalty when she was seven and debuted in New York City in 1852. She performed as a solo pianist and accompanied Patti herself at that time. She was to have been a concert pianist—Thalberg comments on her abilities—until her father's death altered her course.[80]

Herminie's 1919 obituary states that upon the death of her father in 1856, she began a career as a music teacher, married Barbot in 1862, and was "the best of wives, mothers [six children], her marriage did not interrupt her music and her home has always been one of the city's musical centers." She served as organist at the Cathedral of St. John the Baptist from 1882 to 1919, and in the 1870s and 1880s she was the director of the Charleston Musical Association.[81] Perhaps more important, she carried on teaching not only piano but also solfège in Charleston before the war—an unusual choice of subject among women teachers. Nonetheless, we cannot overlook the fact that she was not a native southerner, and her career was one of a teacher first, as it turned out.

PROPER PIANISTS

Dr. James Norcom wrote to Mary B. Harvey on 25 May 1848, "The truth is, Miss Mary, that woman, in her proper sphere & office, is the grace, the ornament, the bliss of life. Out of it, she may shine and dazzle," but "she will soon cease to command attention and admiration, if she lack those characteristics of feminine softness & delicacy & modesty which so eminently distinguish her from our rougher sex. If these divine & love inspiring attributes be wanting, the woman disappears, & we behold in her place, . . . an hermaphrodite, a creature acknowledged by neither sex, & a terror & reproach to both."[82] This advice is close to novelist Sue King's choice of the words "taste," "sweetness," "correctness," and "unpretending" to describe Lily Vere—who was neither a "great musician" nor capable of much "execution"—and her musicality. King provides a keen comparison between her two pianists, for the account of Lily's playing quoted near the beginning of this chapter is followed immediately in the novel with a comparison of her cousin's: "Alicia did not sing, but she played brilliantly, and read music fluently; was rather indifferent about it, and lacked that love of the art which, though restricted from want of *genius*, gave interest to Lily's playing." It is the same Alicia who remarks on the next page: "'What is the use of study? Somehow every one marries so early, and then you give up music and every thing. Look at all the women we know at home [Charleston]. They are taught French, music, drawing, "geography and the use of the globe," and as soon as they marry, they shut the piano, never open a French book, give their paints away, and might a great deal better have had all the money spent on these accomplishments put in the Savings' Bank instead. It is a great waste of time and dollars to study.'"[83]

King judged as Norcom did—Alicia may be one of Upton's "piano thumpers" whereas Lily is one of Huneker's "piano girls." It seems Upton and Huneker describe different types of players: either ones with taste, or ones who "shine and dazzle" and are "brilliant." Many young women took piano—to *not* do so would have been an indicator of bad taste. But that ever-elusive signifier—taste—includes more than a lack of ability; it also includes knowing what to play, when to play, and how much to play for whom. *The Lady's Guide to Perfect Gentility in Manners, Dress, and Conversation, in the Family, in Company, and at the Piano-Forte, the Table, in the Street, and in Gentlemen's Society* gives very explicit advice on matters of taste, as the following excerpts demonstrate:[84]

> *Importance of taste*—Taste is exhibited in the minutest as well as in the most important particulars of conduct; it influences the affections; it gives a bias to the opinions; its control over the inclinations is absolute. (65)

Effect of cultivation—Taste, there can be little doubt, depends, in a great measure, on association. . . . And persons of superior cultivation have not only established for themselves a higher standard of grace or excellence, to which they refer, but they have attained to a quicker perception of the relation of things to each other. (66)

Value of correct taste in society—A correct taste is more properly the result of a general moral and intellectual culture, than of any direct rules or discipline. (67–68)

Naturalness—The first great fundamental rule of good taste is *to be natural*; and it is from an infringement of this that many of our worst mistakes proceed. (68)

Diffidence preferable to ostentation—Beware, also, of an ostentatious manner. By this is meant that kind of manner which savors too much display; which indicates a disposition to make yourself too conspicuous; and which, in short, is the acting out of a spirit of self-confidence and self-conceit. This . . . when seen in a young lady, is quite intolerable. (75)

Considering such disparate items as clothing, social strictures on mixed company, and public display, a multilayered view of southern women pianists begins to emerge. As seen earlier in the chapter, certain types of dresses were worn for specific occasions—fancy dress gowns restricted movement too much to have allowed a woman to perform "Le Réve" on an occasion when such attire was necessary. Even the everyday attire women wore for their requisite calling on friends did not allow for much motion in the upper arms. As such, it is doubtful that in the company of men, women wore clothes that would have allowed them to perform the more demanding pieces. A paragraph in *Godey's Lady's Book* in 1859 promotes that "to instruct on the piano-forte, there must be actual strength, as well as powerful talent," and men should therefore teach piano, whereas women are qualified to teach only singing. This description suggests that "real" piano playing involved serious physical exertion—something ladies did not do.[85] And, as Guion Griffis Johnson noted in his 1937 study on North Carolina social history, "certainly by the [1830s], it had become definitely unfashionable for a lady to exert herself physically."[86]

What is more, in her article "Music and the Feminine Sphere: Images of Women as Musicians in 'Godey's Lady's Book,' 1830–1877," Julia Eklund Koza includes several sections on specific topics, such as women composers and women professional singers, but none on pianists, which further illustrates the lack of a real model of the professional woman pianist in the United States at this time.[87] One might find exceptions to this idea in pianists such as Amy Fay, but certainly not south of the Mason-Dixon Line.[88] The only reference to a potential professional female pianist who was from the South is to Herminie Petit Barbot, who might have had a career as a performer but settled into the role of teacher upon the death of her father. She was foreign-born of professional musician parents, though, and not held to the same rules as a southern lady of the planter class, such as Lily Vere, was.

ON "BRILLIANT EXECUTION"

Evidence from diaries and collections, however, advocates that ladies certainly played a more technically demanding repertory, just not in front of men and perhaps not even in front of other women. The exception might be with teachers (and male teachers were almost always called "professors"), who were presumably of a different social class. Mixed company performances in the parlor were the norm, be it for dancing, singing, or solo performance.

That being said, a careful reading of contemporary commentaries on women and musical performance illuminates a subtler undercurrent of class status that clearly delineates what proper ladies were to play and what performers were to do. *The Lady's Guide to Perfect Gentility* includes a chapter entitled "The Lady at the Piano-Forte," and the advice of the author, Emily Thornwell, gets directly to the issue at hand: "*Invitation to sing or play*—Never exhibit any anxiety to sing or to play. You may have a fine voice, have a brilliant instrumental execution, but your friends may by possibility neither admire nor appreciate either."[89] The use of the term "brilliant instrumental execution" brings back to mind the comment that Lily Vere "had no execution" but did have taste. Modern readers might be tempted to think King's description implies that Lily really couldn't play very well, but what she could manage was to play with feeling or "taste." But this shows a modern bias and how far removed twenty-first-century readers are from the mid-nineteenth century's attitude toward such matters. Contemporary evidence suggests that society preferred the piano girl to play with taste rather than with execution and brilliance. Despite Thornwell's chapter title, the paragraph above is the only recommendation pertaining directly to pianists here. Later, under "Hints and Rules on Polite, Easy, and Graceful Deportment," she counsels young ladies to "let your performance be brief" but nothing further about the actual playing.[90]

More to the point, it seems that "brilliant" did not necessarily imply a positive description but perhaps a crasser one. This interpretation is confirmed by a sarcastic article under the "Centre-Table Gossip" section of *Godey's Lady's Book* of 1852. The following excerpts are taken from this piece, "Directions to Modern Piano-Forte Players": "Always expect to be asked to play in every company. . . . [I]f the invitation to the piano does not come, inquire of your hostess or her daughter if she plays or what the manufacture of the piano is. . . . [I]f the hint is taken, assure the lady you are 'quite out of practice' and 'play little at any rate,' and 'never without your notes' [which you do not have, but after a suitable time searching . . . find them in your muff . . .

where you were keeping them to show to Adelaide]." The author further adds that the young woman should take ten minutes to remove and situate her gloves, fan, bouquet, and the like, and she should never ask about her host-ess's tastes: "You are there to display your own talents, not inquire of theirs." Then, "Commence by a dashing and extemporaneous prelude (learned by heart from Hertz [*sic*])." She should say the piano is out of tune to cover any mistakes she might have made. "Invariably select a piece twenty pages long; it will give you time to make an impression." And "remember that, in the modern school, attention to time, expression, and correctness is not considered essential to brilliant execution."[91]

"Brilliant execution" again, along with the reference to Herz, insinuates that such a performance is undesirable for a true lady—the amateur.[92] It is a marker reserved for professionals, such as the repeated references in reviews of the "execution" of Adelina Patti. Even worse commentary on women pianists is found in a slightly later (1869) piece published by Balmer & Weber in St. Louis. Composed by George W. Brown with words by William Arlington and entitled "She Played on 9 Pianos," the lyrics and the front cover seem to embody the image of Upton's "piano thumper" (figure 5.7):

> Oh couldn't she punish pork and beans,
>   and oysters raw or stew.
> Her size was quite respectable,
>   and her age was twenty-two;
> Her lips were thick like pickled tripe,
>   her parents taught her manners,
> She was the gal to slaughter the notes,
>   and she play'd on nine pianos.
>
> Chorus
> Pianos, pianos,
> She play'd on nine pianos
> One two three four five six seven eight
> Oh! She play'd on nine pianos.
>
> Oh one and all attention give,
>   and a song I now will sing,
> For I've hit upon a subject
>   which I think's the very thing.
> You may talk about your handsome gals
>   your Hetties, Kates, and Hanners,
> But the sweetest gal I ever saw,
>   oh! She play'd on nine pianos.

Her fingers were like lobster claws,
    her thumbs they were both double,
And where she caught them in the keys,
    oh "golly" there was trouble
Her hands were wide, so deep and thick,
    as red as any tanner's;
She was the gal with mice in her hair,
    and she play'd on nine pianos.

Fig. 5.7. "She Played on 9 Pianos," front cover. Permission to reprint kindly provided by The Lester S. Levy Collection of Sheet Music, Special Collections, Sheridan Libraries, The Johns Hopkins University.

The image is not a complimentary one. The publisher may have also intended to extend the insult into racial matters with the textured hair and reference to thick lips.[93] Contrast the vision of the woman pianist in "She Played on 9 Pianos" with that of the young entertainer in the "Happy Family Polka" (figure 5.1). Even though the latter piece dates from slightly later than the period under investigation, I believe it illustrates the ideal situation in which young women played the piano.

A description of a music recital at the Oxford Female Academy in Mississippi in 1842 notes that even though the repertory performed was simple, the students had learned their pieces well. Furthermore, "the style of music preferred in that day was simple melody rather than the class that calls for showy execution—finger gymnastics—or the purely classical." This remark, found in Mrs. I. M. E. Blandin's *History of Higher Education of Women in the South Prior to 1860*, illustrates the distinction between execution and ladylike piano playing.[94] Execution equals finger gymnastics but not pretty music. It also confirms that young women of this class did not play classical music, which would have suggested overexertion.

An article in *Dwight's Journal of Music* of 1856 specifically warns against brilliant execution.

> It should then be your care, at all times and places, when you are requested to play, to lay aside all false modesty, and do your best. Never play carelessly, because only your friends are within hearing, or you are alone.
>
> Try also to play every note as neatly as possible—don't slur over the keys in such haste that you are obliged to leave out half the notes, in aiming for what is so often miscalled a *brilliant execution*. We are aware that to many, this last sentence will seem somewhat heretical; yet we venture to say a "brilliant executionist" may be a very poor musician, if we take this last term as indicating one who makes *music*. A truly great artist scorns the idea of simply "showing off," or "playing for effect," as it is sometimes called—everything in fact, which detracts in any degree from the beauty of the music, in order to display a real of fancied power of execution in himself.[95]

The combined evidence (diaries, collections of sheet music, advice on proper attire and existing costumes, comments from published sources) supports the theory that most southern women did not demonstrate all of their talents when playing in mixed company and probably not even when performing before female acquaintances. Southern women distanced themselves from any activity that might be linked to a career, to earning money, or to being in any way professional. Nor did they allow themselves to be seen as having any other masculine characteristics, such as power. All body movements were restrained so as not to appear to "work" in any way; to do so would be to contravene class boundaries (and "superior cultivation"). The gentle, sweet, correct, and unpretending piano girl would almost never have displayed her abilities, even if she possessed a virtuoso talent. To play the piano with serious physical exertion ("ostentatious" and "conspicuous" display) would be to infringe upon masculine territory, which southern women were extremely reluctant to do. Advice in *Harper's* (1851) directed young women to "practice in private far more difficult [music] than that you play in general society."[96] A young woman who played with "brilliant execution" might cause her to move from the title of "piano girl" to "piano thumper"—hardly a desirable moniker in any period.

6. The Singer

Lily . . . sang with sweetness and correctness,
though her notes were few.

—SUSAN PETIGRU KING, *LILY: A NOVEL*

Next to playing the piano, singing was the most frequently mentioned musical activity in diaries and other references. The idea of singing appealed to the natural simplicity that was inherent in how young women were supposed to behave. The physical act, however, was something different. How one appeared when singing was an aspect that could cause anxiety, for a singer had to face the audience. She had to be careful of how she contorted her mouth as she attempted to produce the proper sounds. Even though clearly performing, she was not to appear to be "on the stage." Furthermore, the repertory itself was open to more scrutiny than that of the piano, for how young girls modeled themselves, or not, on professional singers was dangerous territory. Professional pianists were less threatening because almost all of them were men. Professional singers, on the other hand, included members of both sexes. While most female singers touring in the South carefully guarded their reputations as best they could, a few did not. How young women negotiated association with such models was a complex maze of where to place the self and where to place the other.

Another distinction for singing is its peculiar physicality. Teaching singing may be the most difficult of all music instruction because it is purely physical, personally so. In piano studies, the teacher can give instruction on how to shape the hand while playing or how to practice moving the thumb under the fourth finger. These instructions are easy to demonstrate and also easy to see if erroneously executed on the part of the pupil. Singing is different. It is produced entirely within the body, and the instructor cannot simply describe how to hold the fingers to correct it. Because singing depends on the physical shape of one's bones and how one manipulates the soft and hard palates, tongue placement, and the like, it is a highly personal art. In order to teach voice properly, an instructor must be involved with the physical production of the sound. Singing involves several parts of the body: the face (including sinus cavities, eyes, mouth, teeth, tongue, throat), breathing apparatus, the famous "diaphragm," posture, and chest.

To some degree, voice instructors today usually place their hands on their pupils' bodies. Most often, this is to assist in proper breathing technique or correct posture. Two issues come to mind when considering these physical activities. One is the act of touching the pupil, for such gestures were impossible in the nineteenth century, at least in the situations under discussion. Voice teachers could not simply place their hands on their pupils' bodies, especially not toward the diaphragm. As such, voice instruction was much more dependent on verbal commands than on physical placement. Indeed, elite southern families did not demand much more than singing in tune and a small voice.

Another issue of physicality to consider is attire. The clothing worn by young women during the antebellum period was not conducive to singing, as anyone who has worn a corset for modern productions in period attire can attest. Numerous contemporary articles that try to dissuade young women from wearing such restrictive clothing emphasize that they cannot breathe deeply while cinched tightly. Since breathing is paramount to singing, such strictures must have further hampered singing instruction.[1] As early as the 1820s, Italian opera critic Carlo Ritorni warned women against wearing corsets while singing. To counter these problems, during the mid-nineteenth century, corset-makers designed special garments for professional singers, but it is highly unlikely that the average parlor performer owned one.[2] Southern women, however, would have been loathe to give up this vital part of their costume. Looking their best would outweigh any detriment to singing technique.

Nonetheless, in spite of the physical problems associated with singing, the naturalness of it meant that most everyone could participate. At school, voice instruction was relatively inexpensive compared to piano lessons, and often a singing class was included as part of the regular tuition. Southerners expected that young women could sing with a modicum of success, and being able to do so contributed to their usefulness. Most obviously, the ability of a young mother to soothe her children in the nursery was an expected part of a woman's world and, as such, necessitated some degree of accomplishment.

VOICE LESSONS

Singing lessons were taken either as a group or privately, and teachers often were described as belonging to the "Italian" school. Practitioners acknowledged other styles of singing during the early and mid-nineteenth century, as indicated in a dictionary entry on singing that acknowledges the Italian, German, and French schools of singing:

> The Italian method is distinguished by a peculiar attention to the cultivation of the vocal organs, in order to give the voice the greatest clearness and

flexibility; secondly, by the soft swelling and blending of the tones, which is called *portamento di voce*, and gives to the whole a charm and keeping similar to the effect of a perfect picture; thirdly, by a distinct utterance of the words, though in this the Italian singers are greatly aided by their melodious language. Another advantage of this school is its skill in *recitative*. . . . The defects of this school are, that it often runs into an excess of art and ornament, which among many other causes, is partly owing to the circumstance that, formerly, composers wrote only the fundamental notes for the singers and left them to supply the rest. But Rossini has introduced the fashion of writing all the ornaments in full. The Italian method of singing appears to the greatest advantage in concert and the buffo style in opera. [The authors then describe the German singing technique, but this style does not appear to have been frequently used, at least in the South.] The French method borders on declamation, and shows the proneness of the nation to conversation. The language is very unfavorable for singing, on account of its want of verbal accent.[3]

Of these options, the majority of southern sources refer to the Italian vocal style as the source of instruction. For example, the Southern Female College, in LaGrange, Georgia, was noted as "particularly outstanding, especially in teaching Italian vocal technique."[4] Similarly, Charles A. Dacosta, a voice teacher living in Norfolk by 1812 who later moved to Charleston (1837), advertised that he taught "in the Italian style."[5] (He also taught piano and violin.)

When groups studied together, they apparently used books of music designed for choirs. Mary Terhune mentions singing from *The Boston Academy* in a religious singing group that met at her home. This was probably *The Boston Academy's Collection of Church Music*, which includes beginning sight-singing lessons and progresses to simple hymns and then to anthems. In the hymns, the melody remains in the tenor voice, reflecting an older practice. Of particular interest is a comment concerning the training of female singers:

> In commencing to sing, as the school may now do from a knowledge of the elementary principles of music, let them at first all sing in unison, a single part, say the Base [*sic*], and then the Tenor and Alto, each, separately; afterwards these three parts may be united, and sung together, all the female voices singing Alto. It is highly important that all the female voices should be exercised much on the Alto; that they may have this practice, it is recommended that in the early exercise of the school, the Treble be altogether omitted. When the three parts go well together, a part of the female voices may be required to sing the Treble. It is a very good plan to divide the Treble into two classes, and sometimes require one and sometimes the other, to sing the Alto. Experience proves that if the *low tones* of

female voices are cultivated and brought out, there is no difficulty in the exercise of the *higher tones*, afterward. The best female singers always like to sing Second or Alto. The careless and indolent are usually unwilling to sing this part.[6]

When girls studied privately, they prepared exercises from standard tutors and solo pieces. The advice in *The Boston Academy* to spend time singing alto seems at odds with some of these books, such as the popular *LaBlache's Abridged Method of Singing*. This particular vocal method requires a large amount of high singing, up to high C, and includes exercises in extensive ornamentation, such as one encounters in the works of the bel canto coloratura pieces. Almost none of the literature that exists in surviving collections makes such demands on the singers, which suggests that both professionals and amateurs studied from the same technique methods.

REPERTORY—SONGS

The two major types of pieces that young women sang were songs or arias from popular operas. Many of the songs were by American (or at least living in the United States at the time they were published) or English composers. German *Lieder* rarely appear in the collections, although a work by Franz Abt ("Wenn die Schwalben heimwarts zieh'n," Op. 39, also known as "Agathe") appears in a music book owned by Moravian women at Salem.[7]

One *Lied* that appears to have been well-known is Schubert's famous "Erlkönig." When Miss Helen Underwood lent Sarah Lois Wadley a music book, Sarah found a "beautiful song," the "Erlking." She copied the English text into her diary.[8] With its clamoring accompaniment and different characters to be portrayed, this rather dramatic work does not characterize the typical song that these young women sang. That it should be the only Schubert work besides his "Ave Maria" to be mentioned in an actual performance (the Ladies' Gunboat Musical Evening in Charleston, 1862; see chapter 8) testifies to its long popularity. It also survives in slightly later piano collections in arrangement for piano solo. (Notably, Agnes Graham, in the novel *Agnes*, does sing Schubert's "Wanderer" for Robert; see later in this chapter.)

More representative of the young woman's songbook is that which belonged to the Thornton family of Sussex, Virginia.[9] Most of the publications therein date from the 1840s–1850s. With such pieces as "Rosalie the Prairie Flower" by George F. Root, "When the Moon on the Lake Is Beaming" by Stephen C. Massett, and "I Wandered on the Sea-beat Shore" by J. W. Cherry, the owner of this volume had tastes that resembled those of many other of her peers. When the volume turns to piano music, as it does about halfway through, the repertory there also mirrors that in other collections: popular tunes and schottisches seem to have been favorites.

REPERTORY—OPERA

If young gentlewomen had to sing the operatic repertory, they were encouraged to choose the simpler arias and not to attempt the truly professional repertory. Luckily, the popularity of English opera and Italian bel canto made this a relatively easy task. The more adventurous compositions of the midcentury were not encouraged. An essayist in *Dwight's Journal of Music* (1855) clearly sees no need in one trying to sing Verdi unless one is in the opera house: "We doubt if much singing of Verdi can be nourishing to the voice, or wholesome in respect of style and feeling. Especially in the concert room do some of those dashing cabalettas seem unnatural, there being nothing to justify the excitement indicated in the music, unless it be the excitement of accomplishing a feat."[10] Few works from Verdi appear to have been popular in southern women's vocal collections of the antebellum period, even though some piano books include versions of favorite Verdi melodies and *Ernani* was a particular favorite at the opera house. Rather, the repertory tends to simpler works, some operatic and some not.

An example of how Verdi's pieces appeared in southern women's volumes can be seen in "Oh! Wilt Thou Leave Thy Tranquil Home" from the opera *Nebucadnezzar* (*Nabucco*), published by Benteen in Baltimore (and W. T. Mayo in New Orleans) in the late 1840s and located in the collection owned by Mary Gibson, now housed in the UNC Music Library.[11] The original work is Zaccaria's aria "D'Egitto là su i lidi" and cabaletta "Come notte a sol fulgente" from *Nabucco*. Originally scored for a strong bass voice, the innocuous version in Gibson's book can be sung by any voice type. The arranger (not listed on the sheet music) preserved only a single verse in each part, as opposed to Verdi's setting for soloist and then soloist with chorus.

The text to "Oh! Wilt Thou Leave Thy Tranquil Home," by P. Mordant, Esq., is nothing like that of the original. Verdi set a text in which the character Zaccaria is trying to convince the Hebrews that God will protect them from the Assyrian army (led by Nabucco) and to have no fear. The text of "Oh! Wilt Thou Leave Thy Tranquil Home" is a benign appeal to a lover who has left his home in search of greener pastures. The singer attempts to talk him into remaining at home where they can be together.

Likewise, the music is far from Verdi's original. While retaining the memorable melody of the aria and cabaletta, this version does not require the traditional embellishments one associates with performances of Verdi. It is not known if these were added in the performances in the parlor (instructions on how to do so were certainly in the standard voice tutors), and some degree of improvisation may have indeed taken place. The result, however, of a young woman singing a love song in place of a bass calling the Hebrew people to God is distinctly removed from Verdi's intent.

Similar modifications were made to other opera arias. For "Tutto è gioia" from Bellini's *La sonnambula*, the key has been moved down a third, requiring only high A (and that optional) from the singer, as opposed to high C. In "Ah! non giunge uman pensiero," from the same opera and also in the Gibson collection, the arranger has taken the aria down a fourth, from B-flat to F major, which certainly makes it easier for the average singer. Moreover, the arranger modified some of the coloratura lines so that the high B-flat in the transposed version (high E-flat in the original) is optional. The translation here is close to the original Italian. The arranger for the English version, also published by Benteen and Mayo, is not given, although the work is "as sung by Mrs. Wood."

Perhaps no vocal pieces were as popular as selections from Balfe's *Bohemian Girl*. Balfe's musical gift lay in melody: Johann Strauss Sr. even called him the "King of Melody." With such a talent, Balfe's music naturally rose in popularity among amateur musicians whose primary desire was "sweet singing." Among the most frequently encountered pieces excerpted from *The Bohemian Girl* are "I Dreamt That I Dwelt in Marble Halls" (figure 6.1) and "When Other Lips." The first of these remains one of the most popular melodies from the nineteenth century. It even surfaces frequently in the twentieth; for example, author Willa Cather mentions it (along with several other works from the opera) in her short story "The Bohemian Girl" (1912). A simple song with a relatively small range, the repeated motives and other aspects form a tightly woven expressive piece that has enchanted audiences since its appearance. That it was popular during the period in question is undeniable—numerous versions appeared within a year of its premiere, including arrangements for voice and guitar, piano solo, and voice and piano. All of these were frequently heard in southern parlors.

Not every southerner was enamored of this repertory. A sarcastic article entitled "Music!" by Mr. Sandy Stubblefield (no doubt a pseudonym) makes the following observations about girls' voice studies at "institutions." After informing the reader that he is a widower whose deceased wife had been a consummate singer of the good old songs, he discusses his experiences with his daughters' musical education. The elder daughter, Milly, arrived home from school to a new "splendid rosewood piano—half a dozen octaves or more—it cost me $500." She "dashed off a brilliant prelude" and then proceeded to sing a group of "Ethiopian" songs—much to her father's dismay. He asked her to sing "The Last Rose of Summer" and similar tunes, but she declared them old-fashioned.

Stubblefield's younger daughter, Maggie, remained at school, and he earnestly wrote the lady superintendent that he wished to ensure that she, at least, had a proper musical education. The woman replied that they had hired a "Professor" of "the very highest reputation." When Maggie returned home and sat at the new piano, Stubblefield was initially pleased with her "magnificent execution" but soon displeased with the repertory: "First, she '*dreamt* that she dwelt in marble halls,' till all my *illusions* were most painfully dispelled. Then she was 'a Bayadere'—and next a 'Bohemian Girl'—and so on, through half a dozen transformations, which appeared to me to smack very strongly of stage costume and foot-lights. Finally, she broke into some outlandish dialect (which I am told is Italian), and in which there was a wonderful repetition of 'Pizzicas' and 'Spasimis' and 'ardors,' 'si, si's' and 'tra-

Fig. 6.1. "I Dreamt That I Dwelt in Marble Halls," page 1, from Michael Balfe's *Bohemian Girl.* From the Historic American Sheet Music Collection in the Rare Book, Manuscript, and Special Collections Library, Duke University.

la-las,' absolutely without end. There was evidently a vast amount of *passion* in it, for, in all my life, I have never heard such quavering, and trilling, and screaming, and agony, while the keys of the piano groaned and squeaked, as if in extremest torture."[12]

All of these songs can be associated with Anna Bishop (and others) and were indeed popular among southern young women. Stubblefield clearly admired a different repertory, the older one, from that he frequently heard in southern parlors.

THE SOCIAL CONTEXT

An incident during the voice lessons of Elizabeth Waties Allston Pringle illuminates how elite young women understood singing in the context of their culture. When Madame Togno moved her school from Charleston to Columbia (where she took over the South Carolina Female Collegiate Institute at Barhamville), Elizabeth and her sister Della followed.[13] In both versions of her autobiography, she refers to a remark made by her voice teacher, Monsieur Torriani.[14] She clearly thought highly of Torriani: she describes him as "appreciative" twice in a single paragraph. After six months of singing only exercises, Pringle was finally assigned an aria. She names it "Buona notte, buon dormir" from *Martha*, and in her *Chronicles of Chicora Wood*, she calls it a "very high" song, "Dormi pur ma, il mio riposo tu m'ai tolto, ingrate cor Buone notte, buon dormir."[15]

Pringle sang this song for Angelo Torriani, father of Ferdinand Torriani (who taught Jeanette MacDonald). Angelo reportedly taught the famous star Adelina Patti, but he also conducted various performances of the Italian Opera Company (such as those in 1860 in Columbus, Georgia).[16] In 1874, he and Ernst Eberhard opened a conservatory of music in New York City, and *Dwight's Journal of Music* includes several references to him. Obviously, Torriani had serious musical connections, yet he also taught the daughters of planters in the South.

Pringle's account of her first performance of an entire song for Torriani is illuminating. She berated her singing skills, stating that she was

so overcome by my inability to express what the music said to me that I broke down and was reduced to tears and said : "Oh, Mr. Toiriani [*sic*], there is no use for me to go on: I have no voice and it is useless." He turned fiercely upon me and said: "Voice—what does that matter? You must go on. Vous avez le feu sacré." As I used my handkerchief violently in my effort to suppress the sobs that would come, it seemed to me a poor consolation, for if the said fire found no outlet it must consume and not illuminate; but I dared not answer, only struggled for composure to go on with "Buona notte, buon dormir" in a feeble, quavering, high soprano. But I often think now I understand more what he meant. One is independent of outside things; there is a warmth and a glow and a depth that fills and satisfies, irrespective of results and externals.[17] Whether her initial dissatisfaction is feigned—part of the self-effacement that a demure young woman should affect—cannot be ascertained. If it was, then Torriani also played his part, supporting the young (rich) singer however possible. Pringle would have been about eighteen when this episode occurred and at the prime age for such behavior.

In this excerpt, Pringle learns a key aspect of expectations in the culture, one that is reiterated frequently in other commentaries. As an amateur singer, she did not have—indeed should not have had—a professional quality voice. The best compliment a young female singer could receive was to have a "sweet" voice.[18] Pringle describes her own voice as "very small, sweet" with "high, birdlike qualities."[19] Sarah Lois Wadley also writes approvingly of her brother's fiancée's "sweet" singing.[20] Susan Petigru King describes the musical qualities of her fictional heroine Lily Vere, the morally superior belle, saying, "She was no great musician, but she had taste, if not execution; sang with sweetness and correctness, though her notes were few . . ."[21] A few notes from a sweet voice was exactly what the young belle should possess. Too many notes and one ran the risk of being construed as professional, which was lower class and therefore inappropriate.[22]

Pringle also describes a schoolmate who was sweet in temperament, but her voice was more than that. Not only does Pringle *not* use the word "sweet," she also suggests that the young woman could have been a professional singer. This assessment is not entirely innocent, for it suggests that the girl, Sallie McCullough, was less of a lady. McCullough had a "beautiful, big voice" and was a "sweet, good, simple girl," although she apparently lacked sophistication.[23]

In McCullough, Torriani found an ideal music student who Pringle suspected could have been successful as an opera singer, although Pringle felt that she lacked the ability to act. The girls frequently asked her to sing the famous "Home, Sweet Home" in their dormitory. (This piece, made popular by a number of professional singers, was especially associated with Jenny Lind.)[24] McCullough had the voice to be a professional—hers was not a "sweet" voice—and indeed, she later became a "well-known opera singer of her day."[25]

During the time of the lesson described above (probably 1863), Torriani asked "with a great air of respect" if Pringle had considered going on the stage. He probably did not really expect that she would; rather, it was another way to compliment her singing. Pringle again responded with due modesty, saying her voice was too small (after, predictably, noting that she thought Torriani was making fun of her).[26] He responded that though her voice was small, it was "very sweet," and she would give much pleasure with it, especially in sad songs.[27]

Torriani then inquired about how much she practiced a day. When Pringle replied about half an hour, he demanded that she never practice more than ten minutes at a time and that she always keep her voice down. She should never try to talk from a carriage or car or in a crowd. These instructions are typical of those given to any young lady, whether a singer or not, and demonstrate how musical accomplishment reinforced society's expectations. Indeed, the idea of refinement was almost equal to passivity in southern society; it was the opposite of loud, bold, raucous, and free-spirited. The admonition to be quiet characterized the cultural training of these young women, and exuberance was frowned upon.[28] Loud, emotive, passion-exuberating operatic voices were out of the question.

PROBLEMS WITH SINGING LIKE AN OPERA SINGER

Torriani's question about Pringle's possible intention to sing professionally can only have been a way to commend her, implying that she had a pretty voice. Seeming professional was one of the worst mannerisms young southern women could affect. Even though girls frequently performed at home and at school, their behavior was in no way to resemble that of an actress on the stage. The following excerpt from another of Susan Petigru King's books, *The Actress in High Life*, demonstrates how *not* to perform in the parlor. The main character, Mabel, appears more as an actress than a lady in her desire to use her singing as a method whereby to secure the love of Colonel L'Isle. At a party in which the potential beau is present, she at first refuses to sing but eventually gives in. She pointedly sings "at" him, the word reiterated and emphasized by her father, much to his disgust. The book also exhibits how important the true understanding of "accomplishment" was to this society, sarcastically pointing out at the end that if Mabel continues to behave as she has, she will not be fit for any decent society.

Near the beginning of the party, the hostess, Mrs. Shortridge, declares: "'Now, as the rarest treat that I could offer, I had promised my guests that they should hear Lady Mabel in all her glorious richness of voice; and now she is seized with a sudden fit of modesty, and protests against being exhibited before a motley crowd like an opera singer.'" Although Mabel knows better than to perform as an opera singer, she eventually gives in and goes beyond the bounds of good taste, not wanting to be a "mere singer": "Friendship and flattery at length prevailed, and Lady Mabel promised to do her utmost to charm the ears of the natives, on condition that L'Isle should be at hand as her interpreter, and say to them for her a dozen polite and half as many witty things for every song she sang, in order that these foreigners might not mistake her for a mere singer." The author's intent in the irony of the juxtaposition between "opera singer" and "mere singer" is clear and Mabel's hubris unmistakable. L'Isle "made a list of songs long enough to have cracked her voice forever," but Mabel apparently sings on, undeterred. Unfortunately—or predictably—L'Isle is called away to converse with the men in the company before hearing much of Mabel's singing. As such, the object of her affection (and performance) does not benefit from her display but rather pointedly avoids it.[29]

L'Isle later tells Sir Rowland (an acquaintance) that Mabel sang "Constant My Heart" *at* him. He does not tell Sir Rowland about the other things—kissing, touching her hand under the table, and so on—he is too much of a gentleman. But the author tells the reader. In this case, King reveals how low and unladylike Mabel's behavior was.[30]

By the time Mabel arrives back home, her father has already heard of his daughter's embarrassing behavior. He upbraids the young woman for drawing attention to herself with no regard for propriety. The final straw, however, is Mabel's singing. After hearing a litany of improprieties, she asks:

> "Was that *all* he told you?"
>
> "Why? Was there any thing more to tell?" inquired her father.
>
> Lady Mabel drew a deep, long breath. "Then he said nothing about my—my singing—'Constant my heart' to him?"
>
> "How!" exclaimed Lord Strathern. "Did you sing 'Constant my heart' *at* him?"
>
> "How could I help it, papa, it came in so pat to the purpose?"
>
> "The devil it did! It seems you did not mean to fail, by under acting your part. It is lucky he forgot to mention it. Was there any thing more?"[31]

Lord Strathern has made several items clear to Mabel. He associates her with "acting your part"—which signifies that she has behaved as an actress on the stage. He moves the singing from "to" L'Isle to "at" L'Isle—another indication of improper forwardness. And he puts the finishing touch on these accusations at the end of this conversation: "'Damn his neck!' said Lord Strathern, striding up and down the room. 'Better a neck cracked than a reputation. Things have come to a pretty pass. You singing love-songs at him, he squeezing and kissing your hand—perhaps going further. In these cases, women never tell the whole truth! When he would escape by a leap from your window, you try to keep him by strength of arm. You get on finely, madam! Three months in the army have done wonders for you. Three months more will accomplish you so thoroughly, that you will be fit for no other society through life.'"[32]

Without a doubt, "Lady" Mabel has not negotiated the delicate boundary of knowing how much to perform for people or how a proper young lady should behave. Lord Strathern cynically uses "accomplish" to say that although she may have talent, accomplishment is more than the technical execution of a piece—it implies taste, something Mabel lacks. She learns, to her chagrin, that performing as if she were a professional singer is just about the worst thing she could have done in this situation. (The wrong motives driving this transgression further highlight Mabel's lack of refinement.) Although Mabel knew the difference between being an opera singer and a "mere" singer, she clearly chose to associate herself with the former and lost her reputation in the process. That Lord Strathern declares a broken neck as more favorable than a reputation "cracked" by vulgar display concludes this scene with a voraciousness that is seldom encountered in such stories.

What was the association with professional singers that southern belles might have? Only one "opera star" claimed to have been from the South, and her southern roots are practically nonexistent: Clara Louise Kellogg Strakosch (1842–1916). Although born in Sumterville, South Carolina, where her father was principal of Sumter Academy, the Kellogg family was undoubtedly northern in all other respects. The family hailed from New England, and Clara attended concerts, studied, and debuted in New York City. She was known alternatively as the "Star of the North" (from a role she sang in Giacomo Meyerbeer's opera of that name, *L'étoile du Nord*) and as the "lone Star of the South in the operatic world."[33] While modern authors may describe her as a native South Carolinian, she mentions the state only twice in her autobiography, once to say she was born there and once to note the beginning of the Civil War.[34]

Clearly, southern ladies were not opera singers. Even when they sang opera arias, the music had been modified to make it more suitable for the amateur. The line between amateur and professional was a highly defined one. On the other hand, it is difficult to reconcile the desire to be like professional singers—signified by buying sheet music with a singer's likeness on the front cover, singing the pieces they sang, and attending their concerts—with the extreme censure against behaving anything like them. An examination of some of the most popular songstresses will serve to illustrate the variety of personalities with which young women might have been familiar.

Visual representations play a large role in women's culture of the nineteenth century.[35] The tendency to put portraits of famous singers on sheet music appears in the 1840s; it follows the path of the move from songstress to opera star described in chapter 2. Those who made their name singing in the older style (English opera, as opposed to the "Italian" style mentioned frequently with Anna Bishop and others) did not usually have their pictures on sheet music. Eventually, publishers recognized the marketing potential of famous singers, but rarely did their pictures appear on the covers. A case in point would be the numerous songs associated with Anne Childes (Mrs. Edward Seguin). Most of these have no picture at all, but those that do tend to illustrate the subject of the song rather than the singer herself. Examples of these include "My Love's Been Complaining" (no date) and "The Fisher Boy Merrily Lives" (dated 1840).

An entirely different case may be seen in either Anna Rivière Bishop or Anna Hunt Thillon. In both cases, pictures of these women appeared on several sheet music publications, sometimes in costumes from the operas from which the pieces derived. For example, an actual likeness of Bishop appears on the cover of "Anna Bishop's Polka Rondino" (part of the "Gems of Madame Anna Bishop's Concerts" series; see figure 2.1.) This image is also on several different works from the same series, at least one of which is dated 1849. On another edition of "Anna Bishop's Polka Rondino," she is pictured in costume as Linda di Chamounix. This publication also dates from 1849.

Several other pictures of Bishop survive, some in costume and others in demure, innocent-looking poses. The singer reportedly liked to adorn herself with beautiful gowns and jewelry, although these are not usually pictured on the publications. Such ostentatious display might be considered unseemly, and publishers may have walked a delicate line between using the singer's name to sell pieces but not her reputation (either in her behavior or dress). Indeed, in an 1850 notice entitled "New Music" in the *Southern Quarterly Review*, the editor mentions that on "Anna Bishop's March," "a portrait of Madame Bishop, in the character of Amina, constitutes one of the illustrations of this charming production, which merits general circulation among all fair performers on the piano forte."[36] The visual aspect of the sheet music seems to be as important as the music itself.

Anna Thillon presented such difficulties as well. More than Bishop, Thillon was noted as something of a beauty. Reviewers of nineteenth-century opera inevitably commented on women singers' appearances, which drew attention to them as sexual objects. Obviously, Anna Thillon displayed herself in public and was therefore not a real lady. To have her picture on the parlor piano might indicate approval of the woman, or it might merely connote acquaintance with the latest music. Jenny Lind, the illegitimate Swedish soprano who toured the United States in the 1850s, was also a popular favorite on sheet music covers.

ON "SWEET" SINGING

Southern elite women attended performances in which professional women sang, and they had many opportunities to do so. In this aspect, a sharp distinction can be drawn between their experience with the piano and that with singing. Women sang on the stage, but they were not usually professional pianists. Pianists were not as likely to be construed as professional performers as singers might because southern women had little acquaintance with professional female pianists. This fact conversely made it all the more important that amateur female singers not be seen as anything close to professional status.

The emphasis noted above on "sweet" singing contrasted with the professional tendency to "execute." When George Upton wrote about Adelina Patti, he declared that the audience was "thrown into spasms" by her singing. He qualified this, pointing out how little taste the audience had. He says that Patti "executed" arias from *Linda di Chamounix, La sonnambula, La traviata,* and other "bravura" arias. She sang without feeling or thrill but had an "ease and facility of execution."[37]

In his account of the Patti sisters' performances in Atlanta, musicologist Lee Orr quotes several reviews that use "brilliant" (and "execution") repeatedly, as does his own commentary—the word "brilliant" occurs eight times in four pages.[38] Similarly, descriptions of Anna Bishop's singing often criticize her for her overly technical "brilliant execution." Prior to her arrival, one reviewer commented that she would come to the United States "in order to amuse us with her vocalization."[39] Bishop's tendency to add ornaments, particularly shakes (trills), resulted in her vocal style being mimicked in burlesques.[40]

Richard Grant White, writing for the *Courier & Enquirer* in 1847, said that even before Bishop arrived, "the whole chromatic scale of puffery, from the lowest to the highest semi-tone on the fingerboard, [had] been run up with brilliant variations" and sarcastically added that at soirées in which Bishop sang, "a display of vocalization was given, so brilliantly that nothing could eclipse it, except the diamonds, rubies, pearls, and emeralds displayed in profusion."[41] Critic Henry Cood Watson decried Belgian soprano Madame Laborde's performance in 1848 as "mechanical, cold, and inhuman" with a "finely executed cadenza" that was an "intrusion" and "outrage."[42]

When such vocal fireworks were in the repertory of the amateur southern woman, they tended not to be universally admired. Louisa Gist (1830–1900), a student at the South Carolina Female Collegiate Institute at Barhamville, held something of a reputation as a singer. She is mentioned in various diaries from the period, and at Barhamville, she sometimes took only music lessons (rather than the complete curriculum).[43] When Carey (Jane Caroline) North heard her in 1851 in Hot Springs, she wrote of Miss Gist: "She trills in the most remarkable manner but the voice otherwise is not sweet."[44] Born at Rose Hill Plantation near Union, South Carolina, Louisa was the daughter of William Henry Gist, who would serve as governor of the state from 1858 until 1860.[45] Her mother died just a few days after Louisa's birth. At the early age of eight, Louisa was sent to Salem Female Academy, where she spent one year. (Widowers often sent female children to school at younger ages than other girls.) She probably began her music studies there and continued them while at Barhamville.

LESSONS FROM *AGNES*

A serial novel entitled *Agnes* and published in the *Southern Literary Messenger* in 1863–64 conveys a wealth of information on the importance of singing and singing with good taste. Written by "Filia," it began in June 1863 and ran through March of the following year. The novel opens with Elizabeth Barrett Browning's poem "Perplexed Musician" (untitled in the story), whose first line sets the tone for the story: "Experience, like a pale musician, holds a dulcimer of patience in his hand." Music plays a significant role in the court-ship of the two main characters, and how Filia uses it demonstrates proper music performance among elite southerners.[46]

Agnes Graham and Robert Selman are cousins. The orphaned Agnes has grown up on the plantation owned by her aunt Emeline, her mother's sis-ter. Robert also grew up in this aunt's home. Agnes is consistently painted throughout the novel as the perfect southern belle/lady. She speaks German fluently, having learned it from a German governess, and she translates at sight. She also knows French and Latin and is studying Spanish and Italian at school when the novel opens. The rumor around school is that the head-mistress and the voice teacher, Signor Parini, have determined Agnes to be equal to the mezzo-soprano Maria Malibran—quite a compliment. But Agnes tells her best friend, Elizabeth Hudson, that she studies so much because she is so fond of Robert, and he likes to study too. Thus, the tone is set—Agnes, as is proper, doesn't study for her own pleasure but to please someone else.[47]

Robert moves to Germany for five years to study, and Agnes is left alone with aunts. A family friend, Mr. Danvers, is a "scholar" who has some influ-ence over Agnes, and she writes the following in a letter to Robert: "He is very fond of music, and makes me play the piano for him. I have promised to learn to play the organ. He is to send me some fine sacred music. I am sorry I can't sing for him, but Aunt will not allow me to sing. Signor Parini told her I must not use my voice until after I was fifteen. Aunt says if I practice then I will sing very well. I should like to sing well, so as to sing with you, Robert. I hope you will study that beautiful German music."[48] Again, Agnes is playing the piano *for* Mr. Danvers and will learn to play the organ *for* him, and she wishes to sing with Robert. The last is the only thing she appears to want to do for her own pleasure. And she clearly knows German music, something made more evident later in the story.

Robert was sent to Germany as part of his training to become a medical doctor. The family and their closest friends fear a strain of insanity that runs through the family, and after seeing Robert and Agnes grow so close to each other, they wish to separate them in hopes of avoiding a union between the two. Such a union, it is feared, would yield only deeper madness. Robert had been sent away from his parents because of a mentally disturbed sister, and Agnes's mother had died insane.

Upon Robert's return from Germany, he decides to go to a party incognito, having grown a beard and mustache while abroad.[49] His friend Phil Mathews and he wander around the gathering, commenting to each other on the various young women in attendance. They understand that a musical performance is about to begin, and Phil's anticipation of the performance sets the stage for the entrance of Agnes (who is unidentified at this point in the evening). Their expectations are low and suggest that too many young female vocalists attempted opera arias that were beyond their abilities: "'Stand before me, Selman [Robert], and hide me. I am going to take refuge on this ottoman, in the corner, and put my fingers in my ears! That girl is going to sing! I see my mother leading her to the piano. Now we'll have "Robert, Robert, *toi que j'aime*" in the most *approved* hurdy-gurdy style! It always sets my teeth on edge to hear her!'"

When Robert asks who she is, Phil replies that it is Clara Bell (someone who used to admire Robert). He also comments that "'her voice is as cold as ice, and as high as Teneriffe, and sharp at its peak. She always gives me an ague.'" Not a positive review, to be sure—certainly far-removed from the preferred "sweet" singing of southern belles. Phil continues, "'I wouldn't trust a woman with a voice like that for any consideration, Selman. . . . I believe she would commit murder without a qualm.'" Even if Phil is jesting, this is a dramatic statement and does not paint a positive picture of Clara Bell. It also suggests a correlation between high, piercing operatic tones and questionable character.

Clara does not disappoint their expectations. After a "brilliant" prelude, she embarks on "an exceedingly difficult Bravura." Robert accedes that her voice is "'cold, high, and piercing,'" but he does note that it is also flexible and cultivated. This acknowledgment confirms other satirical writers who criticized the overpolished operatic repertory that some young women learned.[50] Robert goes so far as to stop his ears "before she got through all her trills and roulades."

The hostess quickly thanks her and hurries Clara off. She then finds another performer and has a harp brought to the middle of the room for this young woman to use. The poetic writing that communicates this scene is worth quoting in its entirety because it demonstrates the sheer passion that music could bring forth from the male listener.

> He stood with his eyes fixed upon the young lady, who, after passing her fingers lightly over the strings, took her seat and played a brilliant, merry polka. Robert had a full view of her face now—it was beautiful. The color glowed upon her cheek from the excitement of playing; her large eyes were concealed by their long, black lashes. Phil stooped over, and spoke in a low tone. The lids were lifted, and a radiant smile gleamed like lightning over the lovely face. Striking a few modulations upon the strings, the music changed from the gay polka to a slow, plaintive measure. The red lips parted, and breathed most touchingly the exquisite melancholy strain of Schubert's Wanderer. Robert's heart beat fast—his eyes filled with tears. The deep, rich voice stirred every depth in his soul.

Such intensity of feeling illustrates why music was such a powerful tool in the hands of young women. Wielded with talent and taste, it became an undeniably controlling device. As such, it was also threatening and had to be used carefully.

Before Robert has a chance to move, Phil asks for another song, and the singer proceeds to a "scena and aria" from Weber's opera *Der Freischütz* ("Wie nahte mir der Schlummer bevor ich ihn geseh'n!"). This indulgence in German pieces is at Phil's request. Of course, the only one in the assembled group who is that familiar with German is Agnes, and Robert is astonished to learn that his little cousin has grown into such an engaging young woman.

Needless to say, their relationship blossoms. Interestingly, the most frequent activity that the two share is music. Robert accompanies himself while singing an aria from Bellini's *Beatrice di Tenda* that alludes to one of the characters named "Agnese," and then he accompanies Agnes and himself in the duet "Torna mia di me che m'ami?" This becomes "their song" throughout the remainder of the novel.

When the concerned family questions Robert on his opinion of Agnes the day after this party, he says she is "very pretty," which the family members feel is noncommittal and inaccurate. He chooses to single out, however, that "her voice is superb!" Again, the voice has taken pride of place in accomplishment.

Throughout the rest of her unmarried life, Agnes performs music for various people. Usually she sings. Among the compositions in her repertory that she performs are "old favourites" by Thomas Moore: "Boony Doon," "Mary, When the Wild Wind Blows," "Twilight Dews," and similar pieces for various listeners. She is compared again to Malibran. When Agnes's life takes a downward turn, about midway through the novel, music is rarely mentioned again. Once she is married (not to Robert but to another), music does not appear in the work. This reflects real life in that women usually did not perform much after they married. Musical performance was essentially in the realm of the unmarried young woman; matrons had little time for such activity. But it also suggests that music was the key to her happiness (she is not happy without Robert), and that music can fortify true love.

Elite women such as Elizabeth Waties Allston Pringle strove to be admired for their singing but not to sound too professional. Sue King clearly drew the line between the two in *The Actress in High Life*, noting that a true gentlewoman would not sound like an opera singer. Surviving sheet music collections also indicate that a simple melody, perhaps something from a bel canto opera, served the purposes of the southern lady. "Sweet" singing, not brilliant execution, was the aim of the southern elite woman. The parallels with tasteful piano playing, as opposed to brilliant execution on the piano, confirm cultural expectations that young women should be able to sing or play, but not too well. Most of these young women remained within the expected parameters laid out by society and in so doing participated in the culture of resignation described by several scholars. They sang "sweetly" or with "low, silvery tones," not with cold, hard voices.[51]

Others, however, went too far. They resisted the strictures placed on them and displayed their talent (and hours of practice) unabashedly. Society did not look upon them favorably, but perhaps a sense of personal satisfaction (something not really desired in southern ladies) emboldened them to such extremes. When they sought to display themselves ostentatiously through showy opera arias, southern women stepped out of the bounds of propriety by singing for themselves, not to please others. Again, the tension between a culture of resignation (everyone had to sing some) and resistance (why not sing more difficult repertory if one had the talent?) runs through the use of music by southern women.

7. Women's Composition and Publication in the Antebellum Period

Do not, we beg of you, attempt to write.
—JOHN SULLIVAN DWIGHT, 1856

Upper-class southerners considered a musical education—or at least applied lessons—to be desirable for their daughters; it was a required part of being "accomplished." Such young women were expected to provide soothing music as background entertainment for their families, employing their talents in a variety of ways. Being able to sing and to play the piano or guitar (or maybe the harp) demonstrated that the young performer knew her role in society, proved that her parents had sufficient economic means to support her music lessons, and suggested that she would be a suitable mate. Many of these parents sent their daughters to some sort of institution to be "finished," and an overwhelmingly large number of girls studied voice and piano lessons while at school. Music composition, however, was apparently *not* a desired skill for southern belles of the antebellum period. As far as can be determined, only one of the seminaries and similar schools that existed in almost every southern city and town of any size offered instruction in composition.[1] If composition had been necessary for accomplishment, more emphasis would be found in curricula.[2]

Women composers faced a fundamental dilemma concerning antebellum conceptions of woman as "creator." In *Gender and the Musical Canon*, Marcia Citron discusses gendered theories of creativity and notes historical expectations that men create/produce while women procreate/reproduce. These conventions were particularly delineated in the nineteenth century.[3] Judith Tick describes a debate that began in the 1880s between eminent music critic George Upton and several women journalists. Upton (the same man who described the "piano thumper") stated that woman "will always be the recipient and interpreter but there is little hope that she will be the creator," while women writers (Alice Stone Blackwell, editor of the *Women's Journal*, and Fanny Morris Smith, writing in the *Etude* in 1901) argued against Upton's prejudices.[4]

Nonetheless, a significant number of southern women did indeed compose and publish music during the antebellum period, and over seventy works published by southern women before 1861 have been identified. Most of the works are anonymous. The circumstances of this remarkable body of music are described below. Several elements help to define antebellum women's composition; chief among them is the fact that the majority of music that survives lists the composer as "a lady," not revealing the name of the composer. The few instances that include the composer's name prove to be by professional musicians (with one exception), and almost none of these are indigenous southerners. Other features that characterize antebellum women's composition include styles and genres appropriate to parlor performance, and simplicity is almost always the reigning aesthetic.

As a topic, "southern women's composition" allows for many avenues of investigation. The questions are not always as straightforward as they might seem, and the possibilities surrounding both "southern" and "composition" extend in many directions. For example, how does the actual place of publication figure into the definition of "southern"? In the first half of the nineteenth century, some northern publishers brought out music by southern women; this situation was not at all unusual, as there were few music publishers in the South at that time and it may have been easier to find someone to publish something in an area where a plethora of publishers existed. On the other hand, it might also have been a way of circumventing societal pressures that did not desire a young belle to have her work so publicly displayed. As such, a northern venue might have provided an even surer anonymity. This repertory, as well as music by non-southern women that was published by southern firms, is examined here, for it helps to shed light on southern traditions of what womanhood and ladyhood meant.

Another factor that needs to be considered is that few native southern *men* made their living as composers at this time. The number of compositions published by southern women must be considered against the backdrop of a general scarcity of published southern music. Occasionally, an upper-class man would hire a professional musician to compose music as a gift to a female friend and then publish it as his own. Eliza Ripley describes this practice in *Social Life in Old New Orleans*. After noting that the "Flirtation Polka," dedicated to Madame Lavillebeuvre, was not up to par (she apparently was a "delightful pianist and merited something more inspiring"), Ripley mentions several pieces whose authors were de facto ghostwriters. She says of one, "I don't think Armant wrote music; he 'got it done,' as the saying is. This is not an unusual feat."[5] Whether or not women did the same cannot be determined, but indications are they did not. Whereas the men Ripley mentions deliberately put their names on publications, women almost always remained anonymous. Modesty and propriety deemed it inappropriate to display a young woman's emotions so audaciously.

Another issue to consider is whether or not to include Baltimore as a southern city in a book that extends through the Civil War. Being a slave state, Maryland certainly aligned with many southern views during the antebellum period, and most authors consider Maryland a southern state. In spite of that, when the lines were drawn between North and South upon the creation of the Confederate States of America, Maryland remained with the Union. Its importance as a center for southern music publication, however, justifies treating Baltimore as a southern city in the following discussion, and its significance in publishing women's music, particularly before the war, cannot be ignored.

COMPOSITION VERSUS PUBLICATION

The term "women's composition" needs clarification. Only works in which a woman is credited with the creation of music are discussed below. For years, women wrote the lyrics to songs published in the United States and allowed their names to be published, but their association with music composition remained much more tenuous until about the mid-nineteenth century.[6] Far fewer southern women's musical compositions have been identified to date, and, unlike poets, the composers were rarely named in print. Undoubtedly more manuscripts exist, as indeed more publications also presumably survive in collections that have been neglected because of a lack of funding, interest, or other reasons. But these will not alter the general numbers, and the dearth of identified women's music publications before the war, as compared to the relative explosion after 1860, remains.

Women's composition and publication are surely separate issues, and, as has been the case since music publication began, not everything written was published. So little manuscript evidence for women's composition in the antebellum South survives that it is practically impossible to say much about unpublished composition. The instances of women's composition in manuscripts that do survive are particularly interesting. Examples exist in the Moravian Archives at the Archie K. Davis Center in Winston-Salem, North Carolina. Several volumes in this collection contain examples of women's music from the nineteenth century; those belonging to members of the Van Vleck family are noteworthy because at least one of the sisters, Amelia, participated in music activities in Salem throughout her long life (1835–1929).

An article in the *Winston-Salem Journal* (19 October 1926) describes Amelia as a "musician of note" who "devoted all her time to music, in which she excelled and in which she made for herself a place all her own in the musical life of the church and community." Another writer further comments that "she was a rarely talented musician, a brilliant pianist, and a composer of real merit."[7]

Quite a few pieces in the bound volume SMB.34 of the collection have attributions such as "The Sky Lark by Amelia A[delaide] Van Vleck" (f. 55v) or "Our Words of Love by L[isetta] M[aria] Van Vleck" (f. 51). One of Lisetta's works, "The Mollie March" (f. 58v), was eventually published for band as "Military March." The exact date of the manuscript is unknown; however, since Lisetta (1830–1914) married a local band director named Alexander Meinung in 1868, the pieces attributed to her under her maiden name must predate that year. (Bound volume SMB.58 has the name "Miss Sue Phillips / Salem. 1862" on the cover, and works attributed to the Van Vleck sisters occur therein as well. This information might assist in dating the other book, as the contents are similar.)

Musically, the pieces composed by the Van Vleck women contain many of the same stylistic features as contemporary music published elsewhere. Keys of two to five flats dominate, while the "sharp" key of E major (four sharps) occurs only once in the women's works (in Amelia's "River Waltz" [f. 61]). A surprising amount of chromaticism occurs in several pieces by both Lisetta and Amelia, and it is much more prevalent than in similar works by other composers. Some of the works require more physicality than contemporary parlor pieces, such as the "Lucy Gallop" (f. 53v) or the "Hannah Polka" (f. 60), both of which might have been named for friends of the composer. Therefore, while the music of the Van Vleck women contains many stylistic features that might have been found in most parlor pieces in the United States around 1850, the compositional style of the attributed works in manuscript—technically and stylistically—surpasses most antebellum women composers' works in difficulty.

While this extraordinary collection at first seems to demonstrate a profound interest in women's composition, women's education in the Moravian community differed from that of most of their neighbors. Moreover, the Van Vleck girls began their education in Bethlehem, Pennsylvania, before moving south to the Moravian settlement in Salem, a fact that further distances their experiences from those of other southern girls.

EARLY PUBLICATIONS (1800–1839)

The first publication of a southern woman's music appears to have been printed in Baltimore when John Cole of No. 123 Market Street published "The United States Marine March," composed by "A Lady of Charleston, South Carolina" around 1814 or 1815.[8] This work initiates a trend, for the extant data clearly show that Baltimore became somewhat of a publishing haven for women composers—almost completely unnamed, of course. In 1977, J. Bunker Clark identified the composer as Eliza Crawley Murden (1784–1847), a Charleston poet.[9] She published a book in 1808 whose title page reads "Poems by a Young Lady of Charleston." In 1827, she published *Miscellaneous Poems*, this time by a "Lady of Charleston."[10] (The dedication is to none other than Madame Talvande, the famous schoolmistress.)

"Composed and Dedicated to the Officers of the Marine Corps," "The United States Marine March" is a piano solo in C major that consists of militaristic dotted rhythms and octave flourishes in the right hand. A key change to C minor/E-flat major in the B section and a few ornaments round out the technical requirements of the composition. The fistfuls of chords may seem unladylike to the modern observer, but considering the "pianoforte" of the early nineteenth century, the texture becomes less overtly masculine.

The year 1824 saw unprecedented action in women's composition in Baltimore. No fewer than four pieces appeared in that year, three attributed to "A Lady of Baltimore" and one by an even more anonymous "Lady." Whether or not the three pieces by "A Lady of Baltimore" belong to the same composer cannot be proven, but since two of them seem related by title ("Titus' March" and "Titus' Waltz"), publisher (John Cole), date (1824), and medium (piano), they very likely are the work of the same woman. The "Spanish Rondo" has less obvious connections to this woman but may be her work as well.

"Titus' March" includes full chords in dotted rhythms, octave scales in both hands, and a bit of cross-hand technique. These aspects place the music somewhat above the beginner's level but certainly not at the intensity of professional performers of the period. Tick notes that both the "Titus' March" and "The United States Marine March" appeared throughout the nineteenth century in collections of amateur keyboard pieces. The works appeared anonymously; no doubt part of their attraction lay in the judicious absence of composer attribution and copyright.[11] These works bring to mind the style found in the ever-popular "Battle of Prague"—mimicry of the (supposed) sounds of the battle.

John Cole also published "Colonel William Stewart's March and Quickstep" by "A Lady of Baltimore" in 1824. Why 1824 was such a prosperous year for women composers in Baltimore remains unknown. Only one composition by a southern woman has surfaced for the decade of the 1830s, although more probably appeared. This single work is "No More," by a "Young Lady of Georgia," published in 1836 in J. G. Osbourn's Music Saloon in Philadelphia. Dedicated to "Miss E. V. S.," this composition appeared anonymously, miles away from Georgia.

MIDCENTURY PUBLICATIONS (1840–61)

A noticeable change in the style and number of pieces occurs in the 1840s, when Baltimore firms published several pieces by women. Two houses that produced multiple works in this decade were those of George Willig Jr. and Frederick D. Benteen. Willig produced at least seven pieces by two different women during the 1840s: "Lady Jane Grey" by "A Lady of Virginia," and "La

Capricieuse," "La Gracieuse," "Souvenir de Charleston, valse originale," and "Souvenir de la Saxe, Valse pour le Piano Forte Procidée d'une Introduction Sentimentale," all by Marie R. Siegling. "La Capricieuse" and "La Gracieuse" undoubtedly belong together, and the two "Souvenir" pieces belong to the same genre. A "Miss M. R. Siegling" also composed at least two songs; these are probably the work of the same woman. These compositions by Siegling appear to be the only ones of hers that have survived, and from the capable handling of musical style seen in them, she probably composed more. Presumably she attained some degree of competency from her studies in composition with her paternal grandmother, Regina von Schröder Siegling. Tick draws attention to Siegling's "Chopinesque figurations" in "La Capricieuse" ("valse originale"), noting that her gestures are more virtuoso than those seen in other contemporary women's pieces (figure 7.1).[12]

The composer of "Lady Jane Grey," identified only as a "Lady of Virginia," remains masked, as does her dedicatee, "Miss Leslie"—signs of someone adhering more closely to southern expectations for young women. "Lady Jane Grey" is a vocal duet accompanied by a simple piano part. The piece is marked *Con espressione*, and the pianist's indication is *Dolce*. In the key of E-flat, the introduction lasts ten measures and gives the entire melody before the singers enter. It is an unpretentious little work requiring nothing that would take the performers into anything remotely virtuoso and would be perfectly suitable for a spontaneous parlor performance in mixed company.

Frederick D. Benteen published at least ten pieces by women at this time, and it appears to have been his habit to hold the copyright. The earliest pieces published by Benteen are associated with military officers, places, events, or politicians, and in fact this decade saw several compositions by women celebrating victories in the Mexican war. Both pieces by "A Lady of Cambridge" (probably Cambridge, Maryland) appeared in 1844, and one, the "Dorchester March," is dedicated to the "Whigs of Dorchester" and is connected to Henry Clay's election. Similarly, "A Lady of Baltimore" wrote "General Scott's Grand March" in celebration of his efforts in the war. Later, in 1847, "A Lady of Virginia" published the "Cerro Gordo March and Quickstep" and also dedicated it to General Winfield Scott, through the Benteen firm. This foray into military music wanes in the 1850s and does not surface again until the Civil War, at which time the composer attributions alter significantly.[13]

Among the songs by women that Benteen published is "Why Ask Me Now?" by "Adelene" and "Thou Hast Wounded the Spirit That Lov'd Thee" by "A Lady."[14] As with the others, Benteen held the copyright for "Thou Hast Wounded"; the composer probably did not receive payment for her composition. It would not have been proper for a true lady to be paid for work, even if the work was composition.[15] In both of these cases, each woman was shielded from being too masculine, even though she ventured into the male world of

LA CAPRICIEUSE.

Fig. 7.1. "La Capricieuse," by Marie R. Siegling, page 2. Library of Congress.

creation/composition. Both were allowed to maintain a degree of modesty by not revealing their names, one by being named simply "A Lady" and the other by being eclipsed by the male arranger, Samuel Carusi, who held the copyright to her song. "Thou Hast Wounded" saw at least two printings, and Benteen had the copyright for both. For solo voice and piano, the song stays within a limited range for the singer, and an easy rocking accompaniment lies within the skill level of the amateur pianist; it could have been played and sung simultaneously.

Two other publications by Benteen during the 1840s reveal that he would also publish women's pieces and name the composers. Estelle Hewitt's pieces "Snowdrop Waltz" and "The Sun Was Slowly Setting" both include her full name. She is almost certainly composer John Hill Hewitt's first wife, née Mangin. Born in Jamaica around 1809, Estelle met Hewitt in Boston in 1827 and married him in New York in November of that year. By any account, Estelle Hewitt cannot be said to be representative of elite southern white women. She would not have been called a "lady," in the strictest sense of the word. John Hill Hewitt was not a member of the upper class, and he did not begin the compositional career for which he is famous until 1840. Moreover, neither she nor her husband was of southern birth, for he had been born in New York (but he moved to Augusta, Georgia, in 1823 and reportedly fell in love with the South immediately).[16]

Another 1840s piano solo from Benteen, "Oft in the Stilly Night with Variations for the Piano Forte by a Lady," stylistically resembles other virtuoso sets by women composers. Variation sets were not the most common type of piece for women composers to publish; Tick credits this phenomenon to the lack of female professional pianists before the 1870s.[17] Nonetheless, many surviving collections of sheet music owned by southern women contain variations. Thus, while women perhaps were less likely to compose in the genre, they appear to have played such pieces. In any event, whether or not the composer/arranger of "Oft in the Stilly Night" is southern cannot be certain, but it was published in Baltimore.

Benteen published "'Tis Past—The Spell Is Broken" by "A Lady of Richmond" and dedicated to "John Strobia, Esq." in 1849. This composer remains unknown, but one wonders whether or not the inhabitants of Richmond might have been able to put together the sentiment, dedicatee, and composer. As to style, it resembles other solo songs of the decade, decidedly tuneful and easy. It is in E-flat, it is strophic, and the melodic line encompasses an octave (plus the first pitch, on B-flat).

In 1847, only a year after opening his music publishing business in Charleston, South Carolina, George Oates also published works by a woman: the curious "Keowee Waltzes" composed and arranged by "A Lady of South Carolina." Two sets of waltzes claim this title (by the same composer), and the set forms an interesting commentary on Native Americans by a southern lady. Tick suggests that these pieces may have originally been composed for band and later arranged for piano because "corni" appears at the top of "Eastatoia" (the third waltz of the second set).[18] (On the other hand, in other "battle" pieces of the period, the score sometimes indicates the instrument to be mimicked. Such a case exists in John Schell's "Battle of Resaca de la Palma" [1848, Baltimore] where the "trumpet" and "drum" are listed above the staff.)[19] The various Keowee waltzes, mostly in the key of B-flat major, bear names such as "Amicololah," "Jocassee," "Seneca," and "Toxawau." Both sets have the same frontispiece that unfortunately relates nothing of the Native American associations in the individual titles.

Almost certainly, the composer of the "Keowee Waltzes" is the same as the "Lady of South Carolina" whose "Jasper Guards March" Oates published a year later, also in Charleston. This work, "composed and dedicated to the Officers and Members of the Jasper Guards of Charleston, SC," stylistically resembles the "Keowee Waltzes" closely enough to be attributed to the same composer.

In fact, the composer of these waltzes is none other than Martha Colhoun (or Calhoun, as the name is sometimes spelled), a member of the John C. Calhoun family. Familiarly called "Cuddie," she was the daughter of Colonel John Ewing Colhoun Jr., whose sister Floride married John C. Calhoun (former vice president of the United States and South Carolina senator). Postbellum reports note her accomplishments as an equestrian, musician, and conversationalist. One comments that "Miss Cuddie" was "the airiest of waltzers—she played beautifully on the piano!"[20] That Miss Cuddie was indeed the composer is confirmed by another account by one Dave Sloan. Sloan, who apparently knew the Colhouns, said of her, "People loved to congregate to hear her play at the piano, watch her ride, or marvel at her agility on the dance floor. As a composer, her Keowee waltzes were each given a local Indian name—Jocassee, Cherokee, Seneca."[21]

Keowee was the name of one of Martha Colhoun's homes in South Carolina, and it was reportedly one of the largest and most elegant in an area of beautiful plantations. The cover of the "Keowee Waltzes" has been taken to be an actual drawing of the plantation house (figure 7.2).

Martha Colhoun most definitely belonged to the highest social class in the region, and her aunt Floride once wrote to another family member in a letter that Martha "frequently goes to parties and has extravagant tastes, including lots of nice dresses."[22] Perhaps these extravagant tastes emboldened the young woman to publish her own pieces. She did not, however, indicate her name on any of them (although she gives some clue with the name "Keowee"). That Martha Colhoun, niece of a former vice president of the United States, composed and published music was apparently well known during her lifetime. Her 3 June 1861 obituary in the *Charleston Mercury* credits her

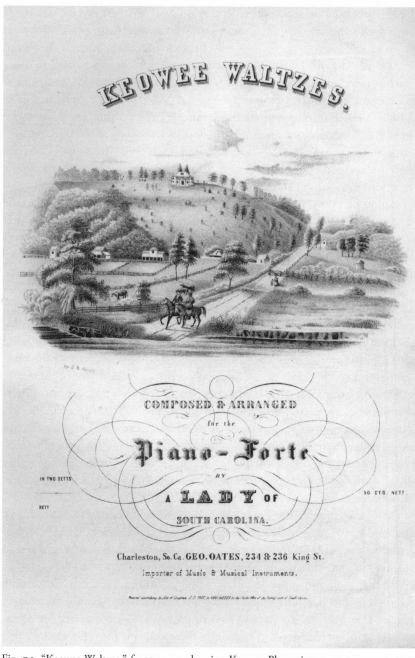

Fig. 7.2. "Keowee Waltzes," front cover, showing Keowee Plantation. Permission to reprint kindly provided by The Lester S. Levy Collection of Sheet Music, Special Collections, Sheridan Libraries, The Johns Hopkins University.

with the composition of the "Keowee Waltzes": "MARTHA CALHOUN, one of the sweetest song birds of Carolina, whose Keowee Waltzes will long linger, with pleasant echoes from memory, in the ears of those who have been so fortunate as to hear her improvise them."[23] Interestingly, the obituary does not mention them as a publication. Moreover, the writer notes that she improvised them, which suggests spontaneity in performance, rather than formal (professional) presentation. Had he said she had "composed" them, it might signify an inappropriate action. The lack of her name on her pieces further suggests that she was not professional, did not need money from the sale of the works, and preserved her reputation.

In 1849, "A Lady of South Carolina" also published the "Iolah Waltzes" but with a New York firm. Whether or not she is Martha Colhoun cannot be proved; however, the compositional style is the same between the two sets. That the composer also presented a "set" of waltzes is indicative. The only other southern woman composer to link pieces together in a similar manner was Mrs. J. M. C., who gathered her works together under the name "James River Waltzes" in the 1850s. Thus, it is most likely that the "Iolah Waltzes" were also composed by Martha Colhoun.

Colhoun's publisher, George Oates, seems to have been a man more than willing to publish music composed by a woman. He did so in Charleston, a city with some of the best musical opportunities in the South at this time, second only to New Orleans.[24] How his views on women and composition fit into Charleston's strict and multilayered social strata is unknown, but Oates moved to Augusta in 1850 and stayed there until the end of the Civil War.[25] Perhaps his modern views on women did not sit so easily with the socioeconomic powers of the city (or with those who would be buying music) and played a part in his move to Georgia. Charleston's conservatism was well known, as a writer known as "Mr. Bingham" noted: "Always conservative, her inhabitants were always slow to admit any innovations in manners."[26] As further evidence of such attitudes in Charleston, consider the case of the Sieglings. Even though publisher John Siegling's daughter, Marie, composed several works during the 1840s, George Willig in Baltimore published them.

Oates later published the "Agnes Polka" by Adèle Hohnstock (d. 1856) in Baltimore. According to an early-twentieth-century writer, Hohnstock immigrated to the United States from Germany in the 1840s and was the sister of pianist and teacher Carl Hohnstock, who had settled in Philadelphia.[27] Adèle Hohnstock taught at the Cherry Valley Seminary in New York, a women's school famous for its emphasis on music studies. (Some of the surviving programs show that Hohnstock's piano pieces were programmed alongside those of Gottschalk.) Her "Concert Polka" (1849) is considered to be the most difficult piano work composed by a woman before 1870 and challenges many preconceptions about the parlor piece.[28] Southerners were familiar with her music, as her arrangement of Vincent A. Schmidt's "Grand Polka Fantastique" received critical acclaim in the *Southern Quarterly Review*. She is described there as a "charming pianist."[29] Like Estelle Hewitt and Marie Siegling, however, Adèle Hohnstock is the exception rather than the rule. She does not represent southern culture, being German and residing in New York.

Other 1840s compositions by southern women are "'Tis Sweet to Muse o'er Memory's Page" by "A Lady of Virginia," published in New York by William Hall & Sons in 1849, and "The Volunteer March" by "A Lady of South Carolina," published in New York by Firth, Hall & Pond in 1847.[30] Why these women chose a New York firm is unknown. The possibilities range from being rejected by local (southern) firms, to trying to remain anonymous (and perhaps to keep their activities hidden from their families), to simply having been in New York at the time, because many southerners spent time in northern cities such as New York.

During the 1840s and 1850s, *Godey's Lady's Book* included several pieces composed by southern women, but it is entirely possible that only four women were involved. Between December 1847 and August 1850, "A Lady of Virginia" published four songs in that magazine; while there is no proof that they all belong to the same composer, the likelihood is great that they do. A single composition by "A Lady of Georgia" appeared in January 1852. The remaining pieces belong to two women, Miss C. M. C. of Baltimore and Mrs. J. M. C. of Virginia, who published in *Godey's* as well as other places. This is not to say that the "Lady of Virginia" and "Lady of Georgia" did not also do so, but it is practically impossible to discern, given the anonymous title of "Lady" in a particular state.

In the September 1854 issue of *Godey's*, Miss C. M. C. of Baltimore published "Summer Wind, Summer Wind," but the work also appeared through the Philadelphia publisher T. C. Andrews in the same year (dedicated to Mrs. Charles Fisk "of Washington City"). A simple work, much like "'Tis Past— The Spell Is Broken," this two-page song requires a vocal range of a twelfth (middle C up to F). The accompaniment is even easier.

Even more enterprising, Mrs. J. M. C. of Virginia published three pieces in *Godey's* in 1856. Without a doubt, these pieces belong with her other "James River Waltzes," published elsewhere. The *Godey's* titles, "Richmond Waltz," "Weyanoke Waltz," and "Powhatan Waltz," relate them to her others: "Dover Waltz," "Elk Hill Waltz," "Blitheville Waltz," and "Belleville Waltz." Almost all of Mrs. J. M. C.'s compositions refer to plantations along the James River.[31]

Benteen published all of Mrs. J. M. C.'s non-*Godey's* pieces. "Dover Waltz (In Imitation of the Tyrolian Air)" by "Mrs. J. M. C." and dedicated to "Mrs. J. Morson of Dover, Virginia" was, like several of her works, also distributed by W. T. Mayo of New Orleans.[32] The "Belleville Waltz" was dedicated to Louisa Mayo.[33] Louisa is described as the composer's niece, which suggests a connection with W. T. Mayo—the middle initial of "Mrs. J. M. C." may stand for Mayo. A relationship with a major distributor of music may explain why Mrs. J. M. C. published more works than any other southern woman before the Civil War. Unfortunately, only the composer's initials are given, not her name, but the connection with Mayo seems likely. The two-page "Belleville Waltz" consists essentially of only two chords, F major and a dominant-seventh chord on C, with the only exception being a G-minor chord in the final cadence.

Mrs. J. M. C. also composed at least two songs, "Each Word Thy Rosy Lip Hath Breath'd" and "Oh! Touch the Chord Yet Once Again." Benteen published both of them. None of Mrs. J. M. C.'s pieces, for piano solo or voice, make use of any accidentals; they remain in a single key throughout. Clearly, while Mrs. J. M. C. felt the need to compose and dedicate works to her friends, her pieces show little evidence of real compositional ability.

Another composer whose name appears even more complete is Fanny Heron, author of "Isadora" (subtitled "Serenade"), which Henry McCaffrey published in Baltimore in 1858. The words of this piece are by E. Donnelly, whose name appears in larger type than the composer's. The music is simply by "Fanny Heron," not "Miss" or "Mrs." A vocal duet with simple piano accompaniment, the composition is more noteworthy for its composer, who is not graced with a proper title for a woman during this period.[34] While this could be a sign that she was not a lady, it might equally be true that the composer is a man.[35] The most familiar instance of this type of gender-masking is with Septimus Winner, who published pieces under the pseudonym "Alice Hawthorne" during this period (no "Miss"). Similarly, in "Music and the Feminine Sphere," Julia Eklund Koza suggests that "Coralie Bell" "sounds suspiciously like a pseudonym" in her discussion of the most frequent women composers found in *Godey's Lady's Book*.[36]

Benteen also published works by two women who gave their complete names: Mrs. Flora Byrne and Miss Virginia E. Evans. Byrne is one of the few women whose works appeared in different places (St. Louis and Baltimore) and both before and during the war. Evans, on the other hand, makes a lone appearance as a composer in 1852.

The firm of Miller & Beacham, also of Baltimore, continued the tradition of publishing a woman's composition anonymously when it produced "Brilliant Variations on the Popular Melody Wild Ashe Deer" by "A Lady of Virginia." (The early publications of Miller & Beacham all carry the phrase "Successors to F. Benteen.") The adjective "brilliant" has been addressed above, and needless to say, these variations fall completely under the description of "brilliant but not difficult." Some of these attributes present in "Wild Ashe Deer" include arpeggios on dominant-seventh chords (on mostly black keys), an Alberti bass in the treble register for the left hand with a double-time in an upper octave, stride-style left hand accompaniments again with a double-time right hand, fast repeated pitches accented with octave leaps, and delightful right-hand chromatic embellishments in the final variation.

Among Miller & Beacham's pieces, two are probably by the same composer. Both works date from 1854, and both are polkas. The "Offering Polka" was composed by "Mary Eugenia C." and dedicated to her father, while "Affection, A Polka" was composed by M. E. C. in a very similar style. Miller & Beacham also published the "Richmond Blues March" by "A Lady" and dedicated to a military group of light infantry.

The final work attributed to a woman that was published in the South before the Civil War is "Bell Knights Waltz," by "Miss. Louisiana Gottheil," dedicated to the "Bell Knights of New Orleans, Louisiana" in 1860. This work, published by A. Elie, raises several questions that might place it out of the scope of this study. Its cover shows images that associate it with the Bell Knights. The period after "Miss" is also unusual. Such issues make it plausible to query whether the composer is genuine—certainly, Miss. Louisiana Gottheil could be a pseudonym, indicating something like "Louisiana, Praise God," with the possibility of Mississippi added. Indeed, although the word "Miss." appears with the composer's name, it is possible that the work is not by a woman at all. If it is, though, it is still possible that "Miss. Louisiana Gottheil" is a nom de plume and not the composer's name. Finally, the case may be that it is in fact her name, although that option is much less exciting than the others.

NON-SOUTHERN COMPOSERS IN SOUTHERN PUBLICATIONS

Consideration must be made of those southern firms that published music by women from places other than the South, for these are enlightening as well and fit other tendencies examined elsewhere in this study. Tick notes that the tradition of publishing music by English women existed in the first half of the nineteenth century in the United States.[37] The woman whose name appears most often in southern music publications and their advertisements is Caroline Norton (1808–77). As seen previously with their seeming approval of Anna Bishop and Ella Wren, southerners apparently did not hold Norton's not-so-private life against her. She was a leading figure in child custody and divorce rights reform in England, and Norton is generally viewed today as a foremost advocate of women's rights during the Victorian era. Norton separated from her husband in the 1830s, and some of her pamphlets greatly influenced the Divorce and Marriage Act of 1857.

Such a character hardly seems to fit into a society so far removed from her behavior and ideals (for example, divorce was impossible in South Carolina at this time), yet her compositions were very popular. How much southern women may have known about her life is unknown, but Norton was discussed favorably in 1852 by the editor of *Godey's Lady's Book*.[38] That some southern women were exceedingly well read and current in foreign affairs has been documented, and Norton's situation cannot have been a secret to all southerners. It is yet another example of the possibility that southern society would permit certain transgressions of "foreigners" but not of their own.

Norton's "Officer's Funeral" was published by John C. Schreiner in Macon, probably between 1860 and December 1861, when Schreiner added Savannah to his imprints.[39] But the list of distributors printed on the title page gives a more accurate picture of how popular this work was: A. E. Blackmar, New Orleans; J. J. Richards & Co. and H. Braumuller, Atlanta; J. W. Burke, Macon; Townsend & North, Columbia; W. S. Barton, Montgomery; J. W. Blandin, Selma; H. Siegling, Charleston; A. Morris, P. H. Taylor, and West & Johnson, Richmond; Charles Catlin, Augusta; and B. B. Baughan, Montgomery. Few works by man or woman enjoyed such immense popularity, and Norton's fame certainly did not hamper sales of her work.[40]

Even more popular than the "Officer's Funeral" was Norton's "Juanita," a work that remains one of the most popular songs associated with this period in American popular music.[41] Like the "Officer's Funeral," it too enjoyed a wide distribution: A. E. Blackmar, Geo. Cates, and Chas. Catlin, New Orleans; Richards & Co., Atlanta; Wm. N. White, Athens; Joseph Bloch and J. W. Snow, Mobile; J. W. Blandin, Selma; T. S. Whitaker, Wilmington; Logemann & Hollenburg, Huntsville; J. W. Burke, Macon; Townsend & North, Columbia; and W. S. Barton, Montgomery.

Faustina Hasse Hodges (1822–95) was another English composer whose works appeared in southern publishing houses. Hodges (named after the famous eighteenth-century singer Faustina Bordoni, who had married composer Johann Adolf Hasse) immigrated to the United States in 1841 and was one of only a few women to receive the title "professor," hers while teaching at Emma Willard's Troy Seminary in New York. She began composing in the 1850s, and several of her works were published in the South as well as in the North—probably without permission.[42] Schreiner published at least one composition, "Dreams," by Hodges in the 1860s. "Dreams" is part of the series "Parlor Gems: A Collection of the Most Popular Songs and Duetts with Piano Accompaniment," which also includes works by "Mrs. Norton." In the place of the lyricist on the first page of the music, Schreiner put "Reverie by H. C. L.," and in the opposite (composer's) corner, "Composed by F. H. Hodges." No place on the publication indicates that "F. H. Hodges" is a woman, nor do ads for her pieces reveal her gender. Stylistically, they do not follow the simple melodic outline of most parlor pieces but require an almost recitative-like interpretation.

So what is one to make of southern women's published compositions before the Civil War? The various components of table 5 (see appendix) illustrate the different ways to consider women and music publication in the South. It seems that Baltimore houses were much more likely than those farther south to bring out music composed by women. New Orleans, home of the most extensive musical life in the entire country, saw only one publication of a woman's composition during the antebellum period, "Bell Knights Waltz."[43] The Gottheil work may not even be by a woman. Charleston, the other city with a substantial musical culture, saw the publication of only two sets of waltzes by presumably the same woman, both in 1847. And the publisher who was responsible for these pieces left Charleston soon after he had arrived. The pieces did not circulate in a variety of music stores, as indicated by the lack of distributors listed on the extant copies. As such, it appears that publication of music composed by women was very limited in the antebellum period, and most of the extant pieces originate from the northernmost city considered in this study.

One of the most meaningful conclusions that one can draw from table 5 is that most of the works simply belong to a "Lady," with or without a broad geographical pointer (see part F). For the seventy-one pieces attributed to southern women (and this includes the nebulous Miss. Louisiana Gottheil), only eleven name the composer completely. Thirteen include a vague identification, such as initials. More than two-thirds of the pieces (forty-eight of seventy-one) are attributed to a "Lady." Clearly, if a southern woman were to publish her own work, the norm was not to put her name on the publication itself, for to do so violated ideas on propriety and blemished the woman's name. Unfortunately, no evidence survives to suggest how southern women felt about this prohibition on music publication, but publication trends throw some light on the subject.

When women did publish music, they usually stayed within the boundaries of the types of music women were most often encouraged and expected to learn, specifically, music for the piano and voice. Two women pianists (Hohnstock and Siegling) composed piano solos that are more challenging than most of the others, and only one other piece approaches theirs in complexity (the anonymous variations on "Wild Ashe Deer").[44] Of course, historical changes in style, especially between "The United States Marine March" and the midcentury works, must be taken into account. Earlier in the century, the technical demands of most solo literature were not challenging. With the coming of the virtuoso solo performer, the difficulty level of piano music rose, and as pianists such as Herz and Thalberg toured in the United States, expectations increased as well.[45]

Not all of the pieces that appeared in the antebellum period under the mask of "Lady" came from different women. As noted above, the "Lady of South Carolina" who composed the "Keowee Waltzes" also probably was responsible for five different publications. The "Lady of Virginia" composed anywhere between one and ten pieces—it is impossible to be certain. "Oft in the Stilly Night," "Thou Hast Wounded the Spirit That Lov'd Thee," and "Why Ask Me Now?" have not been included in these calculations because the identity of their authors cannot be confirmed as southern.[46]

NAMED COMPOSERS

Only five women are listed as composers on sheet music published south of Maryland between 1800 and 1860: Faustina Hasse Hodges, Caroline Norton, Ellen Ervin, Thekla Badarzewska, and Miss. Louisiana Gottheil.[47] Other pieces published south of Maryland include compositions by a "Lady of Richmond, Virginia," a "Lady of Baltimore," and a "Lady of South Carolina." Three pieces are attributed to the "Lady of South Carolina," and circumstances suggest that all three belong to the same composer.[48]

If Maryland is included as a southern place of publication, the list of named composers expands to eleven: Adèle Hohnstock, Fanny Heron, Marie Siegling, Flora Byrne, Estelle Hewitt, Virginia E. Evans, and, from the earlier group, Gottheil, Badarzewska, Ervin, Norton, and Hodges.[49] In addition to "Ladies" of various places, this group of women composers (published in Baltimore or farther south) also includes Mrs. J. M. C. of Virginia, Miss C. M. C. of Baltimore, and Mary Eugenia C. (who may be M. E. C.).[50]

Of the composers whose pieces predate the Civil War and were published in the South, only eleven give enough of their names to identify them. Five of these were definitely not born in the United States: Hewitt, Hodges, Norton, Hohnstock, and Badarzewska. Badarzewska was a Polish composer whose "Maiden's Prayer" became popular in salons in both Europe and the United States.[51] Hodges and Norton were Englishwomen: Hodges from a musical family, Norton famous for her campaigns on behalf of women's rights. Hohnstock, who wrote piano music of considerable difficulty, immigrated to the United States from Germany and taught at Cherry Valley Seminary in New York.[52] Estelle Hewitt was born in Jamaica, grew up in Boston, and married music professor and composer John Hill Hewitt. Others come close to complete identification (Mary Eugenia C., Miss C. M. C. of Baltimore, and Mrs. J. M. C. of Virginia), but details of their lives remain hidden behind their incomplete names.

Other women in this group also appear to be non-southern. Ellen Ervin, a young woman from Ohio who attended school in New Orleans, is possibly the composer who dedicated "La Belle Creole Polka" to Miss Josephine Schreiber of New Orleans in 1852.[53] Two women musicians named Fanny Heron surface during this period. The older woman was a stage performer from Dublin, starring in the title role of *Camille* in 1847 at the Old Park Theatre in New York City. Another female singer by that name made her professional debut in New York City in November 1860. Either woman could be the composer of "Isadora," although the older Fanny Heron is more likely to have published music in the 1850s. A Fanny Heron also published the "Myrtle Waltz" in Philadelphia, in 1854. It is doubtful that the younger singer would have done so before her debut. Whichever of these two she may be (and she may not be either of them, but it seems likely that she is), the woman in question is not an elite southern lady.[54]

Miss Virginia E. Evans composed "The Macon Fair March" and dedicated it to her brother, John J. Evans. Frederick Benteen published the work in 1852, entering the copyright in the district court of Maryland in his name. The work appeared in his store in Baltimore and also in that of W. T. Mayo's in New Orleans. The title suggests Georgia, but the composer's identity remains unknown. That she published in Baltimore and New Orleans further suggests a southern provenance. An unremarkable composition, "The Macon Fair March" is more notable for including its author's name than anything else. That it is one of only two identified compositions published before the Civil War that is *probably* by a southern woman marks it as noteworthy.

Flora Byrne composed "Penitential Hymn," which Benteen published in 1848 (Baltimore), and "Let's Sit Down and Talk Together," published in 1852 in St. Louis by Palmer & Weber. Byrne was born in either 1809 or 1810 in Maryland, then moved with her husband to Missouri and later to Alabama. Her social background prior to marriage is unknown, although her nephew mentioned her fondly several times in his diary, *With Pen and Pencil on the Frontier in 1851; the Diary and Sketches of Frank Blackwell Mayer*.[55]

Marie Siegling is the only other "southern" woman who identified herself in print by first and last name. Marie Siegling is an interesting case: even though she was born in Charleston (in 1824), she was not typically southern in many ways and cannot be seen in any way as representative of a southern *lady*. According to her 1908 autobiography, *Memoirs of a Dowager*, Siegling's parents were reasonably wealthy, her father being John Siegling, the music publisher.[56] He reportedly studied harp with the famous (and somewhat scandalous) Nicholas Bochsa and also sang. Her mother, Mary Schnierle, received a musical education at the Moravian female academy in Bethlehem, Pennsylvania.[57] Mary Schnierle Siegling "made her *début* in Charleston" on a Broadwood piano imported from London by her grandfather for the occasion.[58] If this were indeed a musical debut, as Siegling suggests, the Sieglings were of a different class than most of the women studied here, for *ladies* would not make a public musical debut.

In 1850, Marie Siegling married Edward Schuman-LeClercq of Dresden, and Siegling remained in Europe from that time on. She later called herself Mary Regina Schuman-LeClercq, passing on the name "Marie" to her daughter.

Before her marriage, Siegling's father took her with him on various trips to Havana (where he owned a "musical establishment"), the North, and Europe.

While in Havana, Siegling became acquainted with Countess Fernandina, a cousin of Maria de las Mercedes de Santa Cruz y Montalvo, also known as "La Comtesse de Merlin," to whom her composition "La Capricieuse" is dedicated.[59] Countess Fernandina heard Siegling sing at the festival of Santa Cecelia in Havana. It was in the salon of Countess Merlin that Maria Malibran (1808–36) made her debut, according to Siegling, thereby affording an association with the famous singer.[60]

The Sieglings' frequent tours of Europe and Havana, in addition to Marie's performing career (she claims to have been called the "Charleston Jenny Lind"), also mark Marie Siegling as an atypical southern woman. Even more striking are her compositions. While the bulk of her pieces typify parlor piano music of the period, some aspects set them apart from those works published by women. A comparison of Virginia Evans's "Macon Fair March" with the first page of Siegling's "La Capricieuse" suggests several differences. First is the dedication itself. While Evans modestly dedicated her march to her brother, Siegling's is to "Madame La Comtesse de Ferdinando de la Havane." Other compositions by Siegling carry similarly prestigious dedications, including "La Gracieuse" (dedicated to "La Comtesse de Merlin"), "Souvenir de la Saxe, Valse pour le Piano Forte Procidée d'une Introduction Sentimentale" (dedicated to "Sa Majeste Marie Reine de la Saxe"),[61] and "Souvenir de Charleston, valse originale" (dedicated to a daughter of the Aiken family in Charleston).

Siegling's willingness to publish her own music may have in part stemmed from her exposure to the non-American women she met while touring with her father. Furthermore, her French titles and the types of figuration in her piano music suggest an association with the French school of pianism seen in the works of Thalberg and Herz. Her works evince a confident woman composer who is not afraid to identify herself completely (although sometimes only as "M. R. Siegling," which may be an attempt to shield her identity), who mingles with the Parisian virtuoso professional pianists and Italian singers, and who wants to let people know of her association with the controversial La comtesse Merlin. None of Siegling's pieces are dedicated to men.[62]

In contrast to Siegling, other women composers refrain from exhibiting themselves so blatantly. Three women almost identify themselves in print from this group, but none of them discloses enough information for complete identification. Mary Eugenia C. may be M. E. C., but without a last name, a positive identification is impossible. Miss C. M. C. of Baltimore is probably Mrs. C. McC[onnell], who published "Our Triumph at Manassas: Fantaisie Mazurka" in New Orleans during the war, but again this is a guess, not a certainty. Finally, Mrs. J. M. C. of Dover, Virginia, published several works before the Civil War, but she never used her entire name in print.[63]

Some women found other ways to hide their identities, which assisted them in publishing their music. Works with disguised composers represent southern women's publications before the war much more accurately than those listed above. The title page of "Why Ask Me Now?" by "Adelene" hints that the woman who composed it did not take complete ownership. The work was arranged for harp by Samuel Carusi; since Adelene's surname is not printed, the full name of the arranger suggests that he had more involvement with the publication than did the apparent composer. Was she merely a nice young woman who had almost accidentally created a pretty tune? For her to have labored over it would have been against nineteenth-century mores and would not have lent the work positively to a publisher (even if Benteen were inclined to publish women's music), much less a buying public highly attuned to matters of taste. Indeed, it appears that Carusi rescued Adelene from blemishing her reputation by having his name appear in its entirety on the work.[64]

Thus, very few women who were undeniably southern appear to have published music under their complete names before the Civil War.[65] A few details concerning Flora Byrne have survived; at the time she published the two works that belong to this chapter, she was living in Missouri. Siegling can hardly be seen as representative. (Notably, she did not continue to publish music after her marriage in 1850.) Very little is known about Evans except her brother's name and perhaps where she lived. She was southern, but what her social status was has remained undiscovered. Undoubtedly more pieces will surface by southern women, but their identification will not alter the general finding that these women did not as a rule publish their names on compositions before the Civil War. As Leigh Fought notes regarding the writer Louisa McCord, McCord only identified herself by her initials, L. S. M. While a few people knew her work, the broader audience did not. She hid her gender "behind the assumption of masculinity."[66]

A southern woman who published music under her own name in the North was Mrs. V. G. Cowdin. Her "Mississippi Polka" appeared in Boston (by Oliver Ditson) in 1855. According to the 1860 census, Virginia G. Cowdin was the wife of Thomas G. Cowdin, a physician worth $38,000 in 1860, and lived in Liberty, Amite County, Mississippi. They were married in 1845.[67] There is a Mrs. V. G. Cowdin in the 1870 census who is the mother of Thomas Cowdin, twenty-four, and they also lived in Liberty. No occupation appears beside her name (she is the head of household), but Thomas apparently followed in his father's footsteps and was a physician. Her other children also lived with her.[68] Her birthplace is listed as Virginia, and her worth is accounted at $7,000 in real estate and $1,000 in personal property. The 1880 census yields a Mrs. V. G. Cowdin teaching music in Flatonia, Texas, aged fifty-six. She was born in 1824 in Virginia and in 1880 was living with her son and his family. The census indicates that the son was born in New York, as was the father, but that the son's children (grandchildren of Mrs. V. G. Cowdin) were born in

Mississippi. Flatonia was incorporated as a town only in 1870. These listings probably all refer to the same woman.

A Mrs. V. G. Cowdin published *Ellen; or, The Fanatic's Daughter* in Mobile, Alabama, in 1860, and this may indeed be the same woman who published "Gen. Beauregard's Grand March."[69] (The novelist is assumed to have been the woman who wrote to Jefferson Davis concerning southern literature, quoted in chapter 9.) The copyright for the book was entered by Mrs. Cowdin in Mississippi. Her experience in 1860 as an author suggests a woman who would venture into new territory—first as a novelist (not quite so unusual in the South at this time, particularly since her novel is a pro-slavery response to *Uncle Tom's Cabin*) and later as a composer, publishing another piano composition for the war effort in 1861.

A lengthy commentary by John Sullivan Dwight in 1856 discouraged amateurs from composing, and southerners no doubt heeded such advice—most of the time. He admonished those who had "no idea of the rules of compositions, or any guide except their own imagination," yet who composed and published "pieces which have not even the merit of brevity; generally consisting of four or five pages, written in most unmusical style." He continues:

> Do not, we beg of you, attempt to write; at least not till you have thoroughly learned the rules and principles of composition. You need not fear that the world will grow weary of the old masters, or that without your aid we can have no good modern productions of Art.
>
> As an Amateur of Music, you can best show your devotion to it by keeping within the legitimate sphere of *interpretation*, leaving those who are by nature more gifted than you, to the task of supplying materials for your studies.[70]

Southern women sometimes transgressed upon the hallowed ground of composition, but when they did, an overwhelming number did not put their names on the pieces they composed. Their willingness to remain unidentified, whether for modesty's sake or enforced by society, lasted only until the start of the Civil War, when women began to break many of the rules that had held them in their "proper" place. Their resistance to tradition went only so far—they challenged authority by publishing, but they resigned their lot to anonymity.

8. Becoming Useful

I want to be useful

—IRENE IN *MACARIA*, BY AUGUSTA EVANS

When they entertained their family and other company, southern women fulfilled a designated function. They had been instructed in music in order to perform for others, and they rarely were allowed to express any opposition to these lessons. Young women could have resisted the indications to play or sing just well enough and countered their parents' wishes by displaying too much talent. Such resistance certainly existed in some cases. For southern women, music composition can be interpreted as resistance. They do not mention composing music in their diaries, nor did their schools offer courses in the subject. As such, it was not a sanctioned activity. But as discussed in the previous chapter, several southern women did compose in the antebellum period, which at first glance may be an example of resistance; however, how they composed demonstrates their resignation to society's expectations. Publishing without claiming their work countered that resistance with a resignation to anonymity, as was proper for a lady.

In stark contrast to the antebellum practice of remaining anonymous, most women's music published during the Civil War includes their names. This change coexists with other ways women became useful during the war. That women chose to include their names on public documents cannot simply be explained by a desire to support their country by publishing patriotic music, for they could have done so without including their names. This manner of breaking with tradition must have stemmed from other motives as well.

The courtship, engagement, and marriage of Caroline Davis and Joseph Jones of Augusta make an excellent case in point for both resistance and resignation. Once Davis accepted Jones's proposal, she was reluctant to pinpoint the date of their marriage because she knew that when she married Jones, her individuality would be lost. As she put it, she would "be always ambitious for [his] success in life because we poor women have no name or existence of our own, we pass silently down the stream of time without leaving a single trace behind—we die unknown."[1] This sentiment can be extended to music composition, since most southern women published anonymously before the

Civil War. With the advent of war, however, women changed their ideas and began to put their names on their music compositions. As such, they did not die unknown.

USEFUL ANTEBELLUM LADIES

An accepted understanding of being useful in antebellum southern society was that elite women were *ladies*. In so doing, they fulfilled their assigned role in a highly stratified society; not fulfilling this role would be to transgress societal order. Being a lady meant many things. As the foregoing examination of piano and voice lessons demonstrated, a good deal of time and money went toward the elements deemed necessary in the production of young ladies. They were to be seen and not heard, except when they performed in an acceptable manner in the parlor. To be a lady was to dress in conservative colors and styles, always to speak softly and move with quiet dignity, and constantly to maintain herself as a model of propriety and decorum.[2] A traveler to the region wrote in the *Weekly Post* of Raleigh in 1852 that "the southern lady is naturally easy, unembarrassed and polite"; he further noted her "exquisite taste" in dress and "proverbial affability and urbanity."[3]

Being a lady meant more than a certain socioeconomic position or private behavior; it also held a broader meaning. In a postwar article entitled "Wife, Mistress, Lady" from the journal *Southern Cultivation*, the author notes the differences between each of those titles. He advises men that "who marries for love takes a wife; for fortune takes a mistress; for position takes a lady. You are loved by your wife, regarded by your mistress, tolerated by your lady. You have a wife for yourself, a mistress for your house and friends, a lady for the world and society."[4]

The preservation of society's expectations of a lady and her public duties (which were hardly "public") was paramount for elite southern women. All of their education was directed to that aim. As Alabamian Richard Brumby wrote before the war, "The great object of female education should be the development of the girl into a *lady*."[5] The cult of ladyhood included more than rules on behavior; it also included a distinctive class responsibility and work within the appropriate sphere. Elizabeth Fox-Genovese eloquently observes that "the terms 'woman' and 'lady' evoke mature female identity, but in different forms. 'Woman' suggests at once a more inclusive and more private female nature, whereas 'lady' evokes the public representation of that nature. To be a lady is to have a public presence, to accept a public responsibility. But the essence of that presence and that responsibility consists in recognizing and maintaining a sexual division of labor that relegates any proper woman to the private sphere. No lady would admit that she, and not her husband, ran the plantation."[6] Here she is speaking of Scarlett O'Hara, but the fact that women indeed ran the plantations, especially during the war, is obvious from the primary sources. In fact, being able to run the plantation—from both direct management of supplies, food, clothing, and personnel to the financial planning and accounting for these items—was an expected part of the plantation mistress's domain *before* the war. These were also part of the southern matron's usefulness, although they were rarely touted as desirable attributes. Rather, the real work continued without acknowledgment while the pleasant and agreeable social face defined the lady.

Southern ladies interpreted their usefulness in various ways. Using Joseph Chandler's "Belle of the Opera" as an example, personal beauty constituted "part of the means of her wholesome domestic influence." Her accomplishment in and love of music, "improvement" in drawing, and literary gifts all combined "to give to her consequence and usefulness in the nursery, and to make her beloved and beneficially influential in the domestic circle, and to add attraction to her charms in social life."[7] Southerners certainly worked to produce young women with these accomplishments.

Chandler also notes that as a "woman," the belle has great influence. He consciously chooses to use the word "woman" instead of "belle," but only a lady could have been a belle. "If the great offices of the woman's life, (we are speaking now of the Belle as a *woman*, looking at her higher vocation,) if all these offices are well discharged, if as mother, wife, as friend and neighbor, she stand unimpeachable; if she is as notable in all these relations as in the opera-box, still we want to inquire what is the influence exercised upon all these relations, but those qualities that made her The Belle of the Opera. How stand the opera-box and the nursery related? Because in the complete character of a woman are very few isolated qualities; they all bear upon each other, or exercise mutual influences, and each is less of itself by the qualities which it derives from others."[8] Such attributes contributed to a woman's usefulness during the antebellum period. In an advice manual for young southern women, one Mrs. Hutchinson noted that a "lady could adorn both her home and her husband's name by being able to play piano." Furthermore, she wrote that cultivating a taste for music and drawing was "a means of enlarging the circle of domestic pleasures, so as to raise an additional barrier against that fondness for public amusement, which has so often been the destroyer of domestic comfort."[9]

Traditional expectations of how ladies could be useful altered significantly during the Civil War. Drew Gilpin Faust and LeeAnn Whites, among others, note several ways in which women took over traditionally male activities during the war years. Women not only continued in their time-honored domestic labors but also began to contribute to public life, something previously barred to them.[10] Perhaps the most acceptable of these new public responsibilities was the transformation of previously private domestic labor into public domestic labor, the fashioning of tasks such as sewing for the household into sewing for the army.[11] While many elite white women participated to a degree in clothes production on plantations prior to the war, numerous diaries and letters attest to the fact that during the war years, elite white women also began to sew, knit, and contribute to a degree hitherto unknown to them.

Women entered the war effort in ways that were even more public. In order to raise money for supplies, women organized and ran public fairs and bazaars. They created their own groups, such as the Ladies' Gunboat Society, which in turn held public events for the purpose of raising funds for the Confederates. *Tableaux vivants* and concerts were particularly convenient methods for providing such a service since most women had received some musical training during their lives. *Tableaux vivants* were by far the most popular choice for benefit performances in the South during the war.[12] Approval and preference for this type of public display might have been partially sanctioned because the performers did not make any noise—they were not heard. They simply stood there, looking pretty. This was an exercise to which southern girls were accustomed.

Some women initially resisted the need for public display. Before the war, writer Louisa McCord chose not to reveal her gender when she published her literary works. If she assumed a public voice as a woman, McCord believed she might jeopardize the social order.[13] This resistance to challenging the established order can also be seen in the case of Mary Legg of Florida, who did not believe she should take part in public performances, even for the war effort. Her friends, however, enjoined her to participate in this opportunity to serve her country. Clara MacLean of Columbia, South Carolina, also weighed the need for such performance against her ideas of ladyhood. She keenly noticed that her participation made her feel "quite important," and she discovered an alternative way of thinking about herself and her role.[14]

Some southern men also disdained such activities. They did not feel that the end justified the means but rather that these public appearances destroyed the "true modesty, delicate sensibility" of their women. They raised the question of how such activities truly differed from parlor performances.[15] Public opinion, nonetheless, ruled with those who thought the performances were needed for the war effort, and they remained a popular activity as long as possible.

MUSICAL CONCERTS AND THE PROBLEM
OF PUBLIC PERFORMANCES

Musical concerts were another popular choice for fund-raising, and the public was urged to attend. An advertisement for a Patriotic Musical Festival in Charleston in 1862 attests to the patriotic appeal to the public for such events: "The concert to aid in the construction of the Ladies Gunboat, comes off at Hibernian Hall tonight. The ladies and gentlemen who will take part in the evening entertainment are among the most finished amateur vocalists and musicians whom the city can boast. The programme has been made up with taste and discrimination, and from the musical reputation of those who have undertaken the conduct of the concert, we feel that the pieces will be rendered in excellent style. . . . We know that we need say nothing to urge our citizens to aid the noble exertions of the ladies in the country cause, by attending the concert, and filling the hall to its utmost capacity."[16]

The South Caroliniana Library Manuscript Collection contains what may be a program from this performance.[17] It reveals how such public displays were carefully constructed so as not to damage elite young women's "modesty and delicacy" by flaunting them before an audience. Public concerts had to be prudently created so as not to stretch the bounds of society too far. When women performed, they were almost always listed on the program as "a young lady" or as "a lady amateur." This situation had existed since at least the 1840s, when programs occasionally included a performance by a "lady amateur," unidentified.[18]

The program of a Ladies' Gunboat Musical Evening in Charleston, 1862, represents a typical fund-raising effort.[19] According to the broadside, some "public spirited" ladies of Charleston "will be presented" under the direction of two male musicians in a musical program. The two professors were, of course, lower-middle-class males who taught music for a living. These women were notably public "spirited"—not public actors. They were not "public ladies"—which implied prostitutes in the parlance of the day—but were "public *spirited* ladies." They did not appear on their own but were "presented." Significantly, exactly who was presenting is unclear. By being presented, the ladies were not taking the initiative to exhibit themselves on the public stage.

The program reveals other subtleties. Only the professional musicians are named (male or female): Professor M[atthew] S. Reeves (age forty-three, of South Carolina), Signor Gambati (a local voice teacher), and pupils of "Miss E. Sloman." A harpist, singer, and composer, Elizabeth Sloman belonged to a family of English actors and musicians who performed with some frequency in Charleston.[20]

The pianos for the Charleston concert were lent to the performers by Professor G. F. Cole, who also owned a music shop and whose imprint appears on surviving sheet music. All of the ladies indicated by the program headline are listed as "Young Ladies [and Gentlemen] Amateurs," "Two Young Ladies, Pupils of Miss E. Sloman—Amateurs," "A Lady Amateur," and "A Lady [and Gentleman], Pupils of Sig. Gambati." The "Lady Amateur" may have been a married woman, which distinguishes her from the "Young Ladies" mentioned in other places.

The repertory is interesting. Beginning each part and concluding the whole with patriotic music ("La Marseillaise" being considered a patriotic tune for Confederates), the program contained typical musical pieces for amateurs of this period. A young man performed a *Lied* by Beethoven on the cello, and young ladies played piano duets, one of which was by Herz. Absent are extended works by Thalberg, Gottschalk, or Wollenhaupt—these would not have been appropriate for young ladies to perform in public, being too masculine and/or professional. Opera pieces from *Lucia di Lammermoor, Anna Bolena, La sonnambula*, and *Don Giovanni* reflect typical performance options (fantasy for solo piano, arranged with a small instrumental ensemble, and sung as from the opera). All works appear to be presented in the original languages.

One of Sarah Lois Wadley's favorite songs, Schubert's "Erlkönig," also appears on this program, sung by a woman. This work held a particular appeal to audiences of the period, no doubt because of its dramatic qualities; yet, it is an odd choice for a woman to sing, particularly in a time when gender roles were so defined. (The characters to be portrayed in the *Lied* are narrator, father, son, and the Erlking himself.) "La ci darem la mano" also seems to be an odd choice for such a venue because of its text. In the opera, Don Giovanni sings this duet with Zerlina as he attempts to seduce her on the eve of her marriage to Masetto. This scene hardly seems appropriate for genteel Charlestonians, but the performers—the only unnamed people on the program without "amateur" accompanying their selection—were not quite of the same class as the others. Moreover, since opera arias were often printed in this period with texts entirely unrelated to the originals, audience members may not have been familiar with the context in *Don Giovanni*.

By using their musical abilities for these performances, Confederate women were able to be useful for the Cause. Some women went even further. On 27 September 1861, the *Charleston Mercury* advertised that a group of musical amateurs was traveling to Richmond for a series of concerts to raise money for the war. The leader was none other than Signor Torriani, the man who taught Elizabeth Waties Allston Pringle voice, who was engaged at about the same time at the South Carolina Female Collegiate Institute and who would later open a music school in New York City.

> The Patriotic enterprise, in which this gentleman has been engaged, and to which we have before alluded, is now complete. The ladies and gentlemen who have so generously relinquished the comforts of home in aid of the Soldiers of their country, and who compose this company of musical amateurs, have been for some time rehearsing under the able direction of SIGNOR TORRIANI, are now organized, and leave tonight, en route for Richmond, at which city they will give their first concert next week. We bespeak for these accomplished amateurs a kind reception from the public of Richmond. We cannot give a better guarantee of their ability to the press of that city and throughout the South, than by mentioning that they have been under the direction of SIGNOR TORRIANI,

well known in Charleston as the conductor of the Havana Italian Opera Troupe that has so often delighted our citizens and crowded our Theatre. The purpose is to give a series of attractive concerts throughout the Southern States, commencing in Richmond, Va., proceeding thence to Petersburg, Norfolk, Portsmouth, Lynchburg, &c., and on leaving the Old Dominion the entire profits of the concerts will be handed over to the Ladies Relief Association of that State. The same principle will be pursued in the State of North Carolina, South Carolina, Georgia, Alabama, Louisiana, and wherever else in the South the company may travel. Mr. G. F. MARCH-ANT, of the Charleston Theatre, has obtained a furlough for the purpose of giving his valuable aid as business manager of these concerts.[21]

Women also manipulated how music enabled them to be useful during the war years, and shifts in how women published music in the antebellum period (anonymously) and during the war (under their own names) reflect this change. Whether women deliberately used the idea of supporting the war effort as a mere excuse to suddenly begin putting their names in print on sheet music published in the South or as a sincere attempt to show southern sympathies cannot be determined. There was no real reason why women *had* to put their names on patriotic music, which suggests that the move to signing their own music was part of a growing realization of new possibilities opened before them as the war progressed.

Where to draw the line between what was absolutely *necessary* for women to do and what was *desired* is difficult. Few would argue that for women to take over household duties while men were away was unnecessary. Most would probably agree that assuming responsibility for fund-raising and organization of societies to aid the soldiers' plight was also indispensable. Even performance in public concerts might be seen as obligatory, although some men and women thought this an extreme gesture. In the serial novel *Agnes*, which ran from 1863 to 1864 in the *Southern Literary Messenger*, the main character plays "fantasias and sonatas" when she is alone.[22] How much this reflects the cultural changes in self-perception is unknown, but Agnes clearly ventured into the masculine repertory during the war years. The composition and publication of patriotic songs could likewise have been a significant contribution—but was it necessary for women to put their names on the music now?

9. Confederate Women Composers

A Patriotic Musical Festival proposed by some public-spirited Ladies of Charleston in aid of The Ladies' Gunboat will be presented at the Hibernian Hall.

—*CHARLESTON MERCURY,* 1862

With the advent of the Civil War, women's perceptions of their place in southern culture altered dramatically, and many entered arenas that were hitherto barred to them. One place where a new self-perception can be seen is in the public acknowledgment of music composition by southern women, for the act of naming themselves in print was diametrically opposed to the prewar expectations of elite white women, "ladies." During the war years, some southern women realized their wish to become useful to the Confederacy's cause by publishing patriotic music, signing their names to these works in blatant violation of all cultural norms presented to them prior to 1861. The circumstances that made it possible for such women to even consider this act that was simultaneously beneath them as a class and against them as a sex have been explored in other areas, but not in music.

As the South actively worked toward its independence, several writers tried to encourage the creation of even more original southern literature. A commentator writing in the *Southern Literary Messenger* in October 1861 noted that "a nation cannot live upon bread alone. . . . The moral and intellectual must assist the material, or the whole fabric will fall. . . . The destiny of the South will be but a crude and unfinished attempt, an unmeaning, inconsequential projection into time and space, unless along with her political independence she achieves her independence in thought and education, and in all those forms of mental improvement which by a liberal construction of the word, are included in literature."[1] Women writers continued to pen domestic (plantation) novels that pitted southern virtues against northern shortcomings. Novelist Virginia Cowdin wrote to Jefferson Davis in 1861 that "perhaps the time has now arrived when the South will awaken from her lethargy and appreciate her own literature."[2]

MACARIA

Domestic novelists attempted to provide structure and justification for the changes in what women could and should be doing. One of the most popular of these books was *Macaria*, a novel that is frequently mentioned in connection with southern women's culture of the Civil War. Drew Gilpin Faust suggests that *Macaria* was possibly the most widely read novel in the South during its time.[3] The author, twenty-nine-year-old Augusta Evans, dedicated it in 1864 to the Confederate army, according to a letter she wrote to General P. G. T. Beauregard in 1862, as an "inadequate tribute" from a woman "debarred from the dangers and deathless glory of the 'tented field'" to the "patriotism and sublime self-abnegation of her dear and devoted countrymen." Evans wished to ensure that "the cause of our beloved, struggling Confederacy may yet be advanced through the agency of its daughters" (herself being one) through her "feeble, womanly pen."[4] In Greek mythology, Macaria saves Athens from invasion by sacrificing herself on the altar of the gods. According to Faust (who drew attention to *Macaria* in her work on southern culture), Evans was clearly comparing southern women to this heroine.[5] Evans, like the composers discussed below, used publication as a vehicle for personal expression during the Civil War.[6]

Macaria also makes vivid a desire found throughout women's writings in the South: the need to be useful, or as Evans puts it, "the divinely-appointed goal—Womanly Usefulness." Her character Irene persistently cries out, "I want to be useful," a comment that Faust notes is expressed in almost every extant Confederate woman's diary.[7] Undoubtedly, Evans's novel reflects the general trend of finding alternative ways to contribute to the Confederacy. Evans writes that "in improving the condition of women, it is advisable to give them the readiest access to independent industrial pursuits, and extend the circle of their appropriate occupations."[8] She grappled with the conflicting ideas of transcending the "proper sphere of womanhood" and patriotic duty but in the end found her country's need greater than society's notions of propriety.[9] Similarly, women musicians used composing and publishing patriotic songs as a way to become useful—a way to use their specific skills to advance the Cause.

PUBLISHED MUSIC BY SOUTHERN WOMEN

In examining works by southern women, the definition of who qualifies as "southern" comes into question again. Unfortunately, the biographies of many of the composers remain unknown, and thus the facts of birth, education, and other similar circumstances cannot be used to determine if composers are "southern." Lacking such precise data, sentiments expressed in the title, dedication, and lyrics (if a vocal work) as well as place of publication are guiding factors in such cases. Nonetheless, almost all of the pieces in table 6 (see appendix) can be attributed either to southern women or at least southern sentiments.

Before the war, between 1800 and 1860, most of the seventy-one works by southern women—67 percent—simply belong to a "Lady," with or without initials or a broad geographical pointer.[10] How many of the compositions published under names such as "A Lady of Baltimore" came from the same pen is unknown, so the exact number of women composers cannot be determined.

Seventeen percent of the antebellum pieces have some vague identification, such as initials: Mrs. J. M. C. of Virginia accounts for nine of these twelve pieces. Whether she is the same composer as the "Lady of Virginia" who contributed the first southern pieces to *Godey's Lady's Book* cannot be determined, but she may be. The "Lady of Virginia" pieces appeared between 1847 and 1850, and those by Mrs. J. M. C. appeared in 1856. Two other works with some identification, albeit incomplete, belong to Mary Eugenia C. and M. E. C., who may be the same person as well. Completely identified composers account for 14 percent of the works, and six of these ten pieces belong to Marie Siegling (the daughter of a music publisher).[11] Notably, Siegling did not continue to publish music after her marriage in 1850.

Dramatically, in the 1860s, the situation in the South altered, and most published compositions by women included more identification. The most obvious reason for this change seems to be the advent of war, and most of the extant compositions are patriotic. The question of gender and genre is relevant, for it seems unlikely that women were supposed to be writing patriotic pieces, as most of the music composed by women anywhere in the United States prior to 1860 does not fall under the label of patriotic. Most of the exceptions to the patriotic rule date from the time of the Mexican war and relate to specific battles or commanders. Interestingly, these years, roughly 1846–48, generally saw an increase in the number of publications attributed to women composers (but not specifically named).

PATRIOTIC AND CONFEDERATE MUSIC

A report in the *Raleigh Register* of 16 June 1840 illustrates the genre distinction by gender. Here the writer notes that a small group of prominent men had a separate dinner where they "made toasts and sang patriotic tunes," while the ladies had a tea near town, and "vocal and instrumental music" was the chief entertainment.[12] Emily Thornwell's *Lady's Guide to Perfect Gentility* warns young women not to "sing songs descriptive of masculine passion or sentiment," which suggests that patriotic music would have been inappropriate for women.[13] As with many other things, however, women entered the realm of patriotic music during the war, as the advertisement and concert for the Charleston Patriotic Musical Festival of 1862 demonstrated.

Sarah Morgan reveals how some elite women felt about the subject of patriotism and how it intersected with their ideas of what a lady should be. She notes in 1862 that "the disgust I have experienced from listening to others, I hope will forever prevent me from becoming a 'Patriotic woman.' . . . In my opinion, the Southern women, and some few of the men, have disgraced themselves by their rude, ill mannered behavior in many instances. I insist, that if the valor and chivalry of our men cannot save our country, I would rather have it conquered by a brave race, than owe its liberty to the Billingsgate oratory and demonstrations of some of these 'ladies.'"[14] On the next page, Sarah comments that she wishes she could comfort soldiers in their distress and perform other kind acts, but she cannot do so. She is afraid that she would not be accepted in society after the war was over. Such adherence to society's codes of behavior helps show the audacity that women demonstrated when they broke the rules.

Strikingly, of the thirty-two pieces by southern women published between 1861 and 1865, twenty-one are patriotic.[15] More pieces may be similarly partisan, but only the advertisements still exist for some, so the subject remains unknown.[16] Twenty-four of the publications identify the composer by at least last name and first initial—that is 75 percent, as compared to eleven before the war. The attributions to a "Lady" after 1861 account for only 19 percent of the works, as opposed to 60 percent before 1861. Of these, the "Lady of Kentucky" might have had to shield her identity not because of social customs but from fear of retribution for her pro-Confederate stance.

The numbers bear out a substantial change in the way southern women published before and after April 1861. Other transformations can be noted as well. Before the Civil War, women's music ran along familiar lines. Sentimental songs, polkas, and other simple works typify music by both men and women in the late antebellum period. With the initiation of war, however, southern women's compositions began to take a decidedly different tone. Even as northern cartoonists lampooned southern women in sending their men to war, southern women began to support the Cause with patriotic music. These pieces usually carried dedications to specific commanders or groups of soldiers, such as "General Beauregard's Grand March" or the "Askew Quickstep." Women composed solo songs or piano music, two areas that reflect the most common types of music lessons young women experienced. Some are in familiar styles—polka, waltz, mazurka, and variations—while others draw from militaristic music, such as the march. None of the piano works is slow or sentimental. The songs tend to be strophic and reflect the style of contemporary parlor music composed before the war, but often the sentiments are different in that they relate specifically to the war.[17]

Varying degrees of biographical information are available concerning the women composers of the Confederacy, who came from diverse regions and likewise had different backgrounds. Few can be confirmed as elite women; alternatively, few can be confirmed otherwise. Since the list is relatively short, biographical information available on Confederate women composers is presented below, and the implications for the upper class are considered in the conclusion.[18]

PIECES THAT SPECIFICALLY IDENTIFY MILITARY PEOPLE, GROUPS, OR BATTLES

Nine pieces composed by Confederate women include the names of specific commanders, regiments, or battles in their titles: Mrs. J. B. Henderson's "Askew Quickstep," Mrs. V. G. Cowdin's "Gen. Beauregard's Grand March," Mrs. Flora Byrne's "President Jefferson Davis Grand March," Mrs. C. Mc-Connell's "Tribute to Beauregard Quickstep" and "Our Triumph at Manassas," Mrs. E. Blessey's "Continental Polka Mazurka," Mrs. E. B.'s "Louisiana Guard March," Elizabeth Sloman's "Sumter," and Lizzie C. Orchard's "Maj. General Hampton's Quickstep" (see table 6 in the appendix). Only one of these, "Sumter," is a vocal composition; the rest are for piano solo. That most of these works are marches suggests that the military association with marches also played a role in popularizing this type of piano piece during the Civil War, as it had during the Mexican-American War.

Most of these compositions appeared early in the war, with a number of them being published in 1861. Only Orchard's "Maj. General Hampton's Quickstep" and McConnell's "Our Triumph at Manassas" can be definitely dated after that year. The dearth of new piano works later in the war might be attributed to a number of issues. The lack of materials certainly contributed to this situation, as did the need for more and more women to contribute in more tangible ways (such as sewing and knitting) to the war effort. Another factor might be distribution, for a local publisher such as Bloch in Mobile might have printed a limited number of copies of a new work that has not survived.[19]

An early example of the type of piano music published by southern women during the Civil War is Cowdin's "Gen. Beauregard's Grand March," published in New Orleans in 1861 with her name boldly appearing on the title page. David Thompson mentions it alongside the "President Jefferson Davis Grand March" by Byrne as "fine examples of the grand march by female composers" during the Civil War.[20] One of its most unusual features is the key of E major. Sharp keys are rare for this period of women's literature, and only G major occurs with regularity.[21] Other aspects of this march typify piano music of the period, such as scalar flourishes, hand-crossing, octaves, and dotted rhythms. As with other pieces published by Blackmar in New Orleans in 1861, Cowdin's work appeared in several other cities. It could boast circulation in Henry Siegling's in Charleston, J. H. Snow's in Mobile, W. Nash's in Natchez, E. A. Benson's in Memphis, and the Blackmar & Bros.

store in Vicksburg. Mrs. Cowdin seems to have been more assertive than most southern women because she published another piece, the "Mississippi Polka," and a novel, *Ellen; or, The Fanatic's Daughter*, before the war.

Mrs. J. B. Henderson composed a piano work, the "Askew Quickstep," in honor of the Askew Guards of New Orleans, in 1861. She could be the wife of J. B. Henderson, aged sixty and a widowed physician born in Kentucky, mentioned in the Louisiana (New Orleans) 1880 census. In this census, the couple had daughters aged twenty and sixteen, both born in Louisiana. Blackmar published the piano work there, but it was distributed in several other establishments: J. H. Snow, Mobile; W. Nash, Natchez; Blackmar & Bro., Vicksburg; and White, Pfister & Co., Montgomery. Such a wide distribution occurred for a little less than half of Confederate women's music. Earlier in the war, a composition was more likely to circulate in a number of states; later in the war, most pieces enjoyed only a local reputation. No doubt this was due to reduced circumstances throughout the South.

Flora Byrne's "President Jefferson Davis Grand March," published in 1861 by Werlein & Halsey in New Orleans, includes elements that most nineteenth-century listeners would have expected of a march, including dotted rhythms and a militaristic theme in the main section (characterized by numerous rests, as opposed to lyricism).[22] She had published two works before the war, "Penitential Hymn" in 1848 and "Let's Sit Down and Talk Together" in 1852. Byrne also set to music "Melt the Bells," a pro-Confederate poem, in 1866.[23] Her husband, Edward, a physician, served in the Confederate army as a surgeon. Born in Maryland, Byrne moved to Missouri with her husband upon her marriage. Mary Cooke speculates that the Byrnes left Missouri when it did not secede, which demonstrates a devotion on the part of the family to the Confederacy.[24] In 1880 (at age seventy-one), she was working as a governess for a lawyer with six children. The records do not indicate if reduced circumstances as a result of the war or widowhood prompted this employment.

In all probability, two works can be attributed to Mrs. C. McConnell. Harwell suggests that both "Tribute to Beauregard Quickstep" (no date) and "Our Triumph at Manassas" belong to the same composer. The composer of the latter work is listed on the music as "Mrs. C.McC"; on the former is given a more complete title and name. It is tempting to believe that the more obscurely attributed work might predate the other and that McConnell was emboldened by other women publishing, therefore including a more complete identification on her second piece. The work that refers to Manassas might have been composed near the date of either First or Second Manassas (the last in August 1862), but that remains unknown.[25]

The case of Elizabeth Sloman demonstrates yet a different type of situation for a woman composer. Elizabeth, Ann, and their father taught music in Charleston during the war.[26] (The women are listed in the Ladies' Gunboat

Society program described in chapter 8.) Elizabeth composed songs that suited either northern or southern sentiments during the war, somewhat of an anomaly yet commensurate with the position of a professional musician rather than that of an ardent Confederate.[27] Her "Sumter" clearly belongs to the Civil War songs composed in honor of Confederate victories. She dedicated the work to Beauregard and the "Brave Sons of South Carolina."

Elizabeth Sloman may be the woman listed in the 1860 South Carolina census as Ellen Sloman (age twenty-seven) who was working as a piano teacher in Charleston. She was living with her father, John, and a sister, Mary (age twenty-four). All are listed as musicians from England and are listed with $4,000 in real estate and $4,000 in personal property. Her father was locally known for comic songs composed before the war.[28]

The first appearance of the Sloman women in Charleston is documented in a broadside from 1846, in which "Miss E. Sloman" and "The Misses Sloman" performed a concert with Mr. Sloman at Hibernian Hall. They sang and played harp and piano.[29] They performed several concerts that March, and a farewell concert on the 20th lists "Miss A. Sloman" as well as "Miss E. Sloman." Miss A. played the piano while her sister played the harp. The Slomans, however, did not have elite status but were music teachers. Their participation in such public performances did not carry the same meaning as did that of the "lady amateurs."

Another young composer with links to a professional musician was Lizzie C. Orchard, who also published a work that bears the name of a famous Confederate leader: "Maj. General Hampton's Quickstep." She was an unmarried young woman at the time the work appeared and definitely of not-quite-*lady* status. Lizzie graduated from South Carolina Female Collegiate Institute in Barhamville in 1858, where her father, William H. Orchard, taught music. Like many music professors in the South, William Orchard came to the United States from Europe.[30] Lizzie was the second of at least eight children; in 1850 (at age nine) she was already in school. Lizzie was not in her father's household in 1860 (according to the census).

While the exact date of "Maj. General Hampton's Quickstep" does not appear on the music, it must have been published between Wade Hampton's promotion to major general on 3 August 1863 and his promotion to lieutenant general on 15 February 1865. Since her maiden name appears on the music, Lizzie was not yet married; since she is not listed in her father's house, she may have been earning a living, possibly as a music teacher. In 1857, her school offered a course titled Theory and Practice of Instrumental Music and Vocal Music—quite a find (if it indeed includes what is today considered music theory) among female institutes North or South. Almost certainly, Lizzie Orchard participated in this course, and her work demonstrates her abilities in composition.

PRO-SOUTHERN PIECES (NONMILITARY)

Other types of pieces composed by women in support of the southern cause have more general themes and are not tied necessarily to a single individual or battle. Unlike the militaristic piano marches described above, several of these works are songs for solo voice with piano accompaniment (occasionally a chorus for a mixed ensemble is included). These compositions include "Up with the Flag" by Dr. and Mrs. William B. Harrell (1863), "The Flag of the South" by Anna K. Dixon Hearn (1861), "Farewell to the Star Spangled Banner" by Mrs. E. D. (Francis or Frances) Hundley (186-), "Old Cotton Is King!" by Delia W. Jones (1862), "The Stars of Our Banner" by Alice Lane (1861), "Dixie Doodle" by Mrs. Margaret Weir (1862), "The Southern Soldier Boy" by Sallie Parkington (sometimes spelled Partington, 1863), "You Can Never Win Us Back" by a Lady of Kentucky (1864), "Maryland! My Maryland!" by a Lady of Baltimore (1861), "God Will Defend the Right" by a Lady of Richmond (1861), and "Southern Shout" by Mrs. J. H. Mew (1862?). A number of piano works also carry similar titles: the "Southern Rights Polka" by Mrs. A. G. Warner (1861) and the "Southern Rights March" by Miss C. Lauve (186-).

In contrast to the works published in the antebellum period in which hardly any of the composers was identified, only three of these pieces remain anonymous. How each woman is identified varies, however. One way in which a woman might publish her own "masculine" composition was under the protective care of her husband, and such might be the case with Dr. and Mrs. William B. Harrell's "Up with the Flag."[31] Mrs. Harrell is Ann Judson Battle Harrell, the daughter of a Baptist minister and educator. She was born in Nashville, North Carolina, in 1834 and studied at both Chowan Baptist Female Institute and Rose Bowen Academy (music being mentioned in connection with the latter).[32]

While not a lady of elite status (her father intended Ann to be a missionary), she nonetheless received an education similar to other women recorded in this work. As with many others, after the war Harrell pursued paths not common for women before the war. She and her family performed as the Harrell Family in musical concerts, before her husband was ordained a Baptist minister. She and her husband worked together to produce several songs and hymns throughout their fifty-five-year marriage. Several sources attribute the music to Ann and the lyrics to William.[33]

In the case of "Up with the Flag," Dr. Harrell is credited with having composed the work, and Mrs. Harrell is the one who "arranged" it. The song's attribution is an excellent example of one way women allowed themselves to be perceived. It is difficult to imagine why the person who composed the work could not have arranged it—nothing in the piece indicates any special treatment or issues of setting the tune. The simple accompaniment could have been added by anyone looking at the tune who had any experience at all with accompanying a melody (see figure 9.1.) Might it be possible that the wife completely created the work and that, because of societal pressures, the husband had to receive credit for it? In this example, we would find the wife the ever loyal "helpmeet" supporting her husband in any way possible but never eclipsing his primary judgment and wisdom. She may even have been assisting in validating him, since he was not fighting and may have felt a need to do *something*. Perhaps she became useful by making *him* useful?

Anna K. Dixon Hearn (1828–1910) composed and published "The Flag of the South: A Voice from the Old Academy" in 1861. She dedicated the work to C[ollins] D. Elliott, who was a teacher and the principal of the Nashville Female Academy.[34] Collins Elliott is listed as a "school teacher" in the 1860 census with a combined worth of $175,000 ($90,000 in real estate and $85,000 in personal property). With such a high net worth, he almost certainly was not a music professor. Moreover, Anna's family must have been on somewhat equal footing for her to feel comfortable enough to dedicate a published music composition to Elliott. Hearn, reportedly from a "prominent" family, had married Reverend Isham Garland Hearn, an influential minister in western Tennessee, in 1852. She lost her husband (and brother) at the battle of Shiloh in 1862.[35]

Delia Wright Jones, composer of "Old Cotton Is King!," is one of the more unusual cases in this study. Born in Vermont around 1831, she was not technically a southerner. She moved to the South to teach and by 1856 had married William Borden Jones, a Baptist pastor and educator.[36] An educator herself, Delia Jones publicly presented a paper at the Education Association of North Carolina in Statesville in 1858 and again in New Bern the following year. This work was published as an article, "Manner of Educating Females," in the *North Carolina Journal of Education* in 1859. In this paper, she vehemently criticized the short education girls received (often ending by age fifteen or sixteen) and argued for a longer, more exhaustive study of many subjects and "perhaps music on various instruments."[37]

During the years just before the war, Jones lived with her husband in Warsaw (Duplin County), North Carolina, where he was principal of the Warsaw Baptist Seminary and she taught the women students. Delia published articles and poems that frequently appeared in the *Biblical Recorder*, a vehicle for the state's Southern Baptist Association. The 1860 census lists their worth at $1,100 and names one daughter, Frances. One surviving poem, "To the Duplin Riflemen," appeared on a program when the local troops joined the war effort. On this occasion, the tune was set to the state song, "The Old North State."[38]

Even though Jones saw music only as an option for female education, she must have had some musical training in order to compose and publish her own piece. She also knew something of the other accomplishments, for in the same year that she wrote "Old Cotton Is King!," she advertised as a portrait

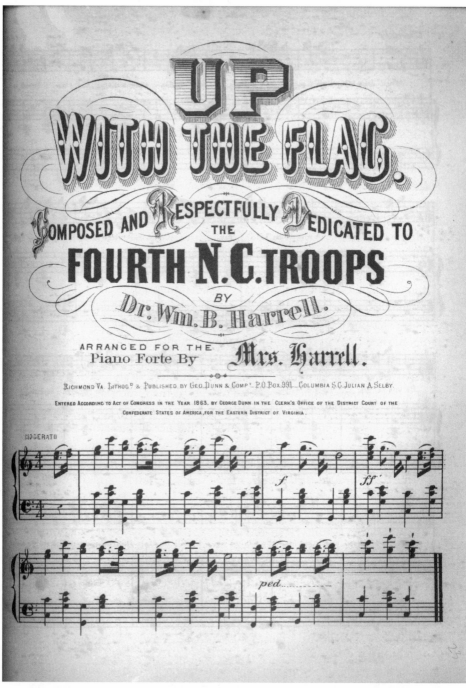

Fig. 9.1. "Up with the Flag," by Dr. and Mrs. William B. Harrell, page 1. From the Historic American Sheet Music Collection in the Rare Book, Manuscript, and Special Collections Library, Duke University.

painter (oils). After the Civil War, the Joneses lived in Greenville, South Carolina, where Delia continued to work, by that time as a photographer.[39]

Cooke describes "Old Cotton Is King!" as "Italianate" in the manner of other pieces from the early nineteenth century. Such a style is an obvious choice because of the numerous bel canto melodies that young women heard in concert and sang at home and at school. More striking is Delia's independent-mindedness at a time when southern women were most restrained. That she should publish a musical composition and sign her name is less unusual when compared to her other public accomplishments. She does not, however, represent the typical southern woman; rather, she was a northerner who traveled south in order to educate southerners.

Little biographical information has been identified concerning Margaret Weir, composer (and lyricist) of "Dixie Doodle." Published in New Orleans by the firm of P. P. Werlein & Halsey in 1862, the sentiments are clearly with the South. Weir dedicated the song to "Our dear soldiers on the Battle Field." Another work attributed to Margaret Weir, "The Lord of the Castle: A Favorite Song," appeared in 1832 from the New York firm of Firth & Hall. Whether or not this is the same Weir cannot be determined. A thirty-year gap between publications is odd, although not insurmountable. In St. Augustine, Florida, a Mrs. Weir advertised to teach piano and guitar in 1829.[40] Just after the war (December 1865), a Mrs. M. Weir advertised to teach music to children in Jacksonville, Florida.[41] The circumstance of two married women with the last name of Weir teaching in such close proximity suggests that the two songs may have been composed by the same woman, *if* this Mrs. Weir composed "Dixie Doodle." Curiously, the first piece appeared at about the same time as the first advertisement to teach music (1832 and 1829), and the second piece at about the same time as the second reference (1862 and 1865).

"Dixie Doodle" celebrates southern victories in general, predicting the eventual defeat of the Union and brazenly acknowledging southern supremacy (figure 9.2). Cooke notes that it is practically the only upbeat composition written by a woman composer during the war, and its jauntiness stems from both lyrics and musical setting.[42] One of the marks of true musical accomplishment is Weir's combination of "Yankee Doodle" and "Dixie," juxtaposing the two tunes in a manner that does not come across as awkward. Weir's method is to alternate measures of each tune under her own lyrics. The clever mixing of both melodies demonstrates a playfulness that is missing from most contemporary songs. The piece must have been popular, for it appeared in music stores in Mobile, Wilmington, Augusta, Macon, New Orleans, and Charleston.

A work similar in conception to Weir's use of two songs in one is Octavie Romey's "La Marseillaise et Bonnie Blue Flag," published in 1864. A much more technically demanding composition than Weir's, Romey's tribute to the Confederacy stylistically resembles her other works. At least two of Romey's

Fig. 9.2. "Dixie Doodle," by Margaret Weir, page 1. From the Historic American Sheet Music Collection in the Rare Book, Manuscript, and Special Collections Library, Duke University.

pieces appeared in New Orleans: "4 mars souvenir; a la memoire de Madame G. T. Beauregard" (also 1864) and the above-mentioned "La Marseillaise et Bonnie Blue Flag."[43] Born in 1828, Romey received notice in the *Allgemeine musikalische Zeitung* (1842) for her *Album des Lys et des Roses*.[44] She was a professional pianist, and her performance of two fantasies ("Jerusalem" by Gottschalk and "Grand Fantasie Dramatique sur des motifs de *Lucia di Lammermoor*" by Strakosch) in New Orleans on 26 July 1862 was favorably reviewed.[45] She was not, however, a native southerner.

In 1861, Alice Lane composed "The Stars of Our Banner," which Armand Blackmar published in his Augusta office. Advertisements on "Old Cotton Is King!" credit Lane with two other works, "Reverie Mazourka" and "La Zaidee Schottisch." Both works appear to have been published by Blackmar in Augusta in 1862. The name "Alice Lane" appears in several stories and plays in the late nineteenth century and may have been a common one.

Perhaps the best example of how women changed their perspective on composing and using their names on sheet music during the Civil War can be found in a work by a wealthy, upper-class woman from Virginia. Mrs. Elijah Dupay (Francis or Frances) Hundley published "Farewell to the Star Spangled Banner" in Richmond sometime during the 1860s, presumably in 1861, when her home state of Virginia seceded. According to the 1860 census, in that year, Francis Yuille Hundley (aged fifty-six) was the wife of a farmer worth approximately $90,000. He also owned fifty slaves. Francis grew up on Rosebank Plantation near Staunton, Virginia, and married Hundley in 1826 when she was twenty.[46] She belonged to the planter class. Her choice of identification contrasts the antebellum publications of Martha Colhoun, another woman undeniably of elite social status who nonetheless chose not to reveal her name. This difference in attitude almost certainly reflects the social disruptions that followed when the South's cultural world was shattered by the Civil War.

"LADY"

The case of "Maryland! My Maryland!" illustrates a different perspective, one much more in line with women's publications in the antebellum period than the examples presented above because the woman involved belonged to the uppermost class in society. The creation of this extremely popular song is rather well documented, and its players are much easier to trace than most of the others. Maryland stands out as somewhat of a paradox: progressive enough to have major publishing houses bringing out women's works while simultaneously a slave state. Public sentiment in Maryland was divided in 1861; being a slave-holding border state in close proximity to Washington, D.C., magnified its significance on both sides of the Mason-Dixon Line.

In 1861, Lincoln suspended habeas corpus along the rail lines between Philadelphia and Washington, especially targeting Maryland, because too few Union troops had arrived in Washington. Lincoln then authorized General Winfield Scott to arrest the opposition (secessionists) in the Maryland state legislature and did not release them in time for the vote on secession. As such, Maryland remained in the Union, although there seems to have been a large percentage of the population that was pro-slavery and pro-Confederacy. In reaction to the pro-southern sentiments of Baltimoreans, James Ryder Randall published his poem "Maryland! My Maryland!" in the *South*, a newspaper for pro-southern residents of Baltimore, on 31 May 1861.

A few days later, the Baltimore Glee Club met at the home of Hetty and Jennie Cary, who were considered two of the most beautiful and influential women in the Confederacy: General P. G. T. Beauregard had named them the "Cary Invincibles." At this gathering, the group decided to find a way to demonstrate their southern sympathies and hit upon the idea of setting "My

Maryland" to music. Captain Francis W. Dawson gave an account: "With a young girl's eagerness to score a success she [Jennie Cary] resolved to secure some new and ardent expression of feelings, by this time wrought up to the point of explosion. In vain she searched through her stock of words, airs, and nothing seemed intense enough to suit the occasion. Aroused by her tone of despair, I [Burton Harrison, her cousin Constance's beau] came to the rescue, with the suggestion that she should adapt the words of 'Maryland! My Maryland!,' which had been constantly on my lips since the appearance of the lyric a few days before in the Baltimore *South*. I produced the paper and began declaiming the verses. 'Lauriger Horatius!' [a familiar tune] she exclaimed, and in a flash the immortal song found voice in the stirring air so perfectly adapted to it."[47]

Several points stand out in this recollection. For one, a young woman receives credit for creating one of the most popular songs of the war. But even more significantly, Dawson suggests that Jennie Cary purposefully wanted to support the war—she wanted to be useful. Jennie wished to "score a success." Such blatant activity would not have been sanctioned before the war, but during and afterward, it apparently warranted praise and admiration.

When the work was published, however, the composer was given only as "A Lady of Baltimore," and that was also the way advertisements listed the piece. At its creation, the Carys and friends noted that they could have been imprisoned for publishing such a work.[48] And later in 1861, the Carys were forced to leave Maryland and flee to Virginia as a result of their pro-Confederate stance. While the first edition of the piece was attributed to "A Baltimorean in Louisianna [*sic*]," subsequent editions, published by Blackmar, list the arranger as "A Lady of Baltimore" and the composer as "A Confederate."[49] The Carys' connection with Blackmar might have been established through a connection with General Beauregard, for he arranged to have the New Orleans Washington Artillery serenade the sisters when they visited him in camp (in Virginia), and they returned the favor with a performance of "Maryland! My Maryland!"[50]

The Carys' influence lived on: a later song, "Close Up the Ranks," carries a curious title page, as well as further associations. It reads:

CLOSE UP THE RANKS
Composed by a Refugee in London / Addressed to
Soldier Comrades in the Field
By Chaplain Cameron
By Permission / Respectfully Inscribed to Miss Constance Cary

The copyright was held by Reverend S. E. Cameron, who must be the chaplain on the title page, and the piece was printed in Richmond, lithography by George Dunn & Company. While many pieces are dedicated to various women (some named, some not) during this period, the composer—a "Refugee in London"—calls attention to the unusual attribution. Refugees were often, though by no means always, women, and the possibility remains that this piece may indeed have been composed by a woman.

The story of "Maryland! My Maryland!" reverts to the use of the term "lady" as a way of publishing a piece without publicly naming the composer and thereby compromising her ladyhood. (One must consider, however, that the possibility of retribution by the United States government might have driven Cary into anonymity.) Just how important this moniker was can be best demonstrated by an incident in New Orleans in 1862. The South's largest city fell to Union forces in April of that year, and it was placed under the governance of General Benjamin Butler. Butler was ruthless in trying to subordinate inhabitants of the city, including such measures as banishing ministers to the North who resisted prayers for the United States president. He even imprisoned anyone who sang "The Bonnie Blue Flag" and went so far as to imprison Blackmar, who had published it *earlier* than the occupation of New Orleans.[51] To quote Butler, "Very soon there was no uncivil treatment received by our soldiers except from the upper class of women." These women were in the habit of spitting or emptying chamber pots on Yankee soldiers in order to humiliate them. In response to these actions, Butler issued General Order No. 28: "As the officers and soldiers of the United States have been subject to repeated insults from the women (calling themselves ladies) of New Orleans . . . it is ordered that hereafter when any female shall, by word, gesture, or movement, insult or show contempt for any officer or soldier of the United States, she shall be regarded and held liable to be treated as a woman of the town plying her avocation."[52]

Butler had hit at the heart of what these women held dearest.[53] As Faust comments, "In ladyhood, southern women accepted gender subordination in exchange for continuing class and racial superiority. Yet their understanding of that bargain had changed profoundly in the course of the war."[54] "Ladies" did indeed change their ideas of how they should function in society during the war, and, not surprisingly, the degree to which their self-perception altered varied from place to place, class to class, and most significantly from personal experience to experience. The appearance of compositions by "a Lady" remained through the 1860s, but the increased number of attributed compositions evinces a change in women's attitudes toward having their names appear in print.

PHILANTHROPY

Regardless of how specifically women chose to reveal their names, their intentions in supporting the war effort are almost always present. Dedications to particular people or groups reveal these goals. Mrs. E. B. dedicated her "Louisiana Guard March" to Captain C. A. Breaux, who is mentioned in a *New Orleans Picayune* article of September 1861 in connection with bringing in prisoners from Virginia.[55] She directed that the proceeds of this publication "be sent to the Continentals now in active service in Virginia." In so doing, she was acting in the interests of the Confederacy, not her own, and seemed to be behaving as Evans suggested southern women should in *Macaria*.

Mrs. E. Blessey's "Continental Polka Mazurka" appeared via the publishing house of Louis Grünewald.[56] (That Mrs. E. B. is the same person as Mrs. E. Blessey is unlikely; the "B." in the former probably stands for "Colonel Breaux," to whom the work was dedicated.) While not obviously Confederate in its title, its dedication, that "the proceeds . . . be sent to the Continentals now in active service in Virginia," indicates a degree of philanthropy (or usefulness) on the part of Blessey.

Another woman's composition published by Grünewald carries a similar sentiment. While not obviously patriotic, Mrs. Francis Fernandez's "Tillie's Waltz" (c. 1861) includes a comment that "the proceeds . . . be appropriated for the benefit of our brave and gallant volunteers now fighting for our liberty."[57] Similarly, Mrs. N. H. Pierce's "A Year Ago" was "sold for the benefit of the poor of Mobile" in 1861. Whether or not these people were poor because of the war (which seems unlikely since it was 1861 and the war had just begun) is an interesting question because if it were a case of general benevolence, why provide for the poor beginning in 1861? Surely there were poor in Mobile before 1861. The most likely answer is that the new circumstances in which women found themselves as a result of the Civil War enabled them to seek new venues of public service, such as this.[58]

That the Civil War necessitated dramatic modifications in women's roles in society cannot be contested. Faust opens her award-winning *Mothers of Invention: Women of the Slaveholding South in the American Civil War* with a quote from Lucy Buck, an eighteen-year-old living in Front Royal, Virginia, who adroitly observed, "We shall never, any of us, be the same as we have been."[59] The conflict altered the way women saw themselves. The advent of published women composers is but one instance of how the strict governances of society were lifted or transformed, if briefly, in the South. The works published in 1861 demonstrate how quickly the attitudes toward publication altered and how the tenor of women's compositions changed from parlor music to patriotic support for the Confederacy. The need to be useful grew exponentially. The effects were not immediate, for the extremely dire circumstances in which the war left the South meant that not only were there few examples of women composers during the 1870s, but there was very little music published in the South at all, by men or women. It would take decades before women could reap the rewards earned during the conflict, but the immediate result was the acceptance of new economic opportunities, such as teaching music.[60] Granted, women teachers had existed throughout the South for decades, but after the war, women from the upper classes worked as teachers—something that did not happen prior to 1861.

How to become useful yet remain a lady challenged fundamental beliefs in the social system in which southern elite women found their identity. As discussed, contributing to "the Cause" as composers of patriotic songs was but one way some women approached this dilemma. Through the publication of musical works, these women had become useful to the Confederate States of America, but they had crossed a line that would eventually contribute to significant shifts of their self-perception and their role in southern society. Women who had held elite status before the war, such as the Pettigrews, became music teachers after the war, just as Augusta Evans declared that she would "make the great end of all my labors in the realm of letters. . . . I must continue to draw support from inkstand."[61] As if music composition/ publication was an extension of the idea that the plantation mistress had redemptive potential—a theme common in plantation novels—Confederate women were able to channel their skills into another area in order to support their men. Elizabeth Moss finds that plantation novelists strove to guard the South from the invasion of northerners; southern women composers attempted the same.[62]

The anxiety some women felt on taking on masculine roles during the Civil War is well documented. At one point in her diary, Sarah Morgan famously asserted that "if some few Southern women were in the ranks, they could set the men an example they would not blush to follow. Pshaw! there are *no* women here! We are *all* men!"[63] But she was not always so sure of herself in this regard. She could not bring herself to try on men's clothing, even though she truly considered the attempt. Even more tellingly, two days after she made the statement that "We are *all* men," she wrote a scathing report of some women's behavior during a patriotic celebration: "After a flag-flying parade: . . . no consolation for the shame I suffered by such a display so totally distasteful to me. How I wished myself away, and chafed at my folly, and hated myself for being there, and every one for seeing me! I hope it will be a lesson to me always to remember a lady can gain nothing by such displays. . . . I came home wonderfully changed in all my newly acquired sentiments, resolved never more to wound their feelings, who were so careful of ours, by such unnecessary display, and hung my flag on the parlor mantle there to wave, if it will, in the shades of private life; but to make a show, make me conspicuous and ill at ease, as I was yesterday—Never again!"[64]

Not all women could easily brush aside their expectations of ladyhood, even during the war, but clearly some of them considered changing their views.

Many of them did. Some commentators considered them "soldiers" for their efforts. Women became useful in many ways, including music composition.

On 22 February 1887, Captain Francis W. Dawson spoke before the 5th Annual Reunion of the Association of the Maryland Line at the Academy of Music, Baltimore, with an address entitled "Our Women in the War." Dawson described how women had but one thought: "to aid, encourage, in every conceivable way, the soldiers of the South." In relating an event that took place in a Confederate hospital, he describes a scene in which a "Lady" says, "Oh! I want to do something for you."[65] The volunteer (lady) wanted to be useful. Women moved from being unnamed piano girls to published Confederate composers. As Dawson closed his address, he drew upon one of the most revered of Confederate icons, Stonewall Jackson, who reportedly said, "Our female soldiers. . . . They are patriots in the truest sense of the word."[66] Undoubtedly, those women composers who crossed the line and acknowledged their works publicly saw themselves as patriots for the Confederacy.

Appendix

Notes

Bibliography

Index

Appendix

Table 1. Contents of Piano Book (1850s–60s) of [Bell]e Hannah McGehee (Burleigh, N.C.)

Composer	Title
Louis Moreau Gottschalk	"The Banjo"
A. Henselt	"La Gondole, op. 13/2"
Richard Hoffman	"By the Sad Sea Waves"
Anon.	"Threeb, Waltz for the Piano" [MS, owner or teacher?]
Gustav Lange	"Pure as Snow, op. 31"
Richard Hoffman	"La Gazelle"
Hermann A. Wollenhaupt	"Grand March de concert, op. 19"
W. Kruger	"La harpe eolienne, op. 25"
J. Blumenthal	"Les deux anges"
James M. Wehli	"March des Amazones"
S. Thalberg	"Home! Sweet Home!, op. 72"
Louis Moreau Gottschalk	"The Last Hope"
Alfred Jaell	"Le carnival de Venise, op. 22"
Hermann A. Wollenhaupt	"Mazeppa, Grand Galop de Concert, op. 43"
William Vincent Wallace	"Grande Polka de Concert"

Source: UNC Music Library, new series, vol. 8.

Table 2. Contents of Vocal Book (1834–47) of Mary Stedman (Fayetteville, N.C.)

1. "Henry Clay's Grand March"; John Bartlett, 1841
2. "Le plaisir de moment, Variations faciles et Brillantes, sur le chant favor (The Watcher)"; Charles Grobe, Op. 97, 1847
3. "Origin of the Harp, Canzonett sung by Mr. Wilson"; Thomas Moore
4. "The Lament of the Irish Emigrant"; William Dempster, 1843
5. "The Rose of Cashmere, Sung by Mr. Wilson"; George Baker
6. "Home! Sweet Home!, A Popular Sicilian Air, Introduction and Variations"; W. R. Coppock
7. "When the Day with Rosy Light, A Celebrated Swiss Air, as Sung by Madame Stockhausen"; F. Stockhausen
8. "Battle of Waterloo"; G. Anderson
9. "Kathleen Mavourneen, Irish Ballad, Sung with rapturous Applause by Mr. Dempster"; E. N. Crouch
10. "Rosita, Grande Valse Espagnole, Composée par Julian Arrangée pour le piano par Gomion"
11. "When for Eternal Worlds We Steer, Pious Song"; 1843
12. "Giraffe Waltz"; Zaleucus
13. "Sentimental Waltz"; Burgmuller
14. "All Things Love Thee So Do I, A Ballad, Sung with rapturous Applause by Mrs. C. E. Horn"; C. E. Horn, 1838
15. "The Harp that Once through Tara's Halls"; Thomas Moore/Sir J. Stevenson
16. "Tulip Waltzes"; Beethoven
17. "Oh! Soon Return, Sung by Mr. Braham"; Thomas Moore, 1814
18. "Waltzes from *La Bayadere* by Auber"; c. 1836
19. "Speed The Plough, A Favorite Dance Arranged with Brilliant Variations," 4th ed.
20. "Gaily The Troubadour Touch'd His Guitar"; T. H. Bayly
21. "Taglioni's Ghirlanda, as danced by Mad. Augusta"; S. A. Cooper
22. "Dumbarton's Bonny Dell, Scotch Ballad with Variations for the Piano Forte"; C. Meineke
23. "Oh! Forget Not the Time When Delighted I Met Thee"; R. G. Shrival, 1843
24. "Begone Dull Care, A Favorite Duett"
25. "Bring Flowers"; James B[ianchi] Taylor, 1834
26. "Oh! 'Twas Sweet to Hear Her Singing, As Sung by Miss Clara Novello"; Alexander Lee
27. "The Blue Juniata [*sic*]"; E. L. White, 1841
28. "Moonlight, Music, Love & Flowers, A Celebrated Duett As Sung by Mrs. Seguin & Mr. Manvers"; John Barnett
29. "Jesus Saviour of My Soul"
30. "Byron's Address to his Sister Augusta"; 1843
31. "The Moon O'er The Mountain Is Beaming, A Serenade as sung with great applause by Mr. Bishop"; Francis H. Brown, 1841

32. "O Would I Were A Boy Again, A Song, Sung with Great Applause By Mr. Ginbelei, at the Theatre Royal, Drury Lane, and At The Nobilities Concerts"; F. Romer, 1840

33. "Where Are Now The Hopes I Cherished? (In Mia Alfin Tu Sei)," [from] *Norma*; Bellini

34. "In The Days When We Went Gipsying, Song, Sung by J. P. Knight, at the Public Concerts and Festivals"; N. J. Sporle, 1839

35. "Meet Me In The Willow Glen, Sung by Miss Shireff"; A. Lee

36. "Ashland Waltz [dedicated to Henry Clay]"; E. L. White

Source: UNC Music Library, new series, vol. 2.

Note: Dates of compositions are given where possible.

Table 3. Contents of Vocal Book (1836–60) of Mary Gibson (Fort Smith, Ark.)

1. "Salut à la France, from Donizetti's Opera of *La Fille du Regiment*"; 1845
2. "Oh! Wilt Thou Leave Thy Tranquil Home from the Opera *Nebucadnezzar*, Performed in London under the Title of Nino"; Verdi
3. "Sounds So Joyful, Cavatina from *La sonnambula*"; Bellini
4. "Ah! Don't Mingle or Ah! non giunge uman pensiero, Sung by Mrs. Wood in the Celebrated Opera of La sonnambula Composed by V. Bellini"
5. "Come Brave With Me The Sea Love (Suoni la tromba intrepide) from the Opera *I Puritani*"; Bellini
6. "I'll Pray For Thee. In the opera of *Lucia di Lammermoor*"; Donizetti
7. "Ever Be Happy! The Pirates Farewell Ballad; Adapted to the celebrated melody The Pirates Chorus in The Enchantress"; Edward L. Walker, 1849?
8. "Not For Gold Or Precious Stones; The Melodies of the Hauseer Family"; 1849
9. "I Am The Bayadere (Je suis le Bajadere). The Tambourine Song. Sung by Madame Bishop"; Arr. N. Chas. Bochsa, 1848
10. "I'm A Merry Zingara. Sung by Madame Anna Thillon in Auber's Opera *Crown of Diamonds*"; Balfe
11. "I'm A Merry Laughing Girl"; C. W. Glover
12. "I Love The Merry Sunshine"; Stephen Glover
13–17. "Songs from Mary, Queen of Scots; Geo. Barker: The Royal Bridal, Farewell Dear France!, The Captivity; Chaterlar To Mary; Chaterlars Farewell"
18. "The Prima Donna Song; Music Arranged from Jullien's"; Thomas Baker, 1853
19. "The Gipsy Countess"; Stephen Glover
20. "Sweetly The Merry Marriage Bells; Arranged for One Or Two Voices from the celebrated Duett in the Opera of *Linda di Chamounix*"; 1849
21. "Something To Love Me"; E. L. Hime, 1853
22. "My Own, My Gentle Mother. Ballad; The Subject taken from the 'Wide, Wide World' Written By W. H. Bellamy"; C. W. Glover
23. "A World Of Love At Home"; Thos. P. I. Magoun, 1853
24. "Home Where Changes Never Come; Ballad; The Subject taken from the 'Wide, Wide World' Written By W. H. Bellamy"; C. W. Glover
25. "Home Sweet Home; Farewell Songs Of Jenny Lind In America"; 1851
26. "'Tis The Last Rose Of Summer"; T. Moore, arr. by Sir John Stevenson
27. "My Boyhood Days"; G. Piccioli, 1854
28. "Kathleen Mavourneen, Irish Ballad, Sung with rapturous Applause by Mr. Dempster"; E. N. Crouch
29. "Jessie Mowbray; Scotch Ballad"; George Linley
30. "Come Dearest, The Daylight Is Done"; B. R., 1853
31. "The Sister's Wedding"; George Linley
32. "Mary, The Village Queen"; William Vincent Wallace
33. "Thou'rt False To Me, Written by a Gentleman of Baltimore and adapted to a favorite Italian Melody by G. F. Cole"; 1836

34. "Thinking Of Thee; Romanza"; Charlie C. Converse, 1853
35. "How Sweet Is The Land; Words by Goethe"; W. Whitmarsh, 1853
36. "Constancy"; Rev. Thomas Dale, A.M., 1852
37. "Origin Of The Harp, Canzonett for One or Two Voices"; Thomas Moore
38. "'Tis Home Where'er The Heart Is"; John Hill Hewitt, 1844
39. "The Female Auctioneer; Orphean Family"; 1850
40. "Oh Boys, Carry Me Along; A Plantation Melody"; Stephen Foster, 1851
41. "The Royal Irish Quadrilles"; Jullien
42. "Virginia Reels, No. 3"
43. "Virginia Reels, No. 2"

Source: UNC Music Library, new series, vol. 5.

Table 4. Contents of Piano Book (1840s–60s) of Mary Gibson (Fort Smith, Ark.)

Composer	Title
Charles D'Albert	"The Bride's Polka"
A. J. Fowler	"Syracuse Polka"
William Vincent Wallace	"Wallace's Polka"
Charles Grobe	"The Aurora Borealis Polka"
A. Goria	"Miranda, polka des salon"
George C. Stenz	"Heliotrope Polka"
Charles J. Merz	"Deliciosa, or Leonore Polka"
Francis H. Brown	"Happy Family Polka"
Carl Bergmann	"Love Polka"
Henri Herz	"Military Polka"
J. A. Fowler	"Cottage Polka"
Johann Strauss	"Tambour Polka"
G. Marcailhou	"La Catalane Polka"
Albert Holland	"Florida Polka"
Johann Strauss	"Kathinka Polka"
Ricardo Linter	"Jenny Lind's Swedish Polka"
Joseph Labitzky	"La Clochette Polka"
C. Lenschow	"Betty Polka"
Johann Munck	"The Atlantic's Return Schottisch"
J. J. Wm. Bruhns	"The Syanna Schottisch"
Allen Dodsworth	"Bolero, or the Dodsworth Schottisch"
Francis H. Brown	"The Rival Schottisch"
George P. Knauff	"Irene Waltz"
Johann Strauss	"Rosabel Waltz"
Charles Grobe	"Couleur de rose Waltz"
Luigi Ricci	"Tadolini's or Ricci's Celebrated Waltz"
Henri Herz	"Lutine Valse brilliante"
Ferdinand Beyer	"Evening Star Waltz"
A. Wallerstein	"The Fairest Maiden Redowa Waltz"
Charles D'Albert	"The New German Redowa"
Henry Bellman	"The Orphean Gallop"
Joseph Munck	"Kossuth Grand March"
Wm. C. Glynn	"Bayeaux's Quick Step"
Gustave Blessner	"The Union Quick Step"
Heinrich Proch	"Alpine Horn, or Le Cor des Alps"
Charles Grobe	"Salut a New-York"
James Bellak	"La Source Valse"
Vincenzo Bellini	"Norma, Selections"
Henri Cramer	"Il Desiderio"
Rossini	"La Cenerentola. Non piu mesta"

Giuseppe Verdi	"Les Charmes de l'Opera *Ernani*. Four hands, one piano"
Friedrich Burgmüller	"Redowa Polka. Four hands, one piano"
Geo. J. Corrie	"Mignonette Polka. Four hands, one piano"
J. B. Duvernoy	"Deux melodies Italliennes. Four hands, one piano"
Aug. Heilmann	"Electric Light Dance" [1894; added later]
Henri Herz	"La Belle Bohemienne. Four hands, one piano"

Source: UNC Music Library, old series, vol. 6.

Table 5. Music Composed by Women and Published before the Civil War

A. Southern Woman Composer, Northern Publication
(incomplete marker: 78%; named: 22%)

	Title	Name Given	Place of Publication	Date
1	"Titus' March"[a]	Lady of Baltimore	New York	1824
2	"No More"	Young Lady of Georgia	Philadelphia	1836
3	"Encouragement; I Will Not Chide"	Miss M. R. Siegling	Philadelphia	1846
4	"The Regall"	Miss M. R. Siegling	Philadelphia	1846
5	"Volunteer March"	Lady of South Carolina	New York	1847
6	"Buena Vista Polka	Lady of Virginia	Boston	1848
7	"Lady Mine"	Lady of Virginia	New York	1848
8	"Thou Art Gone"	Lady	Kentucky[b]	1848
9–13	"Iolah Waltzes" (5)	Lady of South Carolina	New York	1849
14	"'Tis Sweet to Muse o'er Memory's Page"	Lady of Virginia	New York	1849
15	"Why Sad"	Lady of Richmond, Virginia	Philadelphia	1850
16	"Let's Sit Down and Talk Together"	Mrs. Dr. Byrne[c]	St. Louis	1852
17	"Summer Wind, Summer Wind"	Miss C. M. C. of Baltimore	Philadelphia	1854
18	"Mississippi Polka"	Mrs. V. G. Cowdin	Boston	1855

[a] Also published in Baltimore in 1825, and later (such as 1857 in Boston) in arrangements.

[b] Kentucky could count as a northern or southern state, as Maryland does. So few pieces were published there that putting it in one or the other will not alter the results.

[c] Flora Byrne did not live in the South per se but moved there when the war broke out.

B. Southern Woman Composer, *Godey's Lady's Book*
(incomplete marker: 100%; named: 0%)

	Title	Name Given	Place of Publication	Date
1	"New Song"	Lady of Virginia	*Godey's Lady's Book*	12/1847
2	"Magpie Waltz"	Lady of Virginia	*Godey's Lady's Book*	6/1848
3	"Temperance Song"	Lady of Virginia	*Godey's Lady's Book*	11/1849
4	"Song for the Spanish Guitar"	Lady of Virginia	*Godey's Lady's Book*	8/1850
5	"Gondola Waltz"	Lady of Georgia	*Godey's Lady's Book*	1/1852
6	"Summer Wind, Summer Wind"	Miss C. M. C. of Baltimore	*Godey's Lady's Book*	9/1854
7	"Weyanoke Waltz"	Mrs. J. M. C. of Virginia	*Godey's Lady's Book*	2/1856
8	"Powhatan Waltz"	Mrs. J. M. C. of Virginia	*Godey's Lady's Book*	3/1856
9	"Richmond Waltz"	Mrs. J. M. C. of Virginia	*Godey's Lady's Book*	4/1856

C. Non-southern Woman Composer, Southern Publication
(incomplete marker: 0%; named: 100%)

	Title	Name Given	Place of Publication	Date
1	"Snowdrop Waltz"	Estelle Hewitt	Baltimore	1847
2	"The Sun Was Slowly Setting"	Estelle Hewitt	Baltimore	1849
3	"Agnes Polka"	Adèle Hohnstock	Baltimore	1850
4	"La Belle Creole Polka"	Ellen Ervin[d]	Mobile	1854
5	"Dreams"	Faustina Hasse Hodges	Macon	186-
6	"Juanita"	Caroline Norton	Macon, Augusta	186-
7	"Maiden's Prayer"	Thekla Badarzewska	Macon, Savannah, New Orleans, Augusta	186-
8	"The Officer's Funeral"	Caroline Norton	Macon	186-

[d] Northern if Ervin of Ohio is indeed the composer.

D. Southern Woman Composer, Southern Publication
(incomplete marker: 84%; named: 16%)

	Title	Name Given	Place of Publication	Date
1	"The United States Marine March"	Lady of Charleston, S.C.[e]	Baltimore	1815?
2	"Colonel William Stewart's March and Quickstep"	Lady of Baltimore	Baltimore, Charleston	1824
3	"Spanish Rondo"	Lady of Baltimore	Baltimore	1824
4	"Titus' March"	Lady of Baltimore	Baltimore	1824
5	"Titus' Waltz"	Lady of Baltimore	Baltimore	1824
6	"Colonel Pratt's March"	Lady of Cambridge	Baltimore	1844
7	"Dorchester March"	Lady of Cambridge	Baltimore	1844
8	"General Scott's Grand March"	Lady of Baltimore	Baltimore	1844
9	"Lady Jane Grey"	Lady of Virginia	Baltimore	1844
10	"La Capricieuse"	Marie R. Siegling	Baltimore	1845
11	"La Gracieuse"	Marie R. Siegling	Baltimore	1845
12	"Souvenir de Charleston"	Marie R. Siegling	Baltimore	1846
13	"Celebrated Italian Polka"	Lady of Baltimore	Baltimore	1847
14	"Cerro Gordo March and Quickstep"	Lady of Virginia	Baltimore	1847
15–20	"Keowee Waltzes," set 1 (6)	Lady of South Carolina	Charleston	1847
21–26	"Keowee Waltzes," set 2 (6)	Lady of South Carolina	Charleston	1847

D. Southern Woman Composer, Southern Publication (*continued*)

	Title	Name Given	Place of Publication	Date
27	"Sweet Be Thy Dreams!"	Lady of Virginia	Baltimore	1847
28	"Jasper Guards March"	Lady of South Carolina	Charleston	1848
29	"Penitential Hymn"	Mrs. Flora Byrne of Missouri	Baltimore	1848
30	"Polka Song, Come Hie We to the Linden Tree"	Lady of Virginia	Baltimore	1849
31	"Souvenir de la Saxe"	Marie R. Siegling	Baltimore	1849
32	"'Tis Past—The Spell Is Broken"	Lady of Richmond, Virginia	Richmond	1849
33	"Oh! Touch the Chord Yet Once Again"	Mrs. J. M. C. of Virginia	Baltimore	1850
34	"Belleville Waltz"	Mrs. J. M. C. of Virginia	Baltimore	1851
35	"Blitheville Waltz"	Mrs. J. M. C. of Virginia	Baltimore	1851
36	"Dover Waltz"	Mrs. J. M. C. of Virginia	Baltimore	1851
37	"Each Word Thy Rosy Lip Hath Breath'd"	Mrs. J. M. C. of Virginia	Baltimore	1851
38	"Elk Hill Waltz"	Mrs. J. M. C. of Virginia	Baltimore	1851
39	"The Macon Fair March"	Miss Virginia E. Evans	Baltimore	1852
40	"Dream Schottische"	Lady of Baltimore	Baltimore	1853
41	"Affection, A Polka"	M. E. C.	Baltimore	1854
42	"Brilliant Variations on the Popular Melody Wild Ashe Deer"	Lady of Virginia	Baltimore	1854
43	"Offering Polka"	Mary Eugenia C.[f]	Baltimore	1854
44	"Richmond Blues March"	Lady[g]	Baltimore	1855
45	"Bell Knights Waltz"	Miss. Louisiana Gottheil	New Orleans	1860

[e] J. Bunker Clark identifies the composer as Eliza Crawley Murden in his *Anthology of Early American Keyboard Music, 1787–1830* (Middleton, Wis.: A-R Editions, 1977), 129.

[f] Presumed southern because two pieces appeared by Mary Eugenia C. and M. E. C. in Baltimore by the same publishers in the same year. The composer may, of course, be northern, but most northern women whose music appeared from southern publishers were relatively established composers.

[g] Presumed southern because it refers to a local group.

E. Unknown Woman, Southern Publication
(incomplete marker: 50%; identified completely: 25%; other: 25%)

	Title	Name Given	Place of Publication	Date
1	"Oft in the Stilly Night with Variations for the Piano Forte"	Lady[h]	Baltimore	n.d.
2	"Why Ask Me Now?"	Adelene	Baltimore	184-
3	"Thou Hast Wounded the Spirit That Lov'd Thee"	Lady	Baltimore	1846
4	"Isadora"	Fanny Heron	Baltimore	1858

[h] Possibly southern.

F. Southern Women Composers, Summary[i]

Named (4 women, 10 pieces)

Marie R. Siegling	6 pieces	1845, 1846, 1849
Mrs. Flora Byrne	2 pieces	1848, 1852
Miss Virginia E. Evans	1 piece	1852
Mrs. V. G. Cowdin	1 piece	1855

Named, attribution probably pseudonym (1 name, 1 piece)

Miss. Louisiana Gottheil	1 piece	1860

Initials or incomplete marker (3 women, 13 pieces)

Mrs. J. M. C. of Virginia	9 pieces	1850, 1851, 1856
Mary Eugenia C. [M. E. C.]	2 pieces	1854
Mrs. C. M. C.	1 piece	1854
[Mrs. C. McConnell]	(2 places)	

Lady with or without geographic marker
(47 pieces, number of women cannot be determined)

Lady of Charleston, S.C.	1 piece	1815?
Lady of Baltimore	8 pieces	1824, 1844, 1847, 1853
Young Lady of Georgia	1 piece	1836
Lady of South Carolina	3 waltz sets, 2 marches	1847–49, 1847, 1848
Lady of Virginia	8 pieces, 4 pieces in *Godey's Lady's Book*	1844, 1847, 1848, 1849, 1854, 1847–50
Lady of Cambridge	2 pieces	1844
Lady of Richmond, Virginia	2 pieces	1849, 1850
Lady	2 pieces	1848, 1855

[i] Does not include those women mentioned in part E of this table.

Table 6. Music Composed by Women and Published in the South during the Civil War

	Composer[j]	Title of Work	Publisher	Location	Year
1	Mrs. J. B. Henderson	"Askew Quickstep"	Blackmar & Bro.	New Orleans	1861
2	Anna K. Dixon Hearn	"The Flag of the South: A Voice from the Old Academy"			1861
3	Mrs. V. G. Cowdin	"Gen. Beauregard's Grand March"	Blackmar	New Orleans	1861
4	A Lady of Richmond	"God Will Defend the Right"	Blackmar	Augusta, New Orleans	1861
5	A Lady of Baltimore	"Maryland! My Maryland!"	Blackmar	Augusta and New Orleans	1861
6	Mrs. Flora Byrne	"President Jefferson Davis Grand March"	Werlein & Halsey	New Orleans	1861
7	Mrs. A. G. Warner	"Southern Rights Polka"	Werlein	New Orleans	1861
8	Alice Lane	"The Stars of Our Banner"	Blackmar & Bro.	Augusta	1861
9	Elizabeth Sloman	"Sumter: A Ballad of 1861"	H. Siegling	Charleston	1861
10	Mrs. N. H. Pierce	"A Year Ago"	Bloch	Mobile	1861
11	Mrs. E. B.	"Louisiana Guard March"	P. P. Werlein & Halsey	New Orleans	c. 1861
12	Mrs. Francis Fernandez	"Tillie's Waltz"	L. Grünewald	New Orleans	c. 1861
13	Mrs. M. B. Scott[k]	"Bird of Beauty"	J. P. Snow/ Blackmar[l]	Augusta	1862
14	Mrs. Margaret Weir	"Dixie Doodle"	Werlein & Halsey	New Orleans	1862
15	Alice Lane	"La Zaidee Schottisch"	Blackmar	Augusta	1862
16	Delia W. Jones	"Old Cotton Is King!"	Blackmar	New Orleans	1862
17	Alice Lane	"Reverie Mazourka"	Blackmar	Augusta	1862
18	Mrs. J. H. Mew of Louisiana	"Southern Shout"	Blackmar	Augusta	1862?
19	Mrs. E. Blessey	"Continental Polka Mazurka"	L. Grünewald	New Orleans	c. 1862
20	Mrs. C. McConnell	"Tribute to Beauregard Quickstep"	Blackmar & Co.	New Orleans	186-
21	Sallie Parkington	"The Southern Soldier Boy"	George Dunn & Company	Richmond	1863
22	A Lady of Richmond	"T'was Bright but T'was a Dream"	C. T. DeCoëniél	Richmond	1863
23	Mrs. William B. [Ann Judson Battle] Harrell[m]	"Up with the Flag"	George Dunn & Company	Richmond	1863
24	Miss Ella Wren	"We Have Parted"	George Dunn & Company	Richmond	1863

	Composer	Title	Publisher	Place	Date
25	*Octavie Romey*	"4 mars souvenir; a la memoire de Madame G. T. Beauregard"	*A. Elie*	*New Orleans*	*1864*
26	*Octavie Romey*	"La Marseillaise et Bonnie Blue Flag"	*A. Elie*	*New Orleans*	*1864*
27	Lady of Kentucky	"You Can Never Win Us Back"	J. W. Davies & Sons	Richmond	1864
28	Miss Lizzie Tebault	"Home Sweet Home Variations"	[Tebault had copyright]	New Orleans	1865
29	Miss Blossey	"Mazurka"	Louis Grünewald	New Orleans	1865
30	The Veiled Lady	"'No Name' Waltz"	George Dunn & Company	Richmond	1865
31	Miss Emma Wade	"Thine, Ever Thine"	Louis Grünewald	New Orleans	1865
32	Miss Julia Daly	"Dying Camille"	John C. Schreiner	Macon and Savannah	186-[n]
33	A Lady	"My Hopes Have Departed Forever"	A. E. Blackmar	Augusta	186-[o]
34	Lizzie C. Orchard	"Maj. General Hampton's Quickstep"	Gray & Valory	Columbia	Between 8/1863 and 2/1865[p]
35	Mrs. C. McC[onnell][q]	"Our Triumph at Manassas, Fantaisie Mazurka"	P. P. Werlein & Halsey	New Orleans	186- (probably early)
36	Miss C. Lauve	"Southern Rights March"	A. E. Blackmar	New Orleans	186-[r]
37	Mrs. E. D. [Francis Yuille] Hundley	"Farewell to the Star Spangled Banner"	J. W. Davies	New Orleans	186-

[j] Non-southerners are listed in italics.

[k] Where Mrs. Scott lived remains undiscovered. Woodlawn is a popular name for stately homes. The work does not indicate any particular sympathies.

[l] Judith Tick, *American Women Composers before 1870* (Ann Arbor: UMI Research Press, 1973), 239, lists an earlier publication (1856) of this piece in Boston by Oliver Ditson, extant copy in the Boston Public Library. Their records indicate "c. 1856." This version is reproduced on pp. 104–6 of Tick's book. All southern editions have a special comment, such as "The Southern Edition," which is usually reserved for pieces originally published in the North but having a southern imprint as well. Harwell includes the song in his description of songs from the North imported to the South (*Confederate Music*, 95).

[m] On the sheet music, she is said to have arranged to her husband's work.

[n] At least 1861, since Hermann Schreiner, son of John, moved to Savannah in December 1861.

[o] At earliest, November 1862.

[p] Wade Hampton III became major general on 3 August 1863 and was later promoted to lieutenant general on 15 February 1865.

[q] Same woman who wrote "Tribute to Beauregard" of 1862, per Harwell. He lists two editions, one without publisher (*Confederate Music*, 72, 135).

[r] At earliest, fall 1864.

Notes

Abbreviations

SCHS South Carolina Historical Society, Charleston or Columbia

SCL South Caroliniana Library, University of South Carolina, Columbia

SHC Southern Historical Collection, University of North Carolina, Chapel Hill

UNC University of North Carolina, Chapel Hill

PREFACE

1. Mary Cooke's recent dissertation, "Southern Women, Southern Voices: Civil War Songs Created by Southern Women," contains valuable information on southern women who composed both lyrics and music. This is one of the first attempts to separate both women's music and regional music. Cooke discusses both music and lyrics by women.

2. Abel, *Singing the New Nation*, xvi.

INTRODUCTION

1. These materials provide different views of southern women, particularly planters' wives, and it should be noted that a "one size fits all" approach does not do justice to them. The two women whose works served as a catalyst for later scholars, Anne Firor Scott and Elizabeth Fox-Genovese, developed diametrically opposed interpretations of southern elite women. A succinct account of this historiography can be found in Leigh Fought's *Southern Womanhood and Slavery: A Biography of Louise S. McCord, 1810–1879*, 4–5.

2. Silber, "Gender and Civil War Scholarship," 7.

3. Halttunen, *Confidence Men and Painted Women*, 93.

4. Whitaker, "Periodical Press," 52.

5. Mary Pettigrew to William S. Pettigrew, 21 November 1841, Pettigrew Papers, 1.6.85, SHC.

6. Moss, *Domestic Novelists in the Old South*, 14.

7. The role of white men in southern society informed all other interactions. Elite southern women sacrificed independence for male protection and in so doing subjugated themselves to a heavily proscribed system of expectations. Faust, *Mothers of Invention*, 6–7. Catherine Clinton makes the tantalizing assertion that among the parallels to be found between women of the slaveholding class and slaves, white men saw both as "reproductive units, replaceable if necessary." Clinton, *Plantation Mistress*, 61. Moreover, as Clinton observes in *Tara Revisited*, the huge gulf between the myth of the southern lady and the reality of the plantation mistress led many women to equate their status to that of their slaves. She notes that the role of "lady" fitted into society's "chauvinist stereotype" (41). In this particular case, Clinton quotes Susan Dabney Smedes, who wrote in her diary that "the mistress of a plantation was the most complete slave in it." Such thoughts were at the core of some southern women's understanding of their place in the world, but they cannot be seen as normative in the North.

8. Cashin, *Our Common Affairs*, 10.

9. Ibid., 11, 13–15.

10. An illuminating contemporary example of men's perceived differences between northern and southern cultures exists in John William De Forest's *Miss Ravenel's Conversion: From Secession to Loyalty*. De Forest vividly contrasts men from the North with those from the South, and in the novel, Miss Ravenel gradually shifts from her strong desire for and approval of one (southern) to the other (northern) in her personal journey from naive belle (secessionist) to mature woman (Union sympathizer). The values are quite clear, placing the outwardly more attractive southerner in opposition to the refined, gentler, and ultimately better northerner. De Forest generalizes here about southern women and men, but Miss Ravenel's process of growth changes her values. Whether or not these values truly speak for all, they suggest perceived differences between the two cultures. See Stauffer, "Embattled Manhood and New England Writers, 1860–1870," 125–27.

11. [Terhune], *Marion Harland's Autobiography*, 84.

12. Ibid., 241.

13. Painter, introduction to *The Secret Eye*, 3.

14. Burr, *Secret Eye*, 72.

15. Ibid., 74.

16. Ibid., 83.

17. Thursday, 12 July 1855, in ibid., 131.

18. Sarah Josepha Hale (1788–1879) worked as literary editor at *Godey's* from 1837 until 1877.

19. *Godey's Lady's Book*, 1853, 285.

20. Unlike many northern counterparts, most southern schools did not believe it appropriate for young ladies to do domestic chores. Pope, "Preparation for Pedestals," 75.

21. See Thompson, *Education for Ladies 1830–1860*, 67. Thompson specifically lists articles in the *Southern Literary Messenger* (118, no. 2 [1852]: 116–22), *Southern Quarterly Review* (22, no. 42, new series 5, no. 10 [1852]: 507–35), and *DeBow's Review of Southern and Western States* (10, second series 4, third series 2, no. 3 [1851]: 362–63).

22. Christie Anne Farnham, *Education of the Southern Belle*, 3–4.

23. Jabour, *Scarlett's Sisters*, 10–11. A different take on the culture of resistance that Jabour proposes is the culture of resignation that Cashin describes in *Our Common Affairs*. Cashin suggests that these women accepted inequity, did not resist it, and refrained from men's realm of politics (2). The issue of resistance or resignation, beginning with Anne Firor Scott's book *The Southern Lady: From Pedestal to Politics, 1830–1930*, still permeates discussions of southern women in the antebellum period.

24. Jabour, *Scarlett's Sisters*, 14.

25. Halttunen, *Confidence Men and Painted Women*, 72.

26. Another issue that argues for beginning a study of southern women in the 1830s is the political tension that surfaced in that decade concerning the question of slavery in new states.

27. Although she does note that the precise names of such institutions, be they "seminary," "institution," "academy," etc., means little if nothing at all. Farnham, *Education of the Southern Belle*, 21–22.

28. Lott, *From Paris to Peoria*, 7–8. Rakemann was a member of Robert Schumann's Davidsbündler (a group of good musicians who fought against second-rate but popular musicians), where he was called "Walt."

29. Preston, *Opera on the Road*, 5.

30. For example, a collection of sheet music (1839–1909) that belonged to the women in the family of William T. Johnson, a black barber from Natchez, Miss., survives in the

William T. Johnson and Family Memorial Papers, Louisiana and Lower Mississippi Valley Collections, Louisiana State University Libraries, Baton Rouge.

31. Material presented in Fox-Genovese, *Within the Plantation Household*, 78.
32. Ibid., 28.
33. Ibid., 68.
34. See, for example, Cashin, *Our Common Affairs*, 5.
35. Painter, introduction to *The Secret Eye*, 3.
36. Fox-Genovese, *Within the Plantation Household*, 80.
37. Burr, *Secret Eye*, 80.
38. Qtd. in Fox-Genovese, *Within the Plantation Household*, 39.

1. WHY DID NINETEENTH-CENTURY SOUTHERN WOMEN STUDY MUSIC?

1. The volume is currently housed in the UNC Music Library, new series, vol. 8.
2. A short notice in *Debow's Review, Agricultural, Commercial, Industrial Progress and Resources* entitled "The Great Southern Piano Manufactory" notes the successes of the Knabe company, who is "the only rival of the few great piano establishments of the Eastern and Northern states." *Debow's Review* 1, no. 2 (February 1866): 208–9.
3. This story is recounted in an article in the *Durham Morning Herald*, 19 August 1956.
4. "The Report of the Recitation and Deportment of Miss Belle McGehee," Chester Female Academy, 22 December 1865, now housed in the Phifer Papers, SHC. Belle earned 90s and 100s in all subjects except history, for which she received the "barely passable" mark of 70.
5. *Greensboro Daily News*, 20 May 1948.
6. An example of the distinctions in social positions can be seen in the Petigru family's disdain that their governess, Mary Ayme, insisted on sitting with them at the dinner table and in the parlor.
7. Scrapbook, Phifer Papers, SHC.
8. Phifer had reportedly studied piano with the "best teachers in Germany." Scrapbook, vol. 2, #7, Phifer Papers, SHC.
9. UNC Music Library, new series, vol. 1.
10. E. Ripley, *Social Life in Old New Orleans*, 10.
11. Confederate diaries, 6:297, 3 August 1863, Georgia State Archives. Henry also mentions reading as a part of being accomplished.
12. Sarah Lois Wadley Diary, 31 March 1860, Wadley Papers, SHC.
13. Ibid., 18 October 1860.
14. Judith Tick brought the term "piano girl" into modern parlance in several works. Another writer who wrote about female pianists in the nineteenth century is Arthur Loesser, one of the authors of *Men, Women and Pianos: A Social History*; see especially "The Piano as Female 'Accomplishment': The Writers' Testimony," 267–79.

    Tick discusses the reasons parents valued their daughters' musical education, tracing music and feminine accomplishment in American culture from 1770 to the mid-nineteenth century in *American Women Composers before 1870*; see especially chap. 2 ("The Tradition of Music as a Feminine Accomplishment, 1770 to 1830"), and chap. 3 ("Accomplishment Becomes Middle-Class"). Her findings confirm the most commonly stated reasons for studying music, chiefly, to please men (15) and as a cure for loneliness and boredom (16), as well as to attain the broader implications of being accomplished.
15. Fought describes the necessity of social charms for upper-class women, noting in particular Louisa McCord's mother, in *Southern Womanhood and Slavery*, 20.

16. Cashin, *Our Common Affairs*, 2.
17. Louisa McCord wrote in her play *Caius Gracchus* that women should "soothe" their men and

> with self-abnegation nobly lose
> her private interest in the dearer weal . . .
> Of those she loves and lives for. (1.3.1–2, 17)

18. Marcus Cicero Stephens, letter to Mary Anne Primrose, 7 November 1847, qtd. in Engstrom, *Book of Burwell Students*, 181–82.
19. Ibid., 183.
20. Jabour, *Scarlett's Sisters*, 36.
21. Ayer, "Freemasonry and Female Education," 7, 12, 18. Cokesbury opened its doors in Greenwood, S.C., in 1853, remaining a women's college until 1874. By 1859, its enrollment had reached 125 girls. The subjects taught at Cokesbury were languages, natural sciences, philosophy, English, math, music, and painting. See *South Carolina Heritage Corridor*, http://www.knowitall.org/sandlapper/Spring2004/Completed-PDF/SC-Heritage-Corridor.pdf (accessed July 2007). The community of Cokesbury was one of the first planned communities in the South.
22. Pope, "Preparation for Pedestals," 27.
23. Mrs. Caroline H. Butler, "The Little Cap-Maker of Love's Masquerade," *Graham's Magazine*, 1848, 221.
24. "Ups and Downs," *Graham's Magazine*, 1852, 634.
25. Mrs. Mary Scrimzeour Whitaker, "Conrad Clifford; or, the Treacherous Guest. A Southern Tale, Chapters VII–XVI," *Southern Literary Messenger* 33, no. 2 (August 1861): 86.
26. See, for example, a comment in the *New York Mirror* of 1839, qtd. in Tick, *American Women Composers before 1870*, 23.
27. East, *Sarah Morgan*, 1 May 1862, p. 24.
28. "Ups and Downs," 636.
29. Halttunen, *Confidence Men and Painted Women*, 193.
30. On the culture of calling cards, see ibid., 112–15 and 194; also see chap. 2 in ibid., "Hypocrisy and Sincerity in a World of Strangers."
31. Ibid., 104.
32. Ibid., 101.
33. George William Bagby, "It Is Omnipotent," *Southern Literary Messenger* 28, no. 2 (1859): 12.
34. "My First Serenade," *Southern Literary Messenger* 14, no. 8 (1848): 482–83. The incident took place in Florida, based on comments made in the story.
35. Ibid.
36. Chandler, "Belle of the Opera," 3.
37. Ibid.
38. [Terhune], *Marion Harland's Autobiography*, 84. Virginia native Mary Virginia Hawes Terhune (1830–1922) wrote under the pen name Marion Harland. She authored over seventy-five novels, memoirs, travel narratives, domestic manuals, etiquette books, and cookbooks, with her first novel (*Alone*) appearing in 1854. Although she moved with her husband to New Jersey just before the Civil War, Terhune grew up in rural Virginia and attended a boarding school in Richmond in the 1840s. Her memoirs were published in New York in 1910 as *Marion Harland's Autobiography: The Story of a Long Life*.
39. Moss, *Domestic Novelists in the Old South*, 10.
40. Each of these writers forms part of Moss's study, *Domestic Novelists in the Old South*.
41. "Ups and Downs," 637.

42. Jane H. Pease and William H. Pease provide clear genealogical tables in *A Family of Women: The Carolina Petigrus in Peace and War*, 286–96.

43. James Louis changed the spelling of his last name from Pettigrew to Petigru. Mary Boykin Chesnut remarked that he had done so to connect more firmly to his mother's Huguenot roots (the first Huguenots to settle in South Carolina). Woodward, *Mary Chesnut's Civil War*, 377. Jane H. Pease and William H. Pease, however, suggest that James altered the name in rejection of the Scotch-Irish frontier culture that was his father's in favor of his mother's more genteel family. Pease and Pease, *James Louis Petigru*, 17–18.

44. Published in New York in 1914, this book was illustrated by another woman from notable South Carolina families, Alice Ravenel Huger Smith.

45. Jane North to Caroline North, 25 January 1841, Pettigrew Papers, 1.6.82, SHC. Jane wrote all of the letters examined in this section from Badwell and mailed them to Carey in Georgetown, S.C. (the state's third oldest city, near Pawley's Island).

46. Ibid., 4 March 1841.

47. Ibid., 25 January 1841.

48. Ibid., 4 March 1841.

49. Ibid., 23 March 1841.

50. Ibid., 8 December 1840.

51. Mary Pettigrew to William S. Pettigrew, 23 June 1843, Pettigrew Papers, 1.6.94, SHC.

52. Ibid.

53. Ebenezer Pettigrew's father (also called Ebenezer) was the brother of William Pettigrew, who in turn was the father of the William Pettigrew mentioned earlier.

54. "A Few Words to Young Amateurs of Music," by "Daisy" (a pseudonym), *Dwight's Journal of Music*, 39 January 1858, 345.

2. WOMEN'S INTERACTION WITH PUBLIC MUSIC

1. Chandler, "Belle of the Opera," 4.

2. Ravenel, *Charleston, the Place and the People*, 475.

3. S. Dawson, *Confederate Girl's Diary*, 9 July 1863.

4. Stage performers (including opera stars) had been associated with "loose" women for centuries. While women were barred from the stage during Shakespeare's day, the advent of opera—with female voices—caused consternation for many. By the nineteenth century, the stigma of worldliness had not entirely diminished. The act of public display was not something a lady did unless financially forced to do so.

5. Chandler, "Belle of the Opera," 3.

6. Qtd. in Engstrom, *Book of Burwell Students*, 61.

7. Travel book, in Pettigrew Papers, SHC.

8. See Davenport, *Cultural Life in Nashville*, 143.

9. Long, *Florida Breezes*, 27.

10. *Dwight's Journal of Music*, 3 April 1858, 7.

11. Mates, "First Hundred Years of the American Lyric Theater," 23.

12. Mahan, "History of Music in Columbus, Georgia," 33.

13. *Nashville Patriot*, 17–27 January 1860, qtd. in Davenport, *Cultural Life in Nashville*, 142–43.

14. Preston, *Opera on the Road*, 81.

15. The playbill is reproduced in ibid., 97. Auber's work appeared in 1830 and is an example of *opéra comique*. This style of opera is distinguished, among other characteristics, by having spoken dialogue as well as sung material. Today, this sort of juxtaposition of opera and farce on the same program seems unusual but in the nineteenth century was quite common.

16. Preston, *Opera on the Road*, 280.
17. *Spirit*, 25 December 1841, 18, qtd. in ibid., 219.
18. This work was part of a bound collection that Henry Campbell Davis titled "A Barham-ville Music Book," and he says the collection belonged at one time to Nannie McMorris (Francis Morris?). Barhamville Notes, 1:18, SCL. The Library of Congress copy of this work is dated 1846 (M1.A12Z vol. 85 Case Class original bound volumes).
19. Preston, *Opera on the Road*, 219.
20. During the 1840s, only Manhattan and New Orleans could claim Italian opera regularly sung in Italian. Preston, *Opera on the Road*, 220.
21. Interestingly, while Italian singers were the norm for soprano and contralto roles in the Astor Opera Company, the appearance of Miss Virginia Whiting (later Madame Lorini) several times between 5 and 9 April indicates that others were also represented. The singers in this company, regardless of nationality, sang in the Italian style, a distinction often noted in the nineteenth century. An article in *Dwight's Journal of Music* describes Whiting in detail, voice, and beauty, and notes her Italian-styled singing. "Musical Chit-Chat," *Dwight's Journal of Music* 19 (1862): 96.
22. The first American performance of Queen of the Night's famous coloratura aria, "Der hölle Rache kocht in meinem Herzen" (Mozart, *Die Zauberflöte*), was in Nashville in December 1854, sung by Rose DeVries. Davenport, *Cultural Life in Nashville*, 142.
23. Sarah Cunningham's collection in the Georgia Historical Society (Savannah) is unusual because it is a manuscript book, not a bound volume of sheet music. For more on its contents, see Bailey, "Sarah Cunningham's Music Book," forthcoming.
24. They also indicate a connection with Henry Clay, the "Great Compromiser."
25. On the Glovers, Hime, and Linley, see entries in Brown and Stratton, *British Musical Biography*.
26. Using the 1850 census for data, Preston compares Charleston's population of 42,895 (19,523 of whom were slaves) with that of New York City (654,429), Philadelphia (340,045), Boston (208,335), and Baltimore (169,054). Preston, *Opera on the Road*, 199.
27. A list of performances throughout the United States by the Astor Place Opera Company in early 1851 appears in ibid., 195.
28. Mates, "First Hundred Years of the American Lyric Theater," 31.
29. Chandler, "Belle of the Opera," 3.
30. Preston, *Opera on the Road*, 201.
31. Dwight reviewed a performance by Elise Henssler of *Masaniello* in his journal in 1855. Henssler, the soprano whom Terhune heard that night, had made her debut in New York in June 1855 in a concert, not an opera. Dwight describes her as somewhat of an ideal nineteen-year-old. Born in New England and educated in Europe, he notes that "if voice, musical temperament, mind, the first fruits of study, womanly modesty and self-respect [notably linked together], if these are trust-worthy signs, there is an enviable future before her." *Dwight's Journal of Music*, 1855, 102.
32. [Terhune], *Marion Harland's Autobiography*, 280.
33. Some writers refer to Terhune as a southern belle, while others do not. She was born in Virginia and grew up in Amelia County, educated by private tutors. She was a precocious child who at age fourteen began publishing her writing in a weekly paper in Richmond. When she was sixteen, Terhune published "Marrying through Prudential Motives" in England; it was also translated and published in France. Her novel *Alone, A Tale of South-ern Life and Manners*, demonstrates her familiarity with southern upper-class customs. Published in 1854 when she was twenty-four, several reprint editions appeared in later years; the commercial edition reportedly sold more than one hundred thousand copies.

34. The program of a "typical" such performance appears in Preston, *Opera on the Road*, 83.

35. Burr, *Secret Eye*, 99.

36. Mahan, "History of Music in Columbus, Georgia," 34.

37. Albert Stoutamire, "A History of Music in Richmond, Virginia, from 1742 to 1865" (Ph.D. diss., Florida State University, 1960), 179, 193, and 278.

38. *Musical World*, 15 July 1853, 126, qtd. in Preston, *Opera on the Road*, 241–42.

39. Lind's appearances in Nashville are documented in Davenport, *Cultural Life in Nashville*, 145–50.

40. *Nashville Daily Gazette*, 2 April 1851, qtd. in Davenport, *Cultural Life in Nashville*, 147.

41. Barhamville Notes, 1:17, SCL.

42. Harwell, "John Hill Hewitt Collection," 3.

43. Stoutamire, *Music of the Old South*, 182.

44. Concerts announced in broadsides belonging to the Department of Archives and Manuscripts, Louisiana State University, Baton Rouge (Hummel #829 and #866).

45. Mlle. Aniela Niecieska performed as a violinist at Hibernian Hall in Charleston in 1850, and a week later Adèle Hohnstock appeared there as a solo pianist. Reproduced in Hindman, "Concert Life in Ante Bellum Charleston," 2:631.

46. Most of the performers appeared throughout the area, including places like Columbus. See Mahan, "History of Music in Columbus, Georgia," 44.

47. Ibid., 31–32. Hammarskold had also recently sung in Charleston. See Hindman, "Concert Life in Ante Bellum Charleston," 2:600. Leati is described in a program from Charleston in February 1849 as "Prima Donna Assoluta, from the principal Theatres of Italy and the Grand Opera, London." Her husband was a baritone who sang in the same places. Reproduced in Hindman, "Concert Life in Ante Bellum Charleston," 2:618.

48. Hummel, *Southeastern Broadsides*, #2421 and #2490.

49. The splitting of the Mozart symphony into two parts is typical of a nineteenth-century performance.

50. Copies of these works are held in the Dwight Anderson Music Library, Louisville Music Publications of the 19th Century, University of Louisville, Kentucky. A later work, "Speak Gently," 1874, survives in the Library of Congress.

51. Greve, *Centennial History of Cincinnati and Representative Citizens*, 921.

52. Review in *Dwight's Journal of Music*, 1858, 23.

53. The bird flageolet is a small woodwind used to teach birds to sing.

54. Burr, *Secret Eye*, 103.

55. *Milledgeville Daily Federal*, 10 November 1861, qtd. in T. Bryan, *Confederate Georgia*, 189.

56. Mahan, "History of Music in Columbus, Georgia," 41.

57. *Atlanta Daily Intelligencer*, 27 June 1862, qtd. in T. Bryan, *Confederate Georgia*, 190.

58. Although, Housewright notes that the Presbyterians in Florida were particularly strict in their music, not allowing the modern (eighteenth-century) styled hymns, nor music in the streets. Housewright, *History of Music and Dance in Florida*, 139–40.

59. Stoutamire, *Music of the Old South*, 168.

60. Rev. Elias Lyman Magoon, "The Religious Uses of Music," *Southern Literary Messenger* 13, no. 8 (1847): 193–97.

61. Stoops, *Heritage*, 27.

62. Nguyen discussed some of these issues in "'No Church in This Place.'"

63. Stoutamire, *Music of the Old South*, 167.

64. Burton and Brock, *Annals of Henrico Parish*, 248.

65. Stoutamire, *Music of the Old South*, 167.

66. Mrs. John Purcell reported Picot's appointment. Ibid., 167–69.

67. See *Virginia Historical Society* Web site at http://www.vahistorical.org/research/photo_individuals_g.htm (accessed 7 May 2007). Aglia Picot Gaynor was possibly daughter of Giles Picot of the 1820 (Richmond) census.

68. Stoutamire, *Music of the Old South*, 114.

69. *Virginia Gazette and General Advertiser*, 17 September 1803, qtd. in Stoutamire, *Music of the Old South*, 117.

70. *Compiler*, 18 and 20 January 1819, qtd. in Stoutamire, *Music of the Old South*, 120.

71. A copy of the program for one of these in the spring of 1841 is given Stoutamire, *Music of the Old South*, 176–77.

72. The entire reference is quoted in Engstrom, *Book of Burwell Students*, 114–15.

73. Letter to Mrs. Richard H. "Sallie Anderson" (née Gibson), 29 May 1855, Anderson Papers, Box 30-04, SCHS.

74. [Terhune], *Marion Harland's Autobiography*, 109.

75. George Frederick Root (1820–95) was named after the composer George Frideric Handel. Born in Massachusetts, Root was one of the most popular songwriters of the Civil War. Among his compositions are "Tramp, Tramp, Tramp the Boys Are Marching," "Just Before the Battle, Mother," and "Battle Cry of Freedom."

76. [Terhune], *Marion Harland's Autobiography*, 300.

77. Ibid., 234.

78. Ibid., 235. Interestingly, she regrets the adoption of European music by African Americans in the Reconstruction Era: "We have taken great pains to trace the negro folk-lore back to its root. The musical antiquarian is yet to arise who will track to their home the unwritten tunes and chants the liberated negro is trying to forget, and to which his grandparents clung lovingly, all unaware that they were an inheritance more than a dozen generations old."

79. Ibid., 297–98.

80. Ibid., 298.

81. See Hindman, "Concert Life in Ante Bellum Charleston," vol. 2 (the appendix). Hindman has transcribed many programs from the period in question.

82. On public women, see Clinton, "'Public Women' and Sexual Politics in the American Civil War," 62.

3. MUSIC AT HOME: ENTERTAINMENT AND EDUCATION

1. [Terhune], *Marion Harland's Autobiography*, 220.

2. Terhune mentions one in *Marion Harland's Autobiography* (247), and an article in the *Southern Literary Messenger* entitled "A Molasses Stew in the Country" (by Rustic) describes one in more detail (37, no. 3 [1863]: 155–58).

3. Rev. J. M'D. Mathews, "Hints to Young Ladies on Manners," *Ladies' Repository* 12, no. 9 (September 1852): 323.

4. Similarly, the famous—and conservative—general Thomas "Stonewall" Jackson disapproved of the polka.

5. See MacIntosh, *Two Lives*, 49–55.

6. James L. Bryan to Ebenezer Pettigrew, 13 November 1843, and Receipt, 27 December 1843, in Lemmon, *Pettigrew Papers*, 607 and 617, respectively. The Pettigrew daughters were so close to the Bryans that Mary called her father "Pa" and her uncle and aunt Bryan "Mother and Father" (xii).

7. East, *Sarah Morgan*, 9 July 1862, p. 125.

8. Jane Caroline North, First Journal, qtd. in O'Brien, *An Evening When Alone*, 171.

9. Ibid., 176.

10. Ibid., 177 (23 September 1851). Willie Calhoun is probably William Lowndes Calhoun (1829–58), son of Floride Bonneau and John C. Calhoun (the politician).

11. East, *Sarah Morgan*, 9 July 1862, p. 125.

12. Letter of 23 June 1842 in Lemmon, *Pettigrew Papers*, 519–20.

13. Anon., "Julia Grandon: A Coquet's Story," *Graham's Magazine*, 1851, 182.

14. "Clara Gregory," *Graham's Magazine*, 1852, 481–82.

15. On the other hand, Mary Terhune's father, a devout Presbyterian, also played the flute.

16. In comparison with the seemingly impulsive outbreaks that Sarah Morgan describes, Ravenel's account seems rather studied. That the latter is consciously preserving history and tradition undoubtedly plays a role in this distinction.

17. Ravenel, *Charleston, the Place and the People*, 480.

18. Pringle, *Woman Rice Planter*, 89.

19. Although she did participate in an amateur sacred choral group whose intention was to improve the tastes and expectations of the church choir. That Terhune's father played the flute seems to suggest that not all flutists were bad.

20. [Terhune], *Marion Harland's Autobiography*, 114.

21. Terhune then lists some of these illustrious attendees. Ibid., 92–93.

22. Terhune also claims that "almost every household possessed and made frequent use of the *Boston Academy*, the *Carmina Sacra*, the *Shawm*, and other collections of vocal music adapted for the use of societies and churches." This statement comes from a chapter entitled "Family Music" that is full of information and anecdotes on music at home in antebellum Virginia. Harland, *Secret of a Happy Home.*

23. [Terhune], *Marion Harland's Autobiography*, 115.

24. Ibid.

25. In his now-famous quote on the passing of the piano girl, Huneker refers to the more advanced repertory played by young women at the end of the nineteenth century. He implies that the less technically dazzling performances of earlier days suited young ladies much better.

26. [Terhune], *Marion Harland's Autobiography*, 116. The author remarks that her mother, Judith Anna Smith from Olney, Chickahominy Plantation, had "all the womanly accomplishments," noting in particular musical skill and literary tastes (6–7).

27. East, *Sarah Morgan*, 30 January 1863, p. 413.

28. Ibid., 420.

29. Occasionally, married plantation women mention practicing music as part of their regular activities. In describing a typical workday, Eliza Lucas Pinckney (c. 1722–93), responsible for four South Carolina plantations, included music practice as part of her regular routine. She awoke at 5 o'clock and read for two hours. After breakfasting at 7 o'clock, she played music for an hour and then reviewed French or shorthand (lest she forget them). These were accomplishments that Eliza surely learned before she was married, as part of her preparation for her future role as a planter's wife. Before dinner she tutored her sisters; later it was her daughter. She had another hour of music after dinner, then needlework. Going to bed at dusk, she read until bedtime, or wrote letters or other business. Kierner, *Beyond the Household*, 17.

30. S. Dawson, *Confederate Girl's Diary*, 26 June 1862, p. 90.

31. Elanor Adair White of the Monticello Presbyterian congregation (Florida) held services for the slaves of Case Bianca Plantation in which she led the hymn-singing. Housewright, *History of Music and Dance in Florida*, 139.

32. S. Dawson, *Confederate Girl's Diary*, 9 November 1862, p. 233.

33. After the Civil War, Emily opened a "singing school" in Plymouth and organized the music for the Plymouth Methodist Church. Engstrom, *Book of Burwell Students*, 43–44.

34. For an example of how diligently some fathers worked in educating their daughters, see the case of the family of Elizabeth and William Wirt, outlined in Jabour, "'Grown Girls, Highly Cultivated.'"

35. Pease and Pease, *Family of Women*, 40.

36. The following observations concerning the instruction of the Petigru women take as their basis the pioneering work done by the Peases in *Family of Women*, 39–47.

37. On the physical isolation of southern white women, see Cashin, "Into the Trackless Wilderness," 32–35. The remains of the Badwell Cemetery (including the graves of the original Huguenot immigrants, the plantation families, and the slaves from the plantation) are still visible, if now obscured by dense forest, near McCormick, S.C. David Moltke-Hansen makes the case that in many ways, Charleston itself was a city-state inside yet separated from the larger state of South Carolina in "The Expansion of Intellectual Life," 15–16.

38. Adèle Petigru Allston to Mrs. R. Hamilton, 19 May 1853, Pettigrew Family Papers, SHC.

39. Pease and Pease, *Family of Women*, 41.

40. Lemmon, *Pettigrew Papers*, xiv.

41. Ibid., 276.

42. John Hill Hewitt (1801–90) earned the moniker "Bard of the Confederacy" for the popular songs he created. Born in the North, Hewitt moved south early in his career and taught at several girls' schools. After the death of his first wife, Estelle Mangin, Hewitt married a pupil, Mary Smith. Hewitt's sister, Sophia Hewitt Ostinelli (1802–72), was a professional pianist of some renown.

43. Mary Pettigrew to William S. Pettigrew, 23 June 1843, Pettigrew Papers, 1.6.82, p. 94, SHC. "La Parisienne" exists as a duet, published by Willig in Philadelphia, in 1843. Whether this is the same work or not remains unknown.

44. Letter of 23 July 1841 in Lemmon, *Pettigrew Papers*, 476.

45. Letter of 23 June 1842 in ibid., 519–20. James Johnston Pettigrew was the famous North Carolina general who fought at Gettysburg.

46. Burwell, *Girl's Life in Virginia*, 52. Since this book is a retrospective memoir without dates, exactly when the German professor came to Bedford is unknown. Burwell's family home, Avenel, still stands in Bedford, Virginia.

47. Ibid., 193.

48. See Averett University's Web site at http://www.averett.edu/library/collections/presidents/Preot.pdf (accessed 27 February 2006).

49. Nordendorf married Elizabeth L. V. Hooper of Caswell County, N.C., on 24 April 1865. (Caswell County is just over the North Carolina border from Danville.) It is highly likely that Hooper was one of Nordendorf's students. See the James Fenimore Cooper Society Web site at www.oneonta.edu/external/cooper/articles/suny/1999suny-hall.html (accessed 1 March 2006).

50. Robert Phifer, husband of Belle McGehee, later (in the 1870s) performed German music frequently in Danville. Scrapbook, vol. 2, #7, Phifer Papers, SHC. His interests may have stemmed from his study in Germany.

51. Davenport, *Cultural Life in Nashville*, 45.

52. Hambruch spent the war years back in Germany. Elizabeth P. Simons, *Music in Charleston*, 35.

53. The German musical influence began in 1838, when A. Iverson came to Columbus. He was apparently a most popular teacher, being mentioned in accounts a century later. Mahan, "History of Music in Columbus, Georgia," 32, 64–65.

54. *Columbus Enquirer*, 13 November 1844, qtd. in Mahan, "History of Music in Columbus, Georgia," 71.

55. Bernreuter, or Bernrender, previously taught in Apalachicola and Tallahassee, Fla. See Housewright, *History of Music and Dance in Florida*, 116. Other music teachers in Columbus included Catherine Weyman at Glennville College; Charles R. Bewcomb (as well as advertisements for foreign teachers) at LeVert Female College, Talbotton; and Andrew Female College, Cuthbert. Mahan, "History of Music in Columbus Georgia," 76–77.

56. Mahan, "History of Music in Columbus, Georgia," 65.

57. J. Bayard Taylor, "A Recollection of Mendelssohn," *Graham's Magazine*, 1849, 113–14.

58. Reproduction of programs can be found in Hindman, "Concert Life in Ante Bellum Charleston," vol. 2.

59. Upton, *Musical Memories*, 254.

60. An 1880 article in the *New York Times* indicates that in 1870 there were 8,074 foreign-born people in South Carolina, 5,000 of whom resided in Charleston. "Fraud Taking the Census: Startling Analysis of South Carolina Returns," *New York Times*, 17 August 1880.

61. Speissegger was a pianist who performed in Charleston concerts as early as 1840. See Hindman, "Concert Life in Ante Bellum Charleston," 2:498, for a sample program.

62. A portion of the "Buchanan Polka" is reproduced in D. Thompson, "Piano Music in the South," 65.

63. The "Buchanan Polka" is part of the collection at the Charleston Museum. A William Henry Capers (1790–1855) published "Culture of Sea-Island Cotton" in the *Southern Agriculturalist* (8 [1835]: 402–15). He probably was related to the younger man; perhaps he was his father.

64. See Hess, *Lee's Tar Heels*, 62. As a captain during the war, he also composed the "Winder Gallop," dedicated to General John H. Wilder, C.S.A. His brother, Ellison Capers, taught math at the Citadel in 1860.

65. Historic American Sheet Music Collection, b2056, Duke University.

66. Elizabeth Sloman was the composer of "Sumter: A Ballad of 1861."

67. *Augusta Daily Constitutionalist*, 8 May 1864, p. 2, c. 5: "Summary: Masonic Hall—Mr. and the Misses Sloman, a Grand Vocal and Instrumental Concert, May 11th, on which occasion will be introduced, first time this season, the new Musical Instrument the Alexandre Organ."

68. Sarah Lois Wadley Diary, 29 May 1860, Wadley Papers, SHC.

69. Ibid., 6 November 1860.

70. The piece in question, "General Quitman's Grand March," is dedicated to the governor of Mississippi. An incomplete list of Eaton's works is in Panzeri, *Louisiana Composers*, 22.

71. E.g., Sarah Lois Wadley Diary, 3 December 1860, Wadley Papers, SHC.

72. Ibid., 8 December 1860.

73. Ibid., 10 December 1860.

74. Ibid., 14 December 1860.

75. G. A. Gnospelius worked in Savannah as an organist, choir master, and teacher. S. B. King, *Ebb Tide*, 43.

76. Sarah Lois Wadley Diary, 20 March 1861, Wadley Papers, SHC.

77. Ibid., 9 January 1863.

78. Eppes, *Through Some Eventful Years*, 80–81. Damer claimed to be the granddaughter of King George IV by Maria Fitzherbert, a relationship that remains unconfirmed. Housewright, *History of Music and Dance in Florida*, 197.

79. While no confirmation has been found connecting Damer to the royal line, she did marry Benjamin Nicholson White in November 1859 at Parsontown Church, King's County,

Ireland. White was from Limerick County, while Damer is listed in the marriage announcement in the *Baltimore Sun* (6 December 1859) as being of Baltimore. One wonders
if the barrister who brought the news of a "great fortune" was not indeed White.

80. Housewright, *History of Music and Dance in Florida*, 197.

81. "The Governess," *Southern Literary Messenger* 4, no. 2 (1838): 93.

82. Sarah Lois Wadley Diary, 23 September 1863, Wadley Papers, SHC.

83. Ibid., 26 November 1863.

84. Ibid., 14 January 1864.

85. Ibid., 5 February 1865.

86. *Nashville City and Business Directory* 1 (1853): 98, qtd. in Davenport, *Cultural Life in Nashville*, 43.

87. Mahan, "History of Music in Columbus, Georgia," 61.

88. Alexander, *Ambiguous Lives*, 78–79.

89. E. Ripley, *Social Life in Old New Orleans*, 10–11.

90. Winifred Barrington, "Eleonore Eboli," *Graham's Magazine*, 1849, 134.

91. In choosing Princess Marie, Barrington draws attention to another of the arts, for the princess was a widely respected amateur sculptor. Composer Marie Siegling dedicated a piano composition to the same woman.

92. Qtd. in Burr, *Secret Eye*, 74.

93. "Grace Fleming," *Dwight's Journal of Music*, 1846, 25.

94. Barhamville Notes, 1:46, SCL.

4 · MUSIC EDUCATION IN SCHOOLS

1. Farnham, *Education of the Southern Belle*, 2–3.

2. Letter of 7 November 1847, qtd. in Engstrom, *Book of Burwell Students*, 182.

3. "Critical Notices," *Southern Literary Messenger* 2, no. 4 (1836): 289.

4. These included Dr. F. A. Wurm, professor of music.

5. Blandin, *History of Higher Education*, 145–46.

6. Ibid., 194–95.

7. Miles, "Women 'Nobly Planned.'" The Honorable William Porcher Miles (1822–99) was president of the Agricultural College of South Carolina at the time of the lecture. Yorkville opened in 1854. Miles was a well-respected southern intellectual who counted Louisa McCord among his acquaintances.

8. Blandin, *History of Higher Education*, 64.

9. Ibid., 53.

10. The 1850 census records an L. G. Hartge, born c. 1824, living in Claiborne.

11. Blandin, *History of Higher Education*, 38.

12. His age is unclear, having been corrected in the census records. Also, whether it is the Bahamas is also not definitive, as it is somewhat illegible. The transcription lists it as "Baha." Census takers listed the state for United States' births; town, country, or province for foreign.

13. Blandin, *History of Higher Education*, 71–72.

14. Caroline Lee Hentz was a well-known southern novelist whose *Planter's Northern Bride* (1854), a pro-slavery rebuttal to Harriet Beecher Stowe's *Uncle Tom's Cabin* (1852), gar-nered praise from many quarters. She is one of the novelists whose works form the basis of Moss's *Domestic Novelists in the Old South*.

15. Blandin, *History of Higher Education*, 47.

16. Jane H. Pease and William H. Pease's excellent study, *A Family of Women: The Carolina Petigrus in Peace and War*, is one of several studies the Peases have done on this family.

Chapter 4, "Educating the Young," is particularly relevant to the present discussion. The following details of the Petigru women are taken from this volume, pp. 43–47.

17. Jane Caroline Petigru Carson became a noted portrait artist and watercolorist. At the beginning of the Civil War, she moved to Charleston. She later lived in New York City before moving permanently to Rome, where she lived as an artist.

18. Pease and Pease, *Family of Women*, 43. See also William H. Pease and Jane H. Pease, *Roman Years of a South Carolina Artist*.

19. Sue King established herself as a novelist; among her more popular works were *Busy Moments of an Idle Woman* (1854); *Crimes Which the Law Does Not Reach* (1859); *Gerald Gray's Wife* (1864); *Lily: A Novel* (1855); and *Sylvia's World* (1859).

20. Jane North (Badwell, S.C.) to Caroline North (Georgetown, S.C.), 8 December 1840, Pettigrew Papers, 1.6.82, SHC.

21. Della remained for only a short while, for the Allstons found the standards at Mrs. Dupre's school too low for their daughter. Pullum-Piñón, "Conspicuous Display and Social Mobility," 231.

22. Chesnut notes that some girls attended only for a brief time, and Madame Talvande did not expend much time or energy on these girls except to work on manners and deportment. Qtd. in DeCredico, *Mary Boykin Chesnut*, 9.

23. Madame Talvande ran her École pour Demoiselles after the death of her husband, Andrew. See the Charleston County Public Library Web site at http://www.ccpl.org/content.asp?id=15671&action=detail&catID=6025&parentID=5747 (accessed June 2007). Andrew Talvande bought the property in 1819. Because of a law prohibiting aliens from owning property, an act of the assembly was necessary in 1835 to confirm Madame Talvande's right to inherit the property from her husband, who had died without becoming a U.S. citizen. Among its later owners, Mrs. Jessie Lincoln Randolph, a granddaughter of Abraham Lincoln, owned the property in the 1930s but never lived here.

24. A more detailed account of Talvande's as an educational institution can be found in the speech "Educating Daisy: Some Observations on the Education of Women in the Nineteenth Century South" by Elisabeth Showalter Muhlenfeld, ninth president of Sweet Briar College, given at Founder's Day, Sweet Briar College, 3 October 1996, found on the Web site *Gifts of Speech: Women's Speeches from Around the World*, http://gos.sbc.edu/m/muhlenfeld2.html (accessed July 2007).

25. Some girls apparently brought their pianos with them to school, as did Fanny Jones (b. 1837). Although she lived in the same town as the school she attended (the Burwell School in Hillsborough), Fanny nonetheless had her piano delivered to the school in March 1856. Engstrom, *Book of Burwell Students*, 116.

26. Chesnut, *Two Years*, 165.

27. Thalberg to Marie Petit, 1857 and 1858, in Blanch Herminie Petit Barbot (1842–1919) File, 11/68/4, SCHS, Charleston.

28. Greensborough Female College (1837), Floral College (1841), Warrenton Female Collegiate Institute (1846), Carolina Female College (1849), Oxford Baptist Female College (1851), Wesleyan Female College (1852), Goldsboro Female College (1854), Louisburg Female College (1855), Asheville Female College (1855), Jamestown Female College (1855), Statesville Female College (1857), Warrenton Female College (1857), Davenport Female College (1858), Mars Hill College (1859, originally French Broad Baptist Institute, 1856). Pope, "Preparation for Pedestals," 30.

29. Nash, *Ladies in the Making*, 53.

30. Pope, "Preparation for Pedestals," 83.

31. Blandin, *History of Higher Education*, 240.

32. She also comments that her brother must be "very expert" on the violin by now. Letter of 29 October 1843 in Lemmon, *Pettigrew Papers*, 598.

33. Salley, *Life at St. Mary's*, 14.

34. Letter from Kate DeRosset to Dr. A. J. DeRosset, 10 July 1846, DeRosset II Family Papers, SHC.

35. Qtd. in Engstrom, *Book of Burwell Students*, 65–66.

36. Nash, *Ladies in the Making*, 49–50.

37. Barhamville Notes, 1:13, SCL.

38. A letter (13 May 1848) recalled by Mrs. Emilie L. Bacot of Darlington, S.C., noted a performance at Barhamville: "Our concert is to be next Friday night, Mary and myself are to play a duet again." She further commented that these two were also to play a duet at their examination. Barhamville Notes, 2:62, SCL.

39. I am grateful to Sybil McNeil, librarian at the Archives and Special Collections at Wesleyan College, for sending me this information on these performances.

40. Auditor, "Communication," *Hillsborough Recorder*, 4 June 1849.

41. See also Blandin, *History of Higher Education*, 33.

42. Pope, "Preparation for Pedestals," 78.

43. Fries, *Historical Sketch of Salem Female Academy*, 20–21, 23.

44. The first male music professor at Salem was Edward W. Leinbach. Griffin, *Less Time for Meddling*, 256.

45. Ibid., 259.

46. Fries, *Historical Sketch of Salem Female Academy*, 6.

47. Letter of 9 February 1837 from Henry Jones of Tennessee, qtd. in Byrd et al., *Salem Academy and College*, 20.

48. See Kimball, *"True Professional Ideal in America,"* 173.

49. Blandin, *History of Higher Education*, 95. Euhink, or Uhink, Lord, and Massey had all taught the previous year (Euhink as head of music) at the Young Ladies Collegiate Institute at Brownwood, near Columbus. Mahan, "History of Music in Columbus, Georgia," 66. Uhink/Euhink might be related to the Unthank clan of Quakers who lived in the Guilford County region of North Carolina since the Revolution. See Engstrom, *Book of Burwell Students*, 202–3.

50. *Greensborough Female College* (bulletin), 1846–47, 3–5.

51. In 1872, she is listed as principal of the music department there. (See Lander University Web site at http://www.lander.edu/library/jackson/files/Lander_Catalogs/1872_Catalog. pdf+augusta+hagen&hl=en&ct=clnk&cd=2&gl=us, accessed 3 December 2007.) On Hagen's family, see *The Jarvis Family & Other Relatives*, http://www.fmoran.com/hagen. html (accessed 3 December 2007).

52. Francis Hagen was an influential Moravian musician; see Boeringer, *Morning Star*.

53. Reichel, *Moravians in North Carolina*, 128.

54. A sixty-one-year-old woman named Charity Benzien is listed in the 1860 census in Salem, N.C. The close proximity of the two towns as well as the later appearance of another woman music teacher from Salem (Louisa Van Vleck) suggest that Charity may have been related (mother?) to Francisca. Another Benzien is in the 1840 census, Stokes County, N.C. As to Francis Cocheu, the spelling of the first name suggests a man, although the absence of a title is suspicious.

55. She later became Mrs. Fischer. Reichel, *Moravians in North Carolina*, 128.

56. Farnham discusses the problems with such graduation exercises, noting that in some cases, men read girls' essays aloud so as not to cause them the public humiliation. Farnham, *Education of the Southern Belle*, 26. A different situation existed at the Nashville Female

Academy, where a public concert evidently figured into the commencement exercises. John Berrien Lindsley Diary, 8 June 1857, qtd. in Davenport, *Cultural Life in Nashville*, 43.

57. Rau, "John Frederick Peter," 313. Wolle moved to the South in 1853; he also played in a Confederate band during the war. Fix, "Organ in Moravian Church Music," 157.

58. Twelve does not include the preparatory principal. Whether the music teachers also instructed the preparatory students is not indicated, but presumably they could have.

59. In 1848, Karl W. Petersilie, professor of music at the Edgeworth Seminary, composed the music to "'Tis Home Where the Heart Is," in *Graham's Magazine* (176). Miss L. M. Brown wrote the lyrics, and she may have been one of his students there. His "L'artemisie valse" of 1847 is dedicated to her. Petersilie also published the "Monterey Col. Campbell's March" in 1847 and the "Julie Polka" in 1848. The march is the only piece that does not note his position at Edgeworth.

60. On Barhamville in general, see *A Barhamville Miscellany*. The Barhamville Notes, Henry Campbell Davis's collection, fills five volumes in the South Caroliniana Library, Columbia. The South Carolina Female Collegiate Institute in Barhamville apparently produced many music teachers, such as Sally McCullough, who achieved some degree of public acclaim in the 1860s.

61. The following account of the South Carolina Female Collegiate Institute is taken from Blandin, *History of Higher Education*, 258–72. Blandin received this information from Jean Witherspoon in 1909.

62. Ibid., 267.

63. Unless otherwise noted, the information concerning the history of the South Carolina Female Collegiate Institute in the following pages derives from Barhamville Notes, 1:261–65, SCL.

64. One of Warne's sisters married the governor of Vermont. Another became the wife of Dr. Isham, whose grandson became a partner of Robert Lincoln, afterward United States Minister to Great Britain, and whose son, Pierpont Isham, was a judge of the Supreme Court of Vermont. John Pierpont, the poet, was her cousin.

65. Blandin, *History of Higher Education*, 263.

66. Barhamville Notes, 1:49, SCL.

67. These are apparently the observations of Mrs. Jean H. Witherspoon of Columbia, S.C., who provided the background for Blandin's book. Witherspoon wrote for *The State*, published in Columbia. Her account was sent to Blandin by a Mr. Dreher, superintendent of public education in South Carolina, in 1909.

68. A letter to R. F. W. Allston of 13 December 1858, from Mme. R. Acélie Togno to "My dear Friend," seeks his assistance in selling her property at 46 Meeting St., Charleston. Madame Togno operated a school for young ladies in Charleston near the house at 51 Meeting St., known now as the Nathaniel Russell House, which Allston purchased in 1857.

69. Women teachers were paid about half what the men received. Catherine Beecher argues in *Godey's*, January 1853, p. 176, that women could teach for half the salary of men because they had to sustain only themselves. She reversed that opinion later in life. Qtd. in Pope, "Preparation for Pedestals," 202.

70. Information on faculty found in Barhamville Notes, 1:264–70, SCL.

71. F. T. Strawinski was teaching guitar in Norfolk in 1843. Hines, "Musical Activity in Norfolk," 1:50. Strawinski's arrangements were used frequently at Barhamville.

72. Barhamville Notes, 1:46, SCL.

73. Thomas "Blind Tom" Wiggins Bethune (1849–1908) was born blind to slave parents on a plantation in Georgia. His piano abilities carried him into a professional career, one marked by severe exploitation. See Southall, *Blind Tom, the Black Pianist-Composer*.

74. Barhamville Notes, 1:15–16, SCL.

75. Ibid., 1:112.

76. "New Works," *Southern Literary Messenger* 37, no. 12 (1863): 748.

77. Barhamville Notes, 1:19, SCL.

78. Ibid., 1:46. Hermitage Female Seminary in Scottsboro, Ga., described Mr. Walsh as its "scientific" professor of music. See the *Columbus Enquirer*, 15 January 1835. Later, a Mrs. Seaman announced the "scientific teaching of music" in a private school at Eleventh Ave. and Broad St., also in Columbus. Mahan, "History of Music in Columbus, Georgia," 65.

79. *Tallahassee Floridian*, 7 November 1835, qtd. in Housewright, *History of Music and Dance in Florida*, 116.

80. Private communication with Mr. Gary Hardy, a descendant of the family, August 2005.

81. A reference to "Miss A. Bluxome" as instructress in music at the South Carolina Female Collegiate Institute may or may not be the same woman. This woman taught piano, guitar, and organ. *Barhamville Miscellany*, 1:103.

82. Richard Storrs Willis et al., *New York Musical World*, 1857, p. 213.

83. Ping-Robbins, "Musical Criticisms and Attitudes about Music," 58.

84. Barhamville Notes, 1:44, SCL.

85. C. Jones, *Education in Georgia*, 110, 113–14.

86. The 1860 South Carolina census includes a Mary McAliley, aged twenty, daughter of a Charleston lawyer (Sam[ue]l, aged sixty) who was worth $76,000 in real estate and $85,000 in personal property. She is a likely candidate for Párraga's student, being fourteen in 1854.

87. Manuscript I&O, SCL.

88. A Mary Douglas Ancrum, born in 1840, was the daughter of William Alexander Ancrum and Charlotte Elizabeth Douglas. Mary married John Shannon in 1860. This may or may not be the correct family in question. A Mary Ancrum (aged twenty) was living in the household of William A. Ancrum (aged thirty-three) in 1860 in Camden, according to the census. There are several other children in their teens also living at this house. William is listed as a planter.

89. Barhamville Notes, 2:65, SCL.

5. THE PIANO GIRL

1. With this quote, Tick drew the scholarly world's attention to the "piano girl" in several papers published in the 1980s. Tick, "Passed Away Is the Piano Girl," 325. James Huneker's comments originally appeared in the book *Overtones* (New York, 1904), 286. Tick drew attention to Huneker's remarks in "The Emergence of a Professional Ethos for Women Composers," chap. 8 of *American Women Composers before 1870*. For more on Huneker, see Orr, *Alfredo Barili*, 48–49.

2. Tick, "Passed Away Is the Piano Girl," 325. See also works such as Solie, *Music in Other Words*; and J. Smith, "Music, Women, and Pianos."

3. K. Smith, "The Novel," 55.

4. S. P. King, *Lily*, 71.

5. Qtd. in Johnson, *Ante-bellum North Carolina*, 195; *Raleigh Star*, 25 October 1810.

6. *Raleigh Register*, 5 January 1850.

7. David B. Thompson provides images of typical pianos in the South during this period in "Piano Music in the South."

8. Waring, "Confederate Girl's Diary," 281.

9. Sarah Lois Wadley Diary, 29 October 1863, Wadley Papers, SHC.

10. "Mollie Ford to Brother Frank," in SS Women AL, Eleanor S. Brockenbrough Library, Museum of the Confederacy, Richmond, Va.

11. "Emma to Darling Mother," in ibid. She also mentions daily practicing before breakfast and after dinner.

12. Georgia Historical Society, 1361 SM, uncataloged music, which dates from c. 1840 and belonged to Sarah Cunningham of Savannah.

13. Barhamville Notes, 1:19, SCL.

14. SMB 14, Charleston Museum.

15. UNC Music Library, new series, vol. 13.

16. The German practice of numbering the fingers 1–5 gradually became the standard in the United States during the course of the nineteenth century.

17. The UNC Music Library estimate of the date is c. 1822.

18. In the collection of the Charleston Museum, SMB 5.35 and 5.29. Cheves (1810–79) was an influential southern intellectual of many talents, including writing. See Fought, *Southern Womanhood and Slavery*.

19. I am grateful to Rebecca McClure of the Charleston Museum for her assistance in working with this volume.

20. Pease and Pease, *Family of Women*, 61. The difference between playing the dance and dancing the dance has not, to my knowledge, been investigated but is certainly worth consideration.

21. Ibid.

22. Allen Lott persuasively argues in *From Paris to Peoria* that Herz's style of playing was much more delicate than that of other touring pianists, particularly Leopold de Meyer, so it is not surprising to find his works in volumes for young ladies. Moreover, Katharine Ellis discusses a more feminine style of playing (*jeu lié*) in "Female Pianists and Their Male Critics," 379–82.

23. See Preston's comments on the changes in American music, particularly a growing divide between vernacular and cultivated music, at this time. Preston, *Opera on the Road*, 317.

24. Farnham, *Education of the Southern Belle*, 87.

25. Ellis, "Female Pianists and Their Male Critics." In 1819, Sophia Hewitt (daughter of James and sister of John Hill) performed Beethoven's Sonata in A-flat, Op. 26, in Boston, but this was much the exception rather than the rule. Even when Thalberg played the German "classics," he limited his choices to about three: Beethoven's "Moonlight Sonata," Chopin's *Funeral March*, and some of the Mendelssohn *Songs without Words*. Loesser, *Men, Women and Pianos*, 466, 502.

26. Tick notes advice against playing sonatas in the parlor, quoting the *Boston Musical Visitor*, 7 July 1844, p. 113; Tick, *American Women Composers*, 30.

27. Thornwell, *Lady's Guide to Perfect Gentility*, 97. This work was indeed known in the South, as the copy in the SHC attests.

28. SMB 34, f. 72, Moravian Archives, Archie K. Davis Center, Winston-Salem, N.C.

29. This particular source includes works composed by the sisters themselves, as well as several works by Stephen Heller. On the musical education of women in Moravian institutions, see J. Smith, "Music, Women, and Pianos."

30. Other identified collections in the UNC Music Library also originate in sparsely populated areas, such as Clinton and Jonesville, N.C.

31. Interestingly, after the Civil War, Beethoven's sonatas begin to appear in women's collections.

32. Moreover, Belle McGehee married music professor Robert S. Phifer after the war. Composer Frederick Delius spent some time at their home as he made his way north from Florida, marking Burleigh as perhaps not-quite-so-average when it came to music on the plantation.

33. Danville Female College catalog, 1864–65, p. 21, Centre College Library Web site, http://www.centre.edu/web/library/sc/kcw/pdf/d1864.pdf (accessed 2 September 2009).

34. Harp instruction surpassed this at forty dollars each session. Farnham, *Education of the Southern Belle*, 87.

35. Burwell, *Girl's Life in Virginia*, 192.

36. Advertised in the *Hillsborough Recorder*, 25 June 1823. Aykroyd had previously run a music store in New Bern; UNC Music Library, old series, vol. 29, includes several pieces with his dealer's stamp.

37. *Savannah Newspaper Digest*, 1 January 1861.

38. Anita Dwyer Withers Diary, 1860–1865, 21 October 1861, SHC.

39. On the physical isolation of southern white women, see Cashin, "Into the Trackless Wilderness," 32–34.

40. Some of the larger, grander dances composed or arranged for concert performance hardly fit the bill for dancing in the parlor and almost certainly would not have been used as such.

41. Clay-Clopton, *Belle of the Fifties*, 49. In this same entry, Clay comments on how fortunate she was to be able to hear Grisi and Mario, Bozio, Jenny Lind, Parepa Rose, Forrest, Julia Dean, Agnes Robertson, and later (p. 102) Anna Bishop, Ap Thomas, and Bochsa. On the popularity of Gottschalk's "Last Hope," see an anecdote in Starr, *Louis Moreau Gottschalk*, 195. See also Loesser, *Men, Women and Pianos*, 500–501.

42. The cases of Eliza Ripley and Rose Kennedy, below, further support the likelihood that Dimitry played the "Fantaisie."

43. Halttunen, *Confidence Men and Painted Women*, 97.

44. In "Music and the Feminine Sphere," Julia Eklund Koza refers often to musical ability being a path to courtship and on the feminine characteristics of the appropriate music for young women. She does not comment on the issue of physical deportment and piano repertory.

45. Mary Branch Jones Polk also mentions Blind Tom, noting that she brought him to Columbia, S.C., to perform at a benefit for the Hospital Association during the war. Polk, *Memories of a Southern Woman*, 27.

46. Clay-Clopton, *Belle of the Fifties*, 104.

47. Qtd. in Loesser, *Men, Women and Pianos*, 290–91.

48. Ibid., 291–92.

49. Ibid., 291. Loesser dryly remarks that this phrase "could be the slogan of the nineteenth century."

50. Ellis, "Female Pianists and Their Male Critics," 356n.

51. This work is not among Wallace's listed works in biographical references but is part of the collection at the Charleston Museum, SMB 21.29.

52. Strakosch (1825–87) was an American impresario who moved to New York in 1848 from what is now the Czech Republic. He later married Amalia Patti, a noted soprano and sister of Adelina (one of the most popular singers of the century), and he toured with both singers as well as other artists (such as Ole Bull) during the middle years of the century. The latter copy of this work lists its origins as Nashville, and the contemporary owner's name was Martha.

53. E. Ripley, *Social Life in Old New Orleans*, 148.

54. The first lithograph done in New Orleans was for "Sea Serpent," by Xavier Magny. W. T. Mayo published the work. Harwell, *Confederate Music*, 11.

55. E. Ripley, *Social Life in Old New Orleans*, 148.

56. Ibid., 151.

57. Gottschalk based "La Bamboula" on the Créole melody "Quan' patate la cuite."

58. After taking a degree in law from Harvard in 1831, Durell moved to the South in 1834 (Mississippi) and to New Orleans in 1836. He remained there until the secession, which he adamantly opposed. He contributed to periodicals with some frequency and authored several other texts.

59. H. Didimus (Edward Henry Durell), *Graham's Magazine*, 1853, 64–65.

60. E. W. Kemble, *Century Illustrated Monthly Magazine*, February 1886, available at the Louisiana State Museum Web site, http://lsm.crt.state.la.us/cabildo/cab7.htm (accessed July 2008).

61. As with other pieces described in this chapter, "La Bamboula" includes markings of *fff* as well as *tutta la forza* and *pesante*.

62. E. Ripley, *Social Life in Old New Orleans*, 148.

63. When Mary Pettigrew writes how music brings her such pleasure (Mary Pettigrew to William S. Pettigrew, 23 June 1843, Pettigrew Papers, 1.6.94, SHC, qtd. in chapter 1), she makes the most personal statement for music lessons. Mary, however, frequently performed for others also.

64. Jabour, *Scarlett's Sisters*, 10–11.

65. Ibid., 164.

66. Ibid., 180.

67. Anita Dwyer Withers Diary, 4 May 1860, SHC.

68. See, for example, the entry for 15 June 1860.

69. Anita Dwyer Withers Diary, 16 October 1861, SHC. DeCoëniél considered himself to be the musical muse of the Confederacy, and more patriotic music by him survives than by anyone else.

70. Ibid., 1 November 1861.

71. Ibid., 19 November 1861.

72. This is the same melody as seen in "Sleeping I Dream'd, Love," a very popular piece of the period. Since Withers uses the pseudo-French title (neither Withers nor the published version use the circumflex, as in "Le Rêve") and is so focused on her piano lessons, it seems reasonable that she refers to the piano version, not the vocal one with piano accompaniment.

73. Wallace was born in Ireland and died in England, although he spent a considerable amount of time elsewhere, including Australia, New Zealand, Chile, Peru, and the United States, where he toured as both a concert violinist and pianist.

74. Anita Dwyer Withers Diary, 17 January 1862, SHC.

75. Ibid.

76. In "Our Richmond Correspondence," *Charleston Mercury*, 17 October 1861, "Hermes" writes that the recent Torriani concert was "thinly attended," hinting that musical life was indeed falling off in the capital city as a result of the war. These concerts were organized by Signor Torriani and included amateur performances as a morale boost throughout the South. See also the *Charleston Mercury*, 27 September 1861. A bitter comment appears in the *Richmond Enquirer* on 12 February 1864, noting that the winter has been one of "reckless frivolity" and "a carnival of unhallowed pleasure," owing to various dances in the city, and that "all the hideous deformity of Washington society is being fastened upon old Richmond. There was a virtue in the olden hospitality of this city unknown in the hollow formalities of this Yankee custom."

77. Qtd. in Lott, "American Concert Tours," 2:328. The term "piano thumper" was not invented by Upton. An earlier use appears in Tefft, "The Dignity of Music," *Ladies' Repository* 10, no. 6 (June 1850): 180.

78. Letters from Thalberg to Marie Petit, 1857 and 1858, in Barbot (1842–1919) File, 11/68/4, SCHS, Charleston.

79. The *Charleston Tri-Weekly News*, 25 November 1852, describes the father's concert as "one of the rarest displays of instrumental music that we have ever witnessed in this city." On the family, see the Barbot File, SCHS, Charleston.

80. Simons, *Music in Charleston*, 43.

81. *Charleston News & Courier*, 18 December 1919.

82. James Norcom Sr. to Mary B. Harvey, 25 May 1848, James A. Norcum Papers, qtd. in Johnson, *Ante-Bellum North Carolina*, 229.

83. S. P. King, *Lily*, 72.

84. Thornwell, *Lady's Guide to Perfect Gentility*, pages as referenced.

85. The entire quote is worth reviewing: "As a general rule, men are more competent to teach than women, in *routine*; out of routine, women are the best teachers. To instruct upon the piano-forte, there must be actual strength, as well as powerful talent; but in the case of a woman possessing and controlling a fine voice, she is the most orthodox woman-teacher, it stands to reason." *Godey's Lady's Book* 59 (1859): 370–71.

86. Johnson, *Ante-Bellum North Carolina*, 230.

87. Koza also made the observation that women are associated with teaching singing, whereas men are aligned with instrumental music, in "Music and the Feminine Sphere," 117. Adèle Hohnstock is an exception, but her playing was reportedly described by Liszt as "more forcible than those of any lady he had ever heard." *New York Tribune*, 19 December 1848. Nonetheless, such physicality would not have appealed to southern women as something to be emulated. Earlier (22 March 1832) evidence survives of Madame Lonati performing solo piano pieces in Richmond in between "Daguerre's Magical Pictures from Paris," according to Stoutamire's *Music of the Old South*, 136, citing the *Whig*. Other professional women pianists did perform in the United States, and Loesser describes a few in Boston in *Men, Women and Pianos*, 466–67 (see also 472–73), but I have found few records that they performed in the South. One noteworthy female performer was French pianist Octavie Romey (see chap. 9).

88. Although Amy Fay (1844–1928) was born in Mississippi, she was raised by her older sister in the North from the age of twelve.

89. Thornwell, *Lady's Guide to Perfect Gentility*, 97.

90. Ibid., 109.

91. "Centre-Table Gossip: Directions to Modern Piano-Forte Players," *Godey's Lady's Book* 46 (1852): 569.

92. As in *Lily*, a story entitled "The Loves of an Apothecary" contrasts the young woman who plays brilliantly with one who does not, and the brilliant performer is clearly the less desirable of the two. *Graham's Magazine*, 1852, 516.

93. I am grateful to Linda Austern for suggesting the racial stereotyping in this picture.

94. Blandin, *History of Higher Education*, 196.

95. *Dwight's Journal of Music*, 1856, 379.

96. "Mems for Musical Misses," *Harper's New Monthly Magazine*, September 1851, 489.

6. THE SINGER

1. On the other hand, professional singers wore the same types of costume as amateurs, for the most part, which questions how effective they were in executing certain passages.

2. Carlo Ritorni, writing in *L'Eco*, qtd. in Rutherford, *Prima Donna and Opera*, 70. An 1895 book entitled *On Respiration in Singing* purports to prove that women who wear corsets lose a considerable amount of breath. The author, Joseph Joal, highly recommends that female singers not don such attire for performance. Joal, *On Respiration in Singing*, 161.

3. Lieber, Wigglesworth, and Bradford, *Encyclopædia Americana*, 419.

4. This institution held a long, positive reputation. Blandin, *History of Higher Education*, 72–73.

5. *American Beacon Daily*, 24 December 1817, qtd. in Hines, "Musical Activity in Norfolk," 1:56.

6. *Boston Academy's Collection*, 13.

7. These were copied by hand into SMB 34.78 in the Van Vleck Family Folder, Moravian Archives, Archie K. Davis Center, Winston-Salem. This book also includes several piano solos by Stephen Heller, as well as Charles Gounod's "Christmas Morn" ("Noel").

8. Sarah Lois Wadley Diary, 10 August 1860, Wadley Papers, SHC.

9. UNC Music Library, old series, vol. 77.

10. *Dwight's Journal of Music*, 1855, 102.

11. New series, vol. 5, second work in the volume.

12. Stubblefield, "Music!"

13. Elizabeth Waties Allston Pringle was the daughter of planter and politician Robert Francis Withers Allston, who owned one of the largest plantations in South Carolina and served in the state legislature for several years before becoming governor in 1856. Born on Pawley's Island, S.C., in 1845, she left home to attend boarding school in Charleston when she was nine years old. Elizabeth was the younger sister of Della Allston, who is mentioned previously. At the outset of the Civil War, Pringle moved to Columbia and remained there until 1863. Pringle returned to Charleston briefly before settling in Crowley Hill, which Sherman's troops later raided. After the war, she taught at her mother's boarding school in Charleston for three years before she married John Julius Pringle (1870). When her husband died (1876), she famously bought their house and land, as well as her family's farm, Chicora Wood. See Harris Henderson, *Documenting the American South*, http://docsouth.unc.edu/fpn/pringle/summary.html (accessed 21 January 2008).

14. This man was married to the Madame Torriani of the South Carolina Female Collegiate Institute.

15. No work by that title exists in major collections, and none of the arias from *Martha* translates into "Buona notte, buon dormir."

16. *Columbus Enquirer*, 26–31 March 1860.

17. Pringle, *Woman Rice Planter*, 85–86.

18. The opening lines of a poem by Miss M. Sawin even describe Jenny Lind as "a world's sweet enchantress." *Graham's Magazine*, 1849, 269.

19. Pringle, *Chronicles of Chicora Wood*, 180.

20. S. P. King, *Lily*, 71.

21. Ibid.

22. Critics, such as George Templeton Strong and others, tended to dislike virtuoso display. Walt Whitman famously commented on Jenny Lind's singing, saying that her "vocal dexterity" sounded as if "executed . . . in perfect scientific style . . . it was a failure; for it was a vacuum in the head of the performance." Whitman qtd. in Davenport, *Cultural Life in Nashville*, 149.

23. Pringle, *Chronicles of Chicora Wood*, 180.

24. Composed by Sir Henry Bishop (estranged husband of the singer Anna Bishop), this song was reportedly sung by Adelina Patti for President Lincoln in 1863.

25. Federal Writers Project, *South Carolina*, 341.

26. The fact that she belonged to a highly respectable South Carolina family might have made such a suggestion seem absurd. That it occurred during the war years, however, might reflect changes in perceptions. Pringle did spend her adult life in a man's world, as her autobiography, *A Woman Rice Planter*, attests.

27. Pringle, *Chronicles of Chicora Wood*, 180–81.
28. Pope, "Preparation for Pedestals," 159.
29. S. P. King, *Actress in High Life*, 324.
30. Ibid., 390.
31. Ibid., 396.
32. Ibid., 396–98.
33. Qtd. in Strakosch, *Memoirs of an American Prima Donna*, vi.
34. Ibid., 1, 54.
35. The frequency of fashion plates and other images in women's magazines attests to their popularity.
36. "New Music," *Southern Quarterly Review*, 1850, 541.
37. Upton, *Musical Memories*, 39.
38. Orr, *Alfredo Barili*, 30–33.
39. *Spirit of the Times*, 18 June 1847, qtd. in Lawrence, *Strong on Music*, 467.
40. See Lawrence, *Strong on Music*, 530.
41. *Courier & Enquirer*, 11 August 1847, qtd. in ibid., 471.
42. *Albion*, 2 September 1848, qtd. in Lawrence, *Strong on Music*, 507.
43. References to Louisa Gist include the 1841–42 catalog at the South Carolina Female Collegiate Institute, which lists Louisa A. Gist of Union, S.C., taking music as her only elective; and Barhamville Notes, 3:70, SCL. Her father's name (William H. Gist) appears as a signatory to the character of Elias Marks in a letter to the *Laurensville Herald*, December 1851, qtd. in Barhamville Notes, 1:4, SCL.
44. Jane Caroline North 1851–52 Diary, p. 166, Monday, 18 August 1851, Pettigrew Family Papers, SHC.
45. It was Gist who called the Secession Convention upon the election of Abraham Lincoln.
46. Filia, "Agnes," *Southern Literary Messenger* 37, no. 6 (June 1863): 346.
47. Ibid., 351.
48. Ibid., 355.
49. These excerpts are taken from the next installment, which appeared in July 1863 issue, 423–28.
50. See Sandy Stubblefield's remarks earlier in this chapter.
51. The author of "My First Serenade" contrasts the description of a singer with that of the woman he eventually admires by noting the latter's "low and silvery" voice. "My First Serenade," *Southern Literary Messenger* 14, no. 8 (1848): 483.

7. WOMEN'S COMPOSITION AND PUBLICATION IN THE ANTEBELLUM PERIOD

1. The only specific evidence for a course on music, as opposed to music lessons, is one offered in 1857 at the South Carolina Female Collegiate Institute in Barhamville entitled The Theory and Practice of Instrumental Music and Vocal Music.
2. The daughters of Anna Burwell, mistress at the Burwell School, taught music there. These young women signed their names in a copy of *The Piano-Forte Primer; containing the Rudiments of Music: calculated either for Private Tuition, or teaching in Classes*, by J. F. Burrowes, which provides basic theory as well as terminology but no composition instruction. (This copy now resides with the Historic Hillsborough Commission.)
3. Citron, *Gender and the Musical Canon*, 44–45. Citron relies on ideas presented by literary critic Susan Stanford Friedman in "Creativity and the Childbirth Metaphor: Gender Difference in Literary Discourse," in *Speaking of Gender*, ed. Elaine Showalter (New York: Routledge, 1989), 75–76.

4. Tick, *American Women Composers*, 224–26.

5. E. Ripley, *Social Life in Old New Orleans*, 149.

6. Tick acknowledges female poetry of this period and its suitability for the parlor song (the parlor being the women's sphere), quoting critic Henry Tuckerman: "Men do not expect extensive knowledge and active logical powers from a female poet. They do expect to feel the influence and power of the affections." Tick, *American Women Composers*, 93. Tick's work was the first major publication to draw attention to the music of American women composers. See also Cooke, "Southern Women, Southern Voices."

7. See the memoirs of Carl Anton Van Vleck, housed in the Moravian Archives, Archie K. Davis Center, Winston-Salem, N.C.

8. This piece also appeared in a Boston edition, put out by Oliver Ditson. Among the surviving copies is one at the South Caroliniana Library, University of South Carolina, Columbia. It also appeared in *Willig's Musical Magazine*; see the New York Public Library, Performing Arts Division, New York, Wolfe 6361.

9. Clark, *Anthology of Early American Keyboard Music*, 129.

10. Her identity is revealed early in the book (p. 5).

11. Tick, *American Women Composers*, 66.

12. Ibid., 139.

13. The 1848 "Buena Vista Polka," also by "A Lady of Virginia" (but published in New York), is the last of the pieces to mention specific battles until the Civil War.

14. Tick has reproduced "Thou Hast Wounded the Spirit That Lov'd Thee" in its entirety in *American Women Composers*, 109–12. She mentions the collaboration between Adelene and Carusi, in addition to others (p. 75).

15. This is a theoretical statement, of course, as we know that some women authors received remuneration for their efforts. Unfortunately, extremely few financial records of southern music publishers have survived because of various actions on both sides during the Civil War. Domestic novelists of the period, however, do include characters who learn that southern publications depend on voluntary contributions, as editors did not solicit (or pay for) manuscripts. This is the case with one of Augusta Evans's characters, Beulah Benton. See Moss, *Domestic Novelists in the Old South*, 26. Mary Terhune clearly states that she was paid for her work, although she remained anonymous: "'Marion Harland' was, again, a hint of my name, so overt that it was not guessed at by readers in general. The editor, an acquaintance of my father, was informed of my right to draw the money. I continued to send tales and poems to him for two years, and preserved my incognito." [Terhune], *Marion Harland's Autobiography*, 241.

16. The Hewitt family history is replete with anecdotes that reveal much about American musical culture of this period. For example, the father, John, had led an orchestra that performed for George III before the Hewitts left England. John Jr. is linked with several famous Americans, including Edgar Allen Poe. John Hill Hewitt's sister, Sophie Hewitt Ostinelli, incidentally, was a renowned pianist. In 1863, John Hill Hewitt married an eighteen-year-old music student, Mary Alethea Smith, who also published songs.

17. Tick, *American Women Composers*, 139.

18. Ibid.

19. Schell's work appears on the 1852 commencement concert at Georgia Female College, Macon, Ga.

20. Bowen, *Diary of Clarissa Adger Bowen*, 17. Another reference to her musical abilities appears in a letter (10 September 1843) from her aunt Floride, who comments that Martha and her sister both play the piano and guitar very well. Calhoun, *Papers of John C. Calhoun*, 427.

21. Sloan, *Fogy Days*, 77.
22. Calhoun, *Papers of John C. Calhoun*, 427.
23. *Charleston Mercury*, 3 June 1861.
24. At the time of the Civil War, the Siegling Music Company of Charleston, S.C., was the oldest music house in the United States. Established in 1819, it was the second music firm in that city (the first being that of Philip Muck, 1803–22). Harwell notes that during most of the antebellum period, Siegling was "without competition in the South." Harwell, *Confederate Music*, 9. Oddly, Siegling presented his only Confederate composition immediately after South Carolina's secession, although he did join Blackmar and others in later imprints. Ibid., 13.
25. Ibid., 9.
26. Mr. Bingham qtd. in "Notices of New Works," *Southern Literary Messenger*, 1855, 62.
27. *Grove 2nd Edition*, 1904–1910, American Supplement, ed. Waldo Selden Pratt (New York: Macmillan, 1920), 25, qtd. in Tick, *American Women Composers*, 126n.
28. Tick, *American Women Composers*, 43–45, 127–38. Hohnstock's "Agnes Polka" is available in a modern edition in Glickman, *American Women Composers*.
29. "New Music," *Southern Quarterly Review*, 1850, 542.
30. William Hall set up shop in New York in 1820 and in 1821 joined with John Firth to form Firth & Hall. In 1831, they added Sylvanius Pond to their firm. In 1847, Hall left this group to form William Hall & Son with his son James. Whether this "Lady of South Carolina" is Martha Colhoun remains unknown. She did publish at about the same time.
31. Some are still open to the public. The National Register of Historic Places contains information on them, as does the National Park Service Web site, http://www.nps.gov/history/nr/travel/jamesriver/sitelist.htm (accessed June 2008).
32. A James M. Morson, planter, lived in Goochland County, Va., in 1860. (The census lists his worth at $570,000.) He may have been the husband of Mrs. J. Morson. Goochland figures in another of Mrs. J. M. C.'s works: Elk Hill Plantation is also in Goochland County. Randolph Harrison (worth $110,000 according to the 1860 census) owned Elk Hill in 1860.
33. W. T. Mayo succeeded Émile Johns in 1842 and was in turn bought out by Philip Werlein in 1854. "Composers of Music and Music Publishers in New Orleans," *New Orleans Daily Picayune*, 18 February 1912; "Musical History of Louisiana," *New Orleans Times Democrat*, 31 October 1909, 10; also see Harwell, *Confederate Music*, 10.
34. "Fanny Heron" also composed the "Myrtle Waltz," published in Philadelphia by Jas. Couenhoven in 1855.
35. In an ironic twist, Tick finds that Stephen Foster may have published under "A Lady" in order to sell parlor music. Tick, *American Women Composers*, 75.
36. Koza, "Music and the Feminine Sphere," 123.
37. Tick, *American Women Composers*, 79.
38. As Sarah Hale, editor of *Godey's*, put it, "At the head of the living Women of Genius who now make England distinguished as the favored country in Europe for the development of virtues, [are] the talents and the true graces of womanhood. . . . Even the most impassioned passages of her poems are characterized by a sweet feminine delicacy and purity of tone." Hale, *Woman's Record; or Sketches of All Distinguished Women* (New York: Harper & Brothers, 1852), 761, qtd. in Tick, *American Women Composers*, 78.
39. The publisher of these works, Schreiner, opened a music publishing business in Macon, Ga., in 1860. His first pieces are listed in dual imprints with D. P. Faulds of Louisville, Ky., or with Blackmar. The creation of the Confederate States of America resulted in the termination of the relationship with Faulds. (A catalog of Faulds's music publications

during the war years contains numerous pieces named after Union generals, most by the composer C. L. Ward, although a surprising number of Confederate-inspired pieces are also listed.) According to Harwell, the great impetus for music publishing in Georgia began with the fall of New Orleans. At the time the city was occupied, John's son Hermann L. Schreiner was in New Orleans making a purchase. He came back to Macon and established a publishing house there. (One of the more colorful stories of the Civil War involving Schreiner is an incident where he is reported to have traveled to Cincinnati to buy music type from agents of Johnson & Co. of New York in order to set up his own publication company. Federal agents thought he was an Ohioan, and Schreiner got as far as Nashville when he met General Bragg's army and was taken prisoner. They took his pistol but let him keep the type. After one day and night he was allowed to go to Huntsville, Ala., then to Columbus, Ga., and finally to Macon. Harwell, *Confederate Music*, 17, taken from the *Savannah Morning News* and an undated clipping from *Musical Courier*, in Hewitt scrapbooks, Hewitt MSS, Emory University Library.) The Schreiners later moved to Savannah and acquired the music business of W. D. Zogbaum & Co., which was called the "Savannah Firm of Schreiner & Oxenius" but was later altered to "John C. Schreiner & Son." A key to the Schreiners' success was the acquisition of exclusive publication rights for the music of John Hill Hewitt (21 October 1863). Harwell, *Confederate Music*, 17.

40. Undoubtedly, she did not receive remuneration for her works published in the South.

41. This work appears in Tick, *American Women Composers*, 85–87.

42. Tick, "Hodges, Faustina Hasse." Emma Hart Willard (1787–1870) was a pioneer in women's education in the United States. The school at Troy opened in 1821.

43. According to Harwell, New Orleans had an older music tradition than any other southern city. Émile Johns was its first music publisher. In 1824, he is listed as teacher on pianoforte, *maître de piano*. By 1837, Johns was the head of E. Johns & Co., and he published *Album Louisianais* (with Pleyel Publishing Co.), c. 1837. Harwell, *Confederate Music*, 9.

44. While Hohnstock undoubtedly performed as a professional pianist, we cannot be certain that Siegling did. Her compositions indicate that she was probably a capable player, and her dedications to a variety of women associated with music in famous circles also supports exposure to a variety of situations that suggest professional aspiration.

45. This in spite of the continued popularity of the "Battle of Prague."

46. We do not know if Frances Thomas, music teacher at the South Carolina Female Collegiate Institute, was a southerner, nor can Mrs. E. H. Anderson be specifically located in the South. Thomas would not have been a "lady" if she earned her living as a teacher.

47. The exact dates of publication for the Hodges, Norton, and Badarzewska works are unknown, but they are included here because they might have been published in 1860.

48. The two "Keowee Waltzes" sets obviously go together, and the same publisher brought out the "Jasper Guards March."

49. Flora Byrne, as noted earlier, was living in Missouri at the time. Mrs. M. B. Scott's work ("Bird of Beauty") has no date but is given as 186[?]. The entire work appears in Tick, *American Women Composers*, 104–6. Scott's background remains hidden.

50. The "Offering Polka" attributed to Mary Eugenia C. and the "Affection Polka" attributed to M. E. C. were both published in Baltimore by Benteen in 1854. As such, the likelihood is high that they are the same person.

51. On this work and its composer, see Loesser, *Men, Women and Pianos*, 506–7.

52. Tick reproduces Hohnstock's "Concert Polka" in *American Women Composers*, 127–38.

53. Schreiber was born in 1831. No other information has come to light concerning Ellen Ervin. Joseph Bloch published the work in Mobile, Ala.

54. A Fanny Heron is listed as one of the passengers on a steamship landing in New York from Bremen in 1870. *New York Times*, 7 May 1870. In 1860, according to the *New York Tribune*, Miss Fanny Heron, mezzo-soprano, made her singing *début* in November in New York. Qtd. in *Dwight's Journal of Music*, 3 November 1860, 255. The Old Park Theatre and Dublin references are found in Winter, *Vagrant Memories*, 62.

55. Blegen, *With Pen and Pencil on the Frontier*, 78, 82–84, 85.

56. This autobiography makes for a fascinating account of musical culture in the United States, Europe, and Cuba during the nineteenth century. The Marie R. Siegling listed on music publications is indeed the author of this book, Mary Regina Siegling Schuman-LeClercq.

57. I am most grateful to Jewel Smith, who helped identify Marie Siegling's mother and her education (personal correspondence, October 2007).

58. Oddly, the daughter (Marie/Mary Regina) does not mention her mother's name, other than to note that her maiden name was "Schmerle" [*sic*]. The 1860 census for John Siegling lists his wife as Mary, but born in South Carolina. John is listed as Prussian; Marie Siegling puts his place of birth as Stuttgart. The sons of Mary and John have the same names that Mary Regina gives as her brothers in her book. Mary Regina was born in Charleston in 1824. As to Mary Regina's mother, Jewel Smith has graciously shared information on Mary Schnierle that indicates that she entered the Bethlehem Moravian Seminary in 1817 and married John Siegling in 1823 (personal correspondence, October 2007)

59. Born in Cuba, La comtesse Merlin held fashionable salons in France, Switzerland, and Italy (attended by people such as Chopin and Victor Hugo), corresponded with both Chopin and George Sand, and apparently knew many of the celebrated musicians of the day. She also was considered to hold culturally progressive ideas. See Hébert, *La comtesse de Merlin*.

60. Schuman-LeClercq, *Memoirs of a Dowager*, 6–8.

61. Marie Anna Leopoldine, daughter of Karoline Friederike Wilhelmine Princess of Baden and Maximilian I Josef King of Bavaria. Marie married Frédéric-Auguste II in 1833.

62. A "Miss M. R. Siegling" also composed at least two songs (published by Willig); these are probably the work of the same woman. These compositions by Siegling appear to be the only ones of hers that have survived, and from the capable handling of musical style seen in them, she probably composed more.

63. Mrs. J. M. C. left enough clues about her through her dedications and place names, however, that her close acquaintances probably knew who she was.

64. Adelene may or may not have been a southerner.

65. Robert C. Reinders mentions that Mme. E[milie] Lavillebeuvre composed "Reverie," which in 1849 was declared "la première composition musicale écrit par und dame Créole." According to a local review, her songs were comparable to those of Schubert. (He cites *La Violette, Revue Musicale et Littéraire*, December 1849.) Lavillebeuvre is the same woman pianist described in E. Ripley's *Social Life in Old New Orleans*. Reinders also names Mme. Thomas Morphy as a composer in New Orleans from the 1850s. Reinders, *End of An Era*, 192, 195.

66. Fought, *Southern Womanhood and Slavery*, 122.

67. The ages do not figure correctly for the various censuses; however, the ages of the children, their names, and occupations indicate that the 1860, 1870, and 1880 records relate to the same person. Cowdin may have fabricated her age for any of the censuses.

68. Faust discusses women refugees, such as Kate Stone, who read works by Tennyson, Shakespeare, and Scott and particularly *Harper's* in *Mothers of Invention*, 158.

69. The entire text of this book is available at the Institute for Advanced Technology in the Humanities Web site, http://www.iath.virginia.edu/utc/proslav/prfivgca1t.html (accessed 16 April 2006).

70. *Dwight's Journal of Music*, 1856, 372.

8. BECOMING USEFUL

1. Whites, *Civil War as a Crisis in Gender*, 20.

2. Pope, "Preparation for Pedestals," 159.

3. *Weekly Post*, 28 February 1852, qtd. in Johnson, *Ante-bellum North Carolina*, 230.

4. Anon., "Wife, Mistress, Lady," 281.

5. Pope, "Preparation for Pedestals," 27–28, quoting Richard T. Brumby to Ann Eliza Brumby, 3 April 1858, RTB Papers, SHC. See also Jabour, *Scarlett's Sisters*, 52.

6. Fox-Genovese, "Scarlett O'Hara," 398–99.

7. Chandler, "Belle of the Opera," 3.

8. Ibid., 3–4.

9. Qtd. in Pope, "Preparation for Pedestals," 169.

10. Whites, *Civil War as a Crisis in Gender*, 47.

11. Ibid., 56.

12. Faust, *Mothers of Invention*, 26.

13. Fought, *Southern Womanhood and Slavery*, 121.

14. Legg and MacLean qtd. in Faust, *Mothers of Invention*, 26–27.

15. See ibid., 26–28.

16. *Charleston Mercury*, 20 March 1862.

17. The South Caroliniana archivists have dated this performance 20 March 1862, according to Henry G. Fulmer, Curator of Manuscripts, SCL (personal correspondence, January 2008).

18. See various programs listed in Hindman, "Concert Life in Ante Bellum Charleston," vol. 2.

19. Broadside Collection, SCL.

20. Elizabeth Sloman later moved to New York where she taught and gave concerts, as per an announcement of a concert in the *New York Times*, 28 March 1900.

21. Whether or not these are the same women who participated in the concert in Charleston in 1862 is unknown, as is the economic status of the people involved.

22. Filia, "Agnes," *Southern Literary Messenger* 37, no. 8 (August 1863): 437.

9. CONFEDERATE WOMEN COMPOSERS

1. *Southern Literary Messenger* 33 (October 1861): 317.

2. Virginia Cowdin to Jefferson Davis, 17 March 1861, Jefferson Davis Papers, Manuscripts and Archives, Sterling Memorial Library, Yale University.

3. See Faust, *Mothers of Invention*, 157–63. On Evans and *Macaria*, see also Moss, *Domestic Novelists in the Old South*, 174–76.

4. This was somewhat overtly modest, as Evans's previous novel, *Beulah*, was already a best-seller and nationally recognized. See Sexton, *Southern Woman of Letters*, 42.

5. Faust, *Mothers of Invention*, 168–69.

6. Evans's earlier works espouse pro-southern sentiments as tensions mounted before the conflict.

7. Evans, *Macaria*, 380, qtd. in Faust, *Mothers of Invention*, 175; see also p. 172. *Macaria* is available on the Web at *Documenting the American South*, http://docsouth.unc.edu/imls/macaria/menu.html (accessed 3 July 2005).

8. Evans, *Macaria*, 410, qtd. in Faust, *Mothers of Invention*, 173.

9. Sexton, *Southern Woman of Letters*, xxx.

10. Not all of the pieces that appeared in the antebellum period under the mask of "lady" came from different women. See discussion in chap. 8. Another factor that affects the numbers is the appearance of "Summer Wind, Summer Wind" (by Miss C. M. C. of Baltimore) in two places.

11. The two attributed to Flora Byrne of Missouri have not been included in these calculations because of Missouri's status during the war.

12. *Raleigh Register*, 16 June 1840, paraphrased in Johnson, *Ante-bellum North Carolina*, 142.

13. Thornwell, *Lady's Guide to Perfect Gentility*, 97.

14. East, *Sarah Morgan*, 16 June 1862, pp. 121–22.

15. This number does not include the pieces by Sallie Parkington (born in England), Octavie Romey (a professional French pianist and composer), Elizabeth Sloman (a professional English musician), and Mrs. M. B. Scott (whose provenance remains unknown but whose work appeared in Boston and nowhere else). The pieces by Sloman and Romey are pro-Confederate as well. Ella Wren has been included in these numbers. Although she was born in England, she remained in the South throughout the war and entertained troops regularly. For example, Wren toured the South during the war with Charles Morton (a comedian from Richmond) and John Hill Hewitt in places like Macon. Fife, "Confederate Theater in Georgia," 195–96.

16. A total of almost one thousand pieces were published by Confederate houses during the war years. D. Thompson, "Piano Music in the South," 11.

17. Styles and trends in parlor songs are described in Finson, *Voices That Are Gone*.

18. Several of the piano works included here are briefly described in D. Thompson, "Piano Music in the South." Cooke provides information on most of the songs in "Southern Women, Southern Voices."

19. On paper shortages in the South, see Harwell, *Confederate Music*, 18.

20. D. Thompson, "Southern Piano Music during the Civil War," 115.

21. Edward L. Ripley's "Southern Rights Polka" is in B major, but few others venture into that many sharps.

22. Philip Werlein came to the United States in 1831 and worked first as a music teacher, moving into the music business in Vicksburg in 1842. By 1850, he was in New Orleans; in 1853, he was part of Ashbrand & Werlein; and in 1854, Werlein bought a company from W. T. Mayo. In that year, he was the leading music publisher in New Orleans. He did not take the oath of allegiance and ceased publishing after the Union took the city. Mr. and Mrs. Henri Wehrmann, engravers, saved Werlein's pianos during the war, which he sold after the war to re-establish his business. One of the three leading publishers in New Orleans during the Civil War (along with Blackmar and Louis Grünewald), Werlein reopened his business in 1865.

23. Published by Balmer & Weber in St. Louis.

24. Cooke, "Southern Women, Southern Voices," 98–99.

25. She may also be "Miss C. M. C. of Baltimore" who published "Summer Wind, Summer Wind" in 1854, since the titles of "Miss" and "Mrs." were sometimes incorrect. (Mrs. M. B. Scott is listed as "Miss" on at least one printing of the "Bird of Beauty.")

26. On composer Jane Sloman, see Tick, *American Women Composers*, 188–91.

27. Cooke notes that her song expressing northern sentiment, "Barbara Frietche," appeared in 1874 and that all of her songs may have been the result of commissions. Cooke, "Southern Women, Southern Voices," 73.

28. Hoole, "Charleston Theatricals," 541.

29. Program reproduced in Hindman, "Concert Life in Ante Bellum Charleston," 2:580.

30. William Henry Orchard was born 14 August 1811 in Bath, England, and married Helen Zubly Williams on 3 January 1836 at Beech Island, S.C. He died in 1880 in Columbia, S.C., and she in 1909. A descendant of the family has collected a tale of a heroic demonstration before Sherman's troops by W. H. Orchard, in which he stood at the top of the stairs leading into the school daring the Union troops to enter (personal communication with Mr. Gary Hardy, August 2005).

31. The Fourth North Carolina Troops, mentioned on the sheet music, were a regimental brigade from the piedmont and coastal plains area of North Carolina that achieved a great deal of respect, particularly for their efforts at Gettysburg.

32. Her father, Amos J. Battle, was a cofounder of the Chowan Baptist Female Institute and an original trustee of Wake Forest College. Cooke, "Southern Women, Southern Voices," 64.

33. On the Harrells, see *Biblical Recorder*, 19 December 1906, Harrell obituary, p. 15, c. 3; and William Bernard Harrell, "Autobiography," 246, 275–76, in Harrell Family Papers, J. Murray Atkins Library, Special Collections, University of North Carolina at Charlotte. Another of their collaborative works is "Ho! for Carolina," with "Words and music by Dr. William Bernard Harrell" and arrangement by "Ann Battle Harrell." (A roller organ cob for this work exists according to the Web site *Roller Organ Cobology*, http://cobs.rollerorgans.com/cobs/305/home [accessed August 2008]. Its date is unknown.) All of these pieces are described in Cooke, "Southern Women, Southern Voices," 64–66.

34. According to Cooke, Anna Dixon married Reverend Isham G. Hearn in 1852. Cooke, "Southern Women, Southern Voices," 59. Her source for this marriage record is Donahue, *Biographical Sketches of Decatur County*, available at the Tennessee Genealogy and History Web site, http://www.tngenweb.org/goodspeed/decatur/bios.html (accessed March 2008). According to Bobby C. Barnes in *Chester County, Tennessee*, 70, the Hearn men were well-respected Methodist ministers. There is no mention of a marriage to Anna, nor to anyone else, for Isham Garland Hearn.

35. For more on Isham Hearn, see Clayton, *History of Davidson County*.

36. Biographical information on Delia Jones is presented in Cooke, "Southern Women, Southern Voices," 19–20.

37. D. Jones, "Manner of Educating Females," 235.

38. According to Cooke, per the *Biblical Recorder*, 20 (or 26) April 1861 (date partially illegible), in "Southern Women, Southern Voices," 21.

39. Since her husband was married to someone else according to the 1900 census, Delia presumably died sometime in the final decade of the nineteenth century.

40. *Florida Herald*, 22 July 1829, qtd. in Housewright, *History of Music and Dance in Florida*, 115.

41. Advertised in the *Florida Union*, 30 December 1865, qtd. in Williams, "History of Music in Jacksonville," 45.

42. Cooke, "Southern Women, Southern Voices," 75.

43. Popular composer Theodore La Hache also composed a work commemorating Mme. Beauregard: "Elegy on the Death of Mme. G. T. Beauregard," a portion of which is reproduced in Thompson, "Piano Music in the South," 84–85.

44. *Allgemeine musikalische Zeitung* 7 (February 1842): 149.

45. *L'Abeille de la Nouvelle-Orléans*, 28 July 1862.

46. Early, *Campbell Chronicles*. The plantation, later called "Hoveloke" and "Clarkton" and now "Ardross," is part of the Staunton River Tour (see *OldHalifax.com* at http://www.oldhalifax.com/county/ClarktonPlantation:htm, accessed March 2008).

47. F. Dawson, "Our Women in the War," 29–30. This story is also retold in Abel, *Singing the New Nation*, 69–70.

48. Their cousin Rebecca Lloyd Nicholson boasted that she could get it printed, as her grandmother had "The Star-Spangled Banner" fifty years earlier.

49. Armand Edward Blackmar was born in Vermont in 1826. He moved to Cleveland in 1834 and graduated from Western Reserve College in 1845. Shortly afterward, Blackmar moved to the South, working as a music teacher in Huntsville, Ala., until 1852. Between 1852 and 1855, Blackmar served as professor of music at Centenary College, Jackson, La. The man who would be known primarily as a publisher opened his first music store in 1856 in the town of Jackson, Miss. In 1858, Blackmar joined E. D. Patton in the operation of a music store in Vicksburg. Armand's younger brother Henry Clay Blackmar entered business with him, and in 1859 the brothers bought out Patton. Blackmar worked not only as a businessman but also as a composer, publishing under various pseudonyms including A. Noir, A. E. A. Muse, Ye Comic, Dudie Diamonds, and A. Pender.

In 1860, they moved to 74 Camp St., New Orleans, sold pianos and music, and began a music publishing business that would issue more music than any other southern publisher before the end of the Civil War. Upon the occupation of the city by Union troops in April 1862, General Butler raided all Blackmar's goods, and the Confederate States copyrights were confiscated. Harwell, *Confederate Music*, 11, 17, quoting from a letter from Henry C. Blackmar, New Orleans, 9 March 1893, printed in Mildred Lewis Rutherford, *The South in History and Literature*, 254, and quoting [Lizzie Cary Daniel], *Confederate Scrap-Book* (Richmond: J. L. Hill, 1893), 190. At this time, the Blackmars located their business in Augusta, Ga.; from June to November, "A. E. Blackmar & Bros." existed on 255 Broad St. in Augusta, and in November, they moved to 199 Broad St., remaining there until April 1865. Before the Blackmar brothers arrived in Augusta, only one piece (by Beethoven) had been published in that city, by M. M. Cohen & Co., Augusta merchants. While in Augusta, the Blackmars maintained a close connection with the Schreiners for a while. The first advertisement for the Blackmar company in Augusta appeared in the *Daily Constitutionalist* on 15 June 1862. A new store was announced on 5 July 1862 at 255 Broad St. Harwell, *Confederate Music*, 19. Harwell lists specific details of the Blackmar/Schreiner relationship. On 13 September 1862, the firm moved to 199 Broad St., and Henry ran the Augusta branch while Armand remained in New Orleans. At the close of the war, the Blackmar stock remaining in their hands was re-copyrighted under U.S. law, and a notice was overprinted on Confederate-printed title pages. As is well documented elsewhere, Armand Blackmar suffered particularly under the occupation of General Benjamin Butler: even though he took the oath of allegiance, he was imprisoned for publishing "The Bonnie Blue Flag" after Butler's arrival in the city. Naturally, his publishing business suffered, and in time the leading music publisher in Augusta became John Hill Hewitt. On 10 April 1865, before news of Lee's surrender, Hewitt bought the entire stock of Blackmar's Augusta house. The inventory survives in a letter (dated 20 January 1865) to George Dunn, a publisher chiefly located in Richmond, Va., but who also had interests in Columbia, S.C., and Augusta. Harwell states that these are the only Confederate music business records now known to be in existence. Harwell, *Confederate Music*, 20–21.

50. Abel credits the first edition of "Maryland! My Maryland!" to the publishers Miller and Beachem in Baltimore, in an arrangement by C. E. (Charles Ellerbrock—a German music teacher who also wrote several pro-southern songs of his own during the war), 1861. He notes that these editions were out of New Orleans, but the first Blackmar edition clearly states Augusta first. Abel, *Singing the New Nation*, 71.

51. Another consideration in the story of Confederate women's composition is the place of publication, for New Orleans not only produced more extant Confederate music than any other southern city (despite being essentially shut down upon arrival of General Butler) but also allowed a female engraver, Clementine Wehrmann (wife of Henri), to produce music in midcentury. Jumonville, "Set to Music," 103–8.

52. In Butler, *Autobiography and Personal Reminiscences*, 418.

53. See, for example, Sarah Morgan's comments on Butler's proclamation in her diary. East, *Sarah Morgan*, p. 76.

54. Faust discusses the manipulation present in this and other similar incidents, as well as its reverse action of empowering women as political beings, in *Mothers of Invention*, 209, 246–47.

55. *New Orleans Daily Picayune*, 29 September 1861, p. 4. Breaux reached the status of colonel.

56. David Thompson states that because he was a recent immigrant, Grünewald did not publish patriotic music. D. Thompson, "Piano Music in the South," 12. That may be the case, but the "Continental Polka Mazurka" was certainly composed for and dedicated to the aid of soldiers, and Mrs. Francis Fernandez's dedication to "Tillie's Waltz" specifically points to the local volunteers.

57. A portion of this work appears in D. Thompson, "Piano Music in the South," 56.

58. Another example of such a dedication is by Mrs. C. McC[onnell], who asked that the proceeds from "Our Triumph at Manassas" be used "to aid the wounded in Virginia."

59. Lucy Rebecca Buck, *Sad Earth, Sweet Heaven*, 50, qtd. in Faust, *Mothers of Invention*, 3.

60. Clinton observes that after the war, "women who had temporarily assumed roles which had previously been restricted to males, women who had faced adversity and risen to the occasion, were forced back into traditional roles as dependents. Even those who were required by economic necessity to take on wage labor curtsied at the altar of patriarchal hegemony. Traditional sex roles were rigidly reinforced following a brief period of women's agency and achievement." Clinton and Silber, *Battle Scars*, 73.

61. Evans, letter to J. L. M. Curry, 7 October 1865, qtd. in Sexton, *Southern Woman of Letters*, 107.

62. Moss, *Domestic Novelists in the South*, 10.

63. East, *Sarah Morgan*, 9 May 1862, p. 65.

64. Ibid., 11 May 1862, pp. 68–69.

65. F. Dawson, "Our Women in the War," 5–6.

66. Ibid., p. 25.

Bibliography

PRIMARY SOURCES

Manuscript Collections

Alabama Department of Archives and History, Montgomery
> *Mary Rawson Diary*
> *Mary D. Waring Diary*

Dwight Anderson Music Library, University of Louisville, Kentucky
> *Louisville Music Publications of the 19th Century Collection, compiled by Marion Korda*

J. Murray Atkins Library, Special Collections, University of North Carolina at Charlotte
> *Harrell Family Papers*

Charleston Museum, Charleston, South Carolina
> *Sheet Music Bound Collection*

Emory University Library, Atlanta, Georgia
> *Hewitt MSS*
> *Hewitt Scrapbooks*

Georgia Historical Society, Savannah
> *Uncataloged items*

Georgia State Archives, Morrow
> *Confederate Diaries*

Greensboro College Brock Historical Museum

Louisiana and Lower Mississippi Valley Collections, Department of Archives and
> Manuscripts, Louisiana State University Libraries, Baton Rouge
> *William T. Johnson and Family Memorial Papers*

Moravian Archives, Archie K. Davis Center, Winston-Salem, North Carolina
> *Van Vleck Family Folder*

Museum of the Confederacy, Richmond, Virginia
> *Eleanor S. Brockenbrough Library*
> *June Kimble, "The 14th Tenn. Glee Club"*

Rare Book, Manuscript, and Special Collections Library, Duke University, Durham
> *Historic American Sheet Music Collection*

South Carolina Historical Society, Charleston
> *Anderson Papers*
> *Blanch Herminie Petit Barbot File*

South Carolina Historical Society, Columbia
> *Elizabeth Waties (Allston) Pringle Diary*

South Caroliniana Library, University of South Carolina, Columbia
> *Barhamville Notes, compiled by Henry Campbell Davis*
> *Broadside Collection*
> *Ellen Cooper Johnson Memoirs*
> *Manuscript I&O*
> *Louisa McCord Smythe Reminiscences*
> *Moultrie Reid Wilson Papers*

Southern Historical Collection, University of North Carolina, Chapel Hill
> *DeRosset II Family Papers*
> *Pettigrew Family Papers*
> *Robert Smith Phifer Papers*
> *Jane Sivley Letters*
> *Thompson Family Papers*
> *Sarah Lois Wadley Papers*
> *Anita Dwyer Withers Diary*

Sterling Memorial Library, Manuscripts and Archives, Yale University
> *Jefferson Davis Papers*

UNC Music Library, University of North Carolina, Chapel Hill

Newspapers, Magazines, and Related Materials

L'Abeille de la Nouvelle-Orléans
Allgemeine musikalische Zeitung
Arkansas Gazette (Little Rock)
Augusta Daily Constitutionalist
Biblical Recorder
Charleston Mercury
Charleston News & Courier
Charleston Tri-Weekly News
Columbus Enquirer
Confederate Veteran (Elm Springs, Tenn.)
Debow's Review (New Orleans; August, Ga.)
Durham Morning Herald
Dwight's Journal of Music
Florida Herald (St. Augustine)
Florida Union
Godey's Lady's Book
Graham's Magazine
Greensboro Daily News
Harper's New Monthly Magazine
Hillsborough (N.C.) Recorder
Ladies' Repository
Nashville Daily Gazette
Nashville Patriot
New Orleans Daily Picayune
New Orleans Times-Democrat
New York Musical World
New York Times
New York Tribune
Raleigh Register
Raleigh Star
Richmond Enquirer
Richmond Times Dispatch
Savannah Morning News
Savannah Newspaper Digest
Southern Agriculturalist
Southern Literary Messenger

Southern Quarterly Review
Willig's Musical Magazine

Census Records

U.S. Bureau of the Census. Manuscript Census Schedules. Sixth (1840), Seventh (1850),
Eighth (1860), Ninth (1870), and Tenth (1880) Censuses. *Heritagequestonline.com*,
http://www.heritagequestononline.com (accessed 16 October 2009).

Books, Articles, and Related Materials

Anderson, John Q. *Brokenburn: The Journal of Kate Stone, 1861–1868*. Baton Rouge:
Louisiana State University Press, 1955.

Anon. "Wife, Mistress, Lady." *Southern Cultivation* 7 (1873): 281.

Ashkenazi, Elliott, ed. *The Civil War Diary of Clara Solomon: Growing Up in New Orleans,
1861–1862*. Baton Rouge: Louisiana State University Press, 1995.

Ayer, Brother Lewis M. "Freemasonry and Female Education." Address to the Cokesbury
Masonic Female College, Greenwood, S.C., 28 October 1858. Charleston: Burke, 1858.

*A Barhamville Miscellany. Notes and Documents Concerning the South Carolina Female
Collegiate Institute 1826–1865*. Chiefly from the collection of the late Henry Campbell
Davis. Edited by Henning Cohen. Columbia: University of South Carolina Press, 1956.

Blackiston, Henry C. *Refugees in Richmond: Civil War Letters of a Virginia Family*. New
Jersey: Princeton University Press, 1989.

Blandin, Mrs. I. M. E. *History of Higher Education of Women in the South Prior to 1860*.
New York: Neale Publishing, 1909.

Blegen, Theodore C., ed. *With Pen and Pencil on the Frontier in 1851: The Diary and
Sketches of Frank Blackwell Mayer*. St. Paul: Minnesota Historical Society, 1932.

Bonner, James C., ed. *The Journal of a Milledgeville Girl, 1861–1867*. Athens: University of
Georgia Press, 1964.

The Boston Academy's Collection of Church Music . . . Boston: J. H. Wilkins and R. B.
Carter, 1836.

Bowen, Clarissa Adger. *The Diary of Clarissa Adger Bowen, Ashtabula Plantation, 1865:
With Excerpts*. Edited by Mary Stevenson. Pendleton, S.C.: Foundation for Historic
Restoration in Pendleton Area, Research and Publication Committee, 1973.

Brown, James D., and Stephen S. Stratton. *British Musical Biography: A Dictionary of
Musical Artists, Authors, and Composers Born in Britain and Its Colonies*. Birmingham,
U.K.: Chadfield & Son, 1897.

Bryan, Mary Norcott. *A Grandmother's Recollection of Dixie*. New Bern, N.C.: Owen G.
Dunn, 1912.

Buck, Lucy Rebecca. *Sad Earth, Sweet Heaven: The Diary of Lucy Rebecca Buck*. Edited by
William Pettus Buck. Birmingham, Ala.: Cornerstone, 1973.

Burr, Virginia Ingraham, ed. *The Secret Eye: The Journal of Ella Gertrude Clanton Thomas,
1848–1889*. Chapel Hill: University of North Carolina Press, 1990.

Burton, J. *Lectures on Female Education and Manners*. Baltimore: Samuel Jeffries, 1811.

Burton, Lewis William, and Robert Alonzo Brock. *The Annals of Henrico Parish, Diocese of
Virginia*. Richmond: Williams Printing Company, 1904.

Burwell, Letitia M. *A Girl's Life in Virginia before the War*. New York: Frederick A. Stokes, 1895.

Butler, Benjamin F. *Autobiography and Personal Reminiscences of Major-General Benjamin
F. Butler: Butler's Book*. Boston: Thayer, 1892.

Calhoun, John C. *The Papers of John C. Calhoun*. Vol. 28. Edited by Clyde Wilson.
Columbia: University of South Carolina Press, 1993.

Chandler, Joseph. "The Belle of the Opera, Essays upon a Woman's Accomplishment, Her Character and Her Mission." *Graham's Magazine* 34, no. 1 (January 1849): 3–7.

Chesnut, Mary. *Two Years, or The Way We Lived Then*. In *Two Novels by Mary Chesnut*, edited by Elisabeth Muhlenfeld. Charlottesville: University of Virginia Press, 2002.

Clay-Clopton, Virginia. *A Belle of the Fifties: Memoirs of Mrs. Clay, of Alabama, Covering Social and Political Life in Washington and the South, 1853–66*. New York: Doubleday, Page, & Company, 1905.

Clayton, W. Woodford. *History of Davidson County, Tennessee*. Philadelphia: J. W. Lewis and Co., 1880.

Cowdin, Mrs. V. G. *Ellen: or, The Fanatic's Daughter*. Mobile, Ala.: S. H. Goetzel & Company, 1860.

Davis, Varina Howell. *Jefferson Davis: A Memoir by His Wife*. Reprint ed. Vol. 1. Baltimore: Nautical and Aviation Publishing of America, 1990.

Dawson, Captain Francis W. "Our Women in the War." Address, Fifth Annual Reunion of the Association of the Maryland Line at the Academy of Music, Baltimore, 22 February 1887. Charleston, 1887.

Dawson, Sarah Morgan. *A Confederate Girl's Diary*. Boston: Houghton Mifflin, 1913.

De Forest, John William. *Miss Ravenel's Conversion: From Secession to Loyalty*. 1867.

Donahue, David. *Biographical Sketches of Decatur County*. Nashville: Goodspeed Publishing Co., History of Tennessee, 1886.

Eppes, Susan Bradford. *Through Some Eventful Years*. Macon: J. W. Burke Co., 1926.

Evans, Augusta. *Macaria*. Richmond, Va: West & Johnson, 1864.

Fries, Adelaide L. *Historical Sketch of Salem Female Academy*. Salem, N.C.: Crist & Keehlin, 1902.

Garnett, James. *Lectures on Female Education, Comprising the First and Second Series of a Course Delivered to Mrs. Garnett's Pupils, at Elm-Wood, Essex County, Virginia*. Richmond: Thomas W. White, 1825.

Greensborough Female College Established by the North Carolina Conference of the Methodist Episcopal Church 1846. Greensborough: Swaim and Sherwood, 1848.

Greve, Charles Theodore. *Centennial History of Cincinnati and Representative Citizens*. Cincinnati: Biographical Publishing Co., 1904.

Hale, Sarah J. *Woman's Record: or Sketches of All Distinguished Women*. New York: Harper & Brothers, 1852.

Harland, Marion [Mary Virginia Hawes Terhune]. *The Secret of a Happy Home*. New York: Louis Klopsch, 1896.

Jones, Charles Edgeworth. *Education in Georgia*. Washington, D.C.: Government Printing Office, 1889.

Jones, Delia Wright. "Manner of Educating Females." *North Carolina Journal of Education* 2 (1859): 227–37.

Kellogg Strakosch, Clara Louise. *Memoirs of an American Prima Donna*. Introduction by Isabel Moore. New York: Putnam, 1913.

King, Spencer Bidwell, Jr. *Ebb Tide: As Seen through the Diary of Josephine Clay Habersham, 1863*. Macon, Ga.: Mercer University Press, 1987.

King, Susan Petigru [Bowen]. *The Actress in High Life*. New York: Derby & Jackson, 1860.

———. *Lily: A Novel*. Introduction by Jane H. Pease and William H. Pease. Durham: Duke University Press, 1993. Originally published by *Harper's* in 1855.

Lawrence, Vera Brodsky. *Strong on Music: The New York Music Scene in the Days of George Templeton Strong, 1836–1875*. Vol. 1, *Resonances 1836–1850*. New York: Oxford University Press, 1988.

Lieber, Francis, E. Wigglesworth, and Thomas Gamaliel Bradford. *Encyclopædia Americana: A Popular Dictionary of Arts, Sciences, Literature*. Philadelphia: Thomas, Cowperthwait, & Co., 1838.

Long, Ellen Call. *Florida Breezes, or, Florida New and Old*. Jacksonville: Ashmead, 1862.

Longstreet, Helen Dortch. *Lee and Longstreet at High Tide: Gettysburg in the Light of the Official Record*. Published by author, 1905.

MacIntosh, Maria. *Two Lives; or To Seem and To Be*. New York, 1846. Reprint, New York, 1865.

Macon, Emma Cassandra Riely. *Reminiscences of the Civil War*. Cedar Rapids: Torch Press, 1911.

Marks, Elias, M.D. *Hints on Female Education*. Columbia: A. S. Johnston, 1851.

McCord, Louisa. *Caius Gracchus: A Tragedy in Five Acts*. 1851.

Miers, Early Schenck, ed. *When the World Ended: The Diary of Emma LeConte*. New York: Oxford University Press, 1957.

Miles, William Porcher. "Women 'Nobly Planned'—How to Educate Our Girls." Address before the Young Ladies of the Yorkville Female College, Yorkville, S.C. Also in *True Education*. Columbia, S.C.: Presbyterian Publishing House, 1882.

Murray, Elizabeth Dunbar. *My Mother Used to Say: A Natchez Belle of the Sixties*. Boston: Christopher Publishing House, 1959.

Nash, Ann Spotswood Strudwick. *Ladies in the Making (also a Few Gentlemen) at the Select Boarding and Day School of the Misses Nash and Kollock, 1859–1890, Hillsborough, North Carolina*. Hillsborough, N.C.: Ann S. S. Nash, 1964.

O'Brien, Michael, ed. *An Evening When Alone: Four Journals of Single Women in the South, 1827–67*. Charlottesville: University Press of Virginia, 1993.

Our Women in the War: The Lives They Lived; the Deaths They Died. Charleston: News and Courier Book Presses, 1885.

Polk, Mary Branch Jones. *Memories of a Southern Woman "Within the Lines," and Genealogical Record*. Chicago: Joseph G. Branch, 1912.

Pringle, Elizabeth Waties Allston. *Chronicles of Chicora Wood*. New York: Scribner's, 1922.
———. *A Woman Rice Planter*. New York: Macmillan, 1913. Reprinted with an introduction by Charles Joyner. Columbia: University of South Carolina Press, 1992.

Ravenel, Mrs. St. Julian [Harriott Horry]. *Charleston, the Place and the People*. New York: Macmillan, 1912.

Reichel, Rev. Levin T. *The Moravians in North Carolina: An Authentic History*. Salem, N.C.: Keehlin; Philadelphia: Lippincott, 1857.

Ripley, Eliza Moore Chinn McHatton. *Social Life in Old New Orleans, Being Recollections of My Girlhood*. New York: D. Appleton and Company, 1912.

Robertson, Mary D., ed. *A Confederate Lady Comes of Age: The Journal of Pauline DeCaradeuc, 1863–1888*. Columbia: University of South Carolina Press, 1992.
———. *Lucy Breckinridge of Grove Hill: The Journal of a Virginia Girl, 1862–1864*. Columbia: University of South Carolina Press, 1994.

Schuman-LeClercq, Mary Regina Siegling. *Memoirs of a Dowager*. Typescript, South Caroliniana Library, 1908.

Sexton, Rebecca Grant, ed. *A Southern Woman of Letters: The Correspondence of Augusta Jane Evans Wilson*. Columbia: University of South Carolina Press, 2002.

Simons, Elizabeth P. *Music in Charleston from 1732 to 1919*. Charleston: Jno. J. Furlong and Son, Inc., 1927.

Sloan, Dave U. *Fogy Days, and Now: Or, The World Has Changed*. Atlanta: Foote & Davies, 1891.

Smith, Daniel Huger, Alice R. Huger Smith, and Arney R. Childs, eds. *Mason Smith Family Letters, 1860–1868*. Columbia: University of South Carolina Press, 1950.

Snell, William R. *Myra Inman: A Diary of the Civil War in East Tennessee*. Macon, Ga.: Mercer University Press, 2000.

Stubblefield, Sandy. "Music!" *Southern Literary Messenger* 15, no. 1 (January 1849): 23–24.

Sutherland, Daniel E., ed. *A Very Violent Rebel: The Diary of Ellen Renshaw House*. Knoxville: University of Tennessee Press, 1996.

[Terhune, Mary Virginia Hawes]. *Marion Harland's Autobiography: The Story of a Long Life*. New York: Harper Brothers, 1910.

Thornwell, Emily. *The Lady's Guide to Perfect Gentility in Manners, Dress, and Conversation, in the Family, in Company, and at the Piano-Forte, the Table, in the Street, and in Gentlemen's Society*. New York: Derby & Jackson, 1856.

Upton, George P[utnam]. *Musical Memories: My Recollections of Celebrities from the Half-Century 1850–1900s*. Chicago: A. C. McClurg & Co., 1908.

Waring, Malvina. "A Confederate Girl's Diary." In *South Carolina Women in the Confederacy*, vol. 1, edited by Mrs. Thomas Taylor. Columbia, S.C.: 1903.

Whitaker, Daniel K. "The Periodical Press." *Southern Quarterly Review* 1, no. 1 (1842): 52.

Wright, Mrs. D. Giraud. *A Southern Girl in '61: The Wartime Memories of a Confederate Senator's Daughter*. New York: Doubleday Press, 1905.

SECONDARY SOURCES

Books

Abel, Ernest Lawrence. *Singing the New Nation: How Music Helped Shape the Confederacy*. Mechanicsburg, Pa.: Stackpole Books, 1999.

Alexander, Adele Logan. *Ambiguous Lives: Free Women of Color in Rural Georgia, 1789–1879*. Fayetteville: University of Arkansas Press, 1991.

Allgor, Catherine. *Parlor Politics: In Which the Ladies of Washington Help Build a City and a Government*. Charlottesville: University Press of Virginia, 2000.

Ammer, Christine. *Unsung: A History of Women in American Music*. New York: Amadeus Press, 2001.

Andrews, Matthew Page. "History of 'Maryland! My Maryland!'" In *Library of Southern Literature*, edited by Edwin Anderson Alderman, Joel Chandler Harris, and Charles William Kent, 16:68. New Orleans: Martin & Hoyt Co., 1909.

Ash, Stephen V. *When the Yankees Came: Conflict and Chaos in the Occupied South, 1861–1865*. Chapel Hill: University of North Carolina Press, 1995.

Barber, E. Susan. "'The White Wings of Eros': Courtship and Marriage in Confederate Richmond." In *Southern Families at War: Loyalty and Conflict in the Civil War South*, edited by Catherine Clinton, 119–32. New York: Oxford University Press, 2000.

Barnes, Bobby C. *Chester County, Tennessee 1882–1995: History and Families*. Henderson, Tenn.: Chester County Historical Society, Turner Publishing Company, 1998.

Bernhard, Virginia, et al., eds. *Southern Women Histories and Identities*. Columbia: University of Missouri Press, 1992.

Berry, Stephen W. *All That Makes a Man: Love and Ambition in the Civil War South*. New York: Oxford University Press, 2003.

Blanton, DeAnne, and Lauren M. Cook *They Fought Like Demons: Women Soldiers in the American Civil War*. Baton Rouge: Louisiana State University Press, 2002.

Blassingame, John. *The Slave Community: Plantation Life in the Antebellum South*. New York: Oxford University Press, 1972.

Blight, Daniel W. *Race and Reunion: The Civil War in American Memory*. Cambridge: Belknap Press, 2001.

Boeringer, James. *Morning Star: The Life and Works of Francis Florentine Hagen (1815–1907): Moravian Evangelist and Composer*. London: Associated University Presses, 1986.

Bryan, Thomas Conn. *Confederate Georgia*. Athens: University of Georgia Press, 1953.

Bynum, Victoria E. *Unruly Women: The Politics of Social and Sexual Control in the Old South*. Chapel Hill: University of North Carolina Press, 1992.

Byrd, Jess, et al. *Salem Academy and College through the Years*. Winston-Salem, N.C.: Salem College Alumnae Association, 1951.

Campbell, Jacqueline Glass. *When Sherman Marched North from the Sea: Resistance on the Confederate Homefront*. Chapel Hill: University of North Carolina Press, 2003.

Carmichael, Peter S. *The Last Generation: Young Virginians in Peace, War, and Reunion*. Chapel Hill: University of North Carolina Press, 2005.

Cashin, Joan E. "Into the Trackless Wilderness: The Refugee Experience in the Civil War." In *A Woman's War: Southern Women, the Civil War, and the Confederate Legacy*, edited by Edward D. C. Campbell Jr. and Kym S. Rice, 29–54. Richmond: Museum of the Confederacy, 1996.

———. *Our Common Affairs: Texts from Women of the Old South*. Baltimore: Johns Hopkins University Press, 1996.

———. "'Since the War Broke Out': The Marriage of Kate and William McClure." In *Divided Houses: Gender and the Civil War*, edited by Catherine Clinton and Nina Silber, 200–212. New York: Oxford University Press, 1992.

Censer, Jane Turner. *North Carolina Planters and Their Children, 1800–1860*. Baton Rouge: Louisiana State University Press, 1984.

———. *The Reconstruction of White Southern Womanhood, 1865–1895*. Baton Rouge: Louisiana State University Press, 2003.

Chambers-Schiller, Lee Virginia. *Liberty, a Better Husband: Single Women in America; The Generations of 1780–1840*. New Haven: Yale University Press, 1984.

Channing, Steven A. *Crisis of Fear: Secession in South Carolina*. New York: Simon and Schuster, 1970.

Citron, Marcia. *Gender and the Musical Canon*. Urbana: University of Illinois Press, 1993, 2000 (paperback).

Clark, J. Bunker, ed. *Anthology of Early American Keyboard Music, 1787–1830*. Middleton, Wis.: A-R Editions, 1977.

Clinton, Catherine. *The Other Civil War: American Women in the Nineteenth Century*. New York: Hill and Wang, 1984.

———. *The Plantation Mistress: Woman's World in the Old South*. New York: Pantheon Books, 1982.

———. "'Public Women' and Sexual Politics in the American Civil War." In *Battle Scars: Gender and Sexuality in the American Civil War*, edited by Catherine Clinton and Nina Silber, 61–77. New York: Oxford University Press, 2006.

———. *Tara Revisited: Women, War, and the Plantation Legend*. New York: Abbeville Press, 1995.

Clinton, Catherine, and Nina Silber, eds. *Battle Scars: Gender and Sexuality in the American Civil War*. New York: Oxford University Press, 2006.

Cook, Susan C., and Judy S. Tsou, eds. *Cecilia Reclaimed: Feminist Perspectives on Gender and Music*. Urbana: University of Illinois Press, 1994.

Cox, Karen. *Dixie's Daughters: The United Daughters of the Confederacy and the Preservation of Confederate Culture*. Gainesville: University Press of Florida, 2003.

Crofts, Daniel W. *Reluctant Confederates: Upper South Unionists in the Secession Crisis.* Chapel Hill: University of North Carolina Press, 1989.

Davenport, F. Garvin. *Cultural Life in Nashville on the Eve of the Civil War.* Chapel Hill: University of North Carolina Press, 1941.

Davis, Robert Scott, ed. *Requiem for a Lost City: A Memoir of Civil War Atlanta and the Old South.* Macon, Ga.: Mercer University Press, 1999.

Dean, Eric. *Shook over Hell: Post-traumatic Stress, Vietnam, and the Civil War.* Cambridge: Harvard University Press, 1999.

DeCredico, Mary A. *Mary Boykin Chesnut: A Confederate Woman's Life.* Lanham, Md.: Rowman and Littlefield, 2002.

Delfano, Susanna, and Michelle Gillespie, eds. *Neither Lady nor Slave: Working Women of the Old South.* Chapel Hill: University of North Carolina Press, 2002.

Early, R. H. *Campbell Chronicles and Family Sketches: Embracing the History of Campbell County, Virginia, 1782–1926.* Lynchburg, Va.: J. P. Bell Company, 1927.

East, Charles, ed. *Sarah Morgan: The Civil War Diary of a Southern Woman.* New York: Touchstone, 1991.

Edwards, Laura F. *Gendered Strife and Confusion: The Political Culture of Reconstruction.* Urbana: University of Illinois Press, 1997.

———. *Scarlett Doesn't Live Here Anymore: Southern Women in the Civil War Era.* Urbana: University of Illinois Press, 2000.

Engstrom, Mary Claire. *The Book of Burwell Students: Lives of Educated Women in the Antebellum South.* Hillsborough, N.C.: Hillsborough Historical Commission, 2007.

Epstein, Dena. *Sinful Tunes and Spirituals.* Urbana: University of Illinois Press, 2003.

Farnham, Christie Anne. *The Education of the Southern Belle: Higher Education and Student Socialization in the Antebellum South.* New York: New York University Press, 1994.

Faust, Drew Gilpin. *The Creation of Confederate Nationalism: Ideology and Identity in the Civil War South.* Baton Rouge: Louisiana State University Press, 1988.

———. *Mothers of Invention: Women of the Slaveholding South in the American Civil War.* Chapel Hill: University of North Carolina Press, 1996.

Federal Writers Project. *South Carolina: A Guide to the Palmetto State.* New York: Oxford University Press, 1941.

Fife, Iline. "The Confederate Theater in Georgia." In *Music in Georgia*, edited by Frank W. Hoogerwerf, 189–99. New York: Da Capo Press, 1984. Originally published in *Georgia Review* 9 (Fall 1955): 305–15.

Finson, Jon W. *The Voices That Are Gone: Themes in 19th-Century American Popular Song.* New York: Oxford University Press, 1994.

Fix, Lou Carol. "The Organ in Moravian Church Music." In *The Music of the Moravian Church in America*, edited by Nola Reed Knouse, 133–68. Rochester, N.Y.: University of Rochester Press, 2008.

Ford, Lacy K. *Origins of Southern Radicalism: The South Carolina Upcountry, 1800–1860.* New York: Oxford University Press, 1991.

Fought, Leigh. *Southern Womanhood and Slavery: A Biography of Louisa S. McCord, 1810–1879.* Columbia: University of Missouri Press, 2003.

Fox-Genovese, Elizabeth. *Within the Plantation Household: Black and White Women of the Old South.* Chapel Hill: University of North Carolina Press, 1988.

Frankenberg, Ruth. *White Women, Race Matters: The Social Construction of Whiteness.* Minneapolis: University of Minnesota Press, 1993.

Fraser, Walter J., Jr., R. Frank Saunders Jr., and John L. Wakelyn, eds. *The Web of Southern Social Relations: Women, Family and Education.* Athens: University of Georgia Press, 1985.

Friedman, Jean E. *The Enclosed Garden: Women and Community in the Evangelical South, 1830–1900*. Chapel Hill: University of North Carolina Press, 1985.

Fries, Adelaide L. *Historical Sketch of Salem Female Academy*. Salem, N.C.: Crist & Keehlin, 1902.

Gallagher, Gary. *The Confederate War: Popular Will, Nationalism, and Strategy*. Cambridge: Harvard University Press, 1997.

Gallagher, Gary, and Alan T. Nolan, eds. *The Myth of the Lost Cause and Civil War History*. Bloomington: Indiana University Press, 2000.

Gardner, Sarah E. *Blood and Irony: Southern White Women's Narratives of the Civil War, 1861–1937*. Chapel Hill: University of North Carolina Press, 2004.

Genovese, Eugene D. *Roll, Jordan, Roll: The World the Slaves Made*. New York: Vintage Books, 1974.

Glickman, Sylvia, ed. *American Women Composers: Piano Music from 1865–1915*. Bryn Mawr, Pa.: Hildegard, 1990.

Glover, Lorri. *All Our Relations: Blood Ties and Emotional Bonds among the Early South Carolina Gentry*. Baltimore: Johns Hopkins University Press, 2000.

Green, Elna C. *Southern Strategies: Southern Women and the Woman Suffrage Question*. Chapel Hill: University of North Carolina Press, 1997.

Greve, Charles Theodore. *Centennial History of Cincinnati and Representative Citizens*. Cincinnati: Biographical Publishing Co., 1904.

Griffin, Frances. *Less Time for Meddling—A History of Salem Academy and College 1772–1866*. Winston-Salem, N.C.: John F. Blair, 1979.

Grimsley, Mark. *The Hard Hand of War: Union Military Policy toward Southern Civilians, 1861–1865*. New York: Cambridge University Press, 1995.

Halttunen, Karen. *Confidence Men and Painted Women: A Study of Middle-Class Culture in America, 1830–1870*. New Haven: Yale University Press, 1982.

Harwell, Richard Barksdale. *Confederate Music*. Chapel Hill: University of North Carolina Press, 1950.

Hébert, Jacques. *La Comtesse de Merlin*. Montreal: VLB Editeur, 2004.

Hess, Earl J. *Lee's Tar Heels: The Pettigrew-Kirkland-MacRae Brigade*. Chapel Hill: University of North Carolina Press, 2002.

Hill, Lois, ed. *Poems and Songs of the Civil War*. New York: Gramercy Books, 2000.

Historical and Cultural Resources Survey of the Clemson University Experimental Forest. 2006. Study directed by Will Hiott. Clemson University Web site, http://www.clemson.edu/cef/pdf%20documents%20for%20cef%20website/Historic%20and%20Cultural%20Resources%20Survey.pdf (accessed July 2008).

Housewright, Wiley L. *A History of Music and Dance in Florida, 1565–1865*. Tuscaloosa: University of Alabama Press, 1991.

Hummel, Ray Orvin, ed. *Southeastern Broadsides before 1877: A Bibliography*. Richmond: Virginia State Library, 1971.

Jabour, Anya. *Marriage in the Early Republic: Elizabeth and William Wirt and the Companionate Ideal*. Baltimore: Johns Hopkins University Press, 1998.

———. *Scarlett's Sisters: Young Women in the Old South*. Chapel Hill: University of North Carolina Press, 2007.

Joal, Joseph. *On Respiration in Singing*. N.p.: F. J. Rebman, 1895.

Johnson, Guion Griffis. *Ante-bellum North Carolina: A Social History*. Chapel Hill: University of Carolina Press, 1937.

Jumonville, Florence M. "Set to Music: The Engravers, Artists, and Lithographers of New Orleans Sheet Music." In *The Cultivation of Artists in Nineteenth-Century America*, edited by Georgia Brady Barnhill, Diana Korzenik, and Caroline F. Sloat, 103–8. Worcester, Mass.: American Antiquarian Society, 1997.

Jones, Jacqueline. *Labor of Love, Labor of Sorrow: Black Women, Work, and the Family from Slavery to the Present*. New York: Vintage Books, 1985.

Kelley, Bruce C., and Mark A. Snell, eds. *Bugle Resounding: Music and Musicians of the Civil War*. Columbia: University of Missouri Press, 2004.

Kett, Joseph F. *Rites of Passage: Adolescence in America, 1790 to the Present*. New York: Basic Books, 1977.

Kierner, Cynthia. *Beyond the Household: Women's Place in the Early South, 1700–1835*. Ithaca: Cornell University Press, 1998.

Kimball, Bruce A. *The "True Professional Ideal in America": A History*. Lanham, Md.: Rowman and Littlefield, 1995.

Klatch, Rebecca E. *A Generation Divided: The New Left, the New Right, and the 1960s*. Berkeley: University of California Press, 1999.

Lebsock, Suzanne. *The Free Women of Petersburg: Status and Culture in a Southern Town, 1784–1860*. New York: W. W. Norton, 1984.

Lemmon, Sarah McCulloh, ed. *The Pettigrew Papers*. Vol. 2, *1819–1843*. Raleigh: North Carolina Department of Cultural Resources Division of Archives and History, 1988.

Litwack, Leon F. *Been in the Storm So Long: The Aftermath of Slavery*. New York: Knopf, 1979.

Loesser, Arthur. *Men, Women and Pianos: A Social History*. New York: Simon and Schuster, 1954. Reprint, New York: Dover, 1990.

Lott, R. Allen. *From Paris to Peoria: How European Piano Virtuosos Brought Classical Music to the American Heartland*. New York: Oxford University Press, 2003.

Marten, James. *The Children's Civil War*. Chapel Hill: University of North Carolina Press, 1998.

Massey, Mary Elizabeth. *Bonnet Brigades*. New York: Knopf, 1966.

———. *Refugee Life in the Confederacy*. Baton Rouge: Louisiana State University Press, 1964.

McArthur, Judith N. *Creating the New Woman: The Rise of the Southern Women's Progressive Culture in Texas, 1893–1918*. Urbana: University of Illinois Press, 1998.

McCurry, Stephanie. *Masters of Small Worlds: Yeomen Households, Gender Relations, and the Political Culture of the Antebellum South Carolina Low Country*. New York: Oxford University Press, 1995.

McMillen, Sally G. *Motherhood in the Old South: Pregnancy, Childbirth, and Infant Rearing*. Baton Rouge: Louisiana State University Press, 1990.

McPherson, James M. *Battle Cry of Freedom: The Civil War Era*. New York: Oxford University Press, 1988.

———. *For Cause and Comrades: Why Men Fought in the Civil War*. New York: Oxford University Press, 1997.

Mohr, Clarence L. *On the Threshold of Freedom: Masters and Slaves in Civil War Georgia*. Athens: University of Georgia Press, 1986.

Moltke-Hansen, David. "The Expansion of Intellectual Life: A Prospectus." In *Intellectual Life in Antebellum Charleston*, edited by Michael O'Brien and David Moltke-Hansen, 3–44. Knoxville: University of Tennessee Press, 1986.

Moss, Elizabeth. *Domestic Novelists in the Old South: Defenders of Southern Culture*. Baton Rouge: Louisiana State University Press, 1992.

Oakes, James. *The Ruling Race: A History of American Slaveholders*. New York: Knopf, 1982.

———. *Slavery and Freedom: An Interpretation of the Old South*. New York: Knopf, 1990.

O'Brien, Michael, and David Moltke-Hansen, eds. *Intellectual Life in Antebellum Charleston*. Knoxville: University of Tennessee Press, 1986.

Orr, Lee. *Alfredo Barili and the Rise of Classical Music in Atlanta*. Atlanta: Scholars Press, 1996.

Painter, Nell Irvin. Introduction to *The Secret Eye: The Journal of Ella Gertrude Clanton Thomas, 1848–1889*, edited by Virginia Ingraham Burr, 1–67. Chapel Hill: University of North Carolina Press, 1990.

Panzeri, Louis. *Louisiana Composers*. New Orleans: Dinstuhl, 1972.

Pease, Jane H., and William H. Pease. *A Family of Women: The Carolina Petigrus in Peace and War*. Chapel Hill: University of North Carolina Press, 1999.

———. *Ladies, Women and Wenches: Choice and Constraint in Antebellum Charleston and Boston*. Chapel Hill: University of North Carolina Press, 1990.

Pease, William H., and Jane H. Pease. *James Louis Petigru: Southern Conservation, Southern Dissenter*. Columbia: University of South Carolina Press, 2002.

———. *The Roman Years of a South Carolina Artist: Caroline Carson's Letters Home, 1872–1892*. Columbia: University of South Carolina Press, 2003.

Potter, David M. *The South and the Sectional Conflict*. Baton Rouge: Louisiana State University Press, 1968.

Preston, Katherine K. *Opera on the Road: Traveling Opera Troupes in the United States, 1825–60*. Urbana: University of Illinois Press, 1993, 2001 (paperback).

Rable, George. *Civil Wars: Women and the Crisis of Southern Nationalism*. Urbana: University of Illinois Press, 1989.

Ransom, Roger L., and Richard Sutch. *One Kind of Freedom: The Economic Consequences of Emancipation*. 2nd ed. New York: Cambridge University Press, 2001.

Reinders, Robert C. *End of an Era: New Orleans, 1850–1860*. New Orleans: Pelican, 1964. Reprint, 1989.

Remson, Michael K. *The Songs of Septimus Winner*. Lanham, Md.: Scarecrow Press, 2003.

Richard, Patricia L. "'Listen Ladies One and All': Union Soldiers Yearn for the Society of Their 'Fair Cousins of the North.'" In *Union Soldiers and the Northern Home Front*, edited by Paul A. Cimbala and Randall M. Miller, 143–81. New York: Fordham University Press, 2002.

Ripley, Peter C. *Slaves and Freedmen in Civil War Louisiana*. Baton Rouge: Louisiana State University Press, 1976.

Roark, James L. *Masters without Slaves: Southern Planters in the Civil War and Reconstruction*. New York: Norton, 1977.

Roberts, Giselle. *The Confederate Belle*. Columbia: University of Missouri Press, 2003.

Rothman, Ellen K. *Hands and Hearts: A History of Courtship in America*. New York: Basic Books, 1984.

Royster, Jacqueline Jones. *Southern Horrors and Other Writings: The Anti-lynching Campaign of Ida B. Wells, 1892–1900*. Bedford Series in History and Culture. Boston: Bedford/St. Martin's, 1997.

Rubin, Sarah Anne. *A Shattered Nation: The Rise and Fall of the Confederacy, 1861–1868*. Civil War America. Chapel Hill: University of North Carolina Press, 2005.

Rutherford, Susan. *The Prima Donna and Opera, 1815–1930*. Cambridge: Cambridge University Press, 2006.

Salley, Katherine Batts, ed. *Life at St. Mary's*. Chapel Hill: University of North Carolina Press, 1942.

Schwalm, Leslie. *A Hard Fight for We: Women's Transition from Slavery to Freedom in South Carolina*. Urbana: University of Illinois Press, 1997.

Scott, Anne Firor. *The Southern Lady: From Pedestal to Politics, 1830–1930.* Chicago: University of Chicago Press, 1970.

Silber, Nina. "Colliding and Collaborating: Gender and Civil War Scholarship." In *Battle Scars: Gender and Sexuality in the American Civil War*, edited by Catherine Clinton and Nina Silber, 3–18. New York: Oxford University Press, 2006.

———. *The Romance of Reunion: Northerners and the South, 1865–1900.* Chapel Hill: University of North Carolina Press, 1993.

Simkins, Francis Butler, and James Welch Patton. *The Women of the Confederacy.* Richmond: Garrett and Massie, 1936.

Smith, Karen Manners. "The Novel." In *The History of Southern Women's Literature*, edited by Carolyn Perry and Mary Louise Weaks, 48–58. Baton Rouge: Louisiana State University Press, 2002.

Solie, Ruth A. *Music in Other Words: Victorian Conversations.* California Studies in 19th-Century Music 12. Berkeley: University of California Press, 2004.

Southall, Geneva Handy. *Blind Tom, the Black Pianist-Composer (1849–1908): Continually Enslaved.* Lanham, Md.: Scarecrow Press, 1999.

Starr, S. Frederick. *Louis Moreau Gottschalk.* Urbana: University of Illinois Press, 2000.

Stauffer, John. "Embattled Manhood and New England Writers, 1860–1870." In *Battle Scars: Gender and Sexuality in the American Civil War*, edited by Catherine Clinton and Nina Silber, 120–39. New York: Oxford University Press, 2006.

Sterkx, H. E. *Partners in Rebellion: Alabama Women in the Civil War.* Teaneck, N.J.: Fairleigh Dickinson University Press, 1970.

Stevenson, Brenda. *Life in Black and White: Family and Community in the Slave South.* New York: Oxford University Press, 1996.

Stoops, Martha. *The Heritage: The Education of Women at Saint Mary's College, Raleigh, North Carolina, 1842–1982.* Raleigh: The College, 1984.

Stoutamire, Albert. *Music of the Old South: Colony to Confederacy.* Teaneck, N.J.: Fairleigh Dickinson University Press, 1972.

Stowe, Steven M. *Intimacy and Power in the Old South: Ritual in the Lives of the Planters.* Baltimore: Johns Hopkins University Press, 1987.

Stowell, David W. "A Family of Women and Children: The Fains of East Tennessee." In *Southern Families at War: Loyalty and Conflict in the Civil War South*, edited by Catherine Clinton, 155–73. New York: Oxford University Press, 2000.

Tawa, Nicholas. *American Solo Songs through 1865.* Vol. 1 of *Three Centuries of American Music.* Boston: G. K. Hall and Co., 1989.

Thompson, David B. "Southern Piano Music during the Civil War." In *Bugle Resounding: Music and Musicians of the Civil War*, edited by Bruce C. Kelley and Mark A. Snell, 106–18. Columbia: University of Missouri Press, 2004.

Thompson, Eleanor Wolf. *Education for Ladies 1830–1860: Ideas on Education in Magazines for Women.* Morningside Heights, N.Y.: King's Crown Press, 1947.

Tick, Judith. *American Women Composers before 1870.* Ann Arbor: UMI Research Press, 1983.

———. "Passed Away Is the Piano Girl: Changes in American Musical Life, 1870–1900." In *Women Making Music: The Western Art Tradition, 1150–1950*, edited by Jane Bowers and Judith Tick, 325–48. Urbana: University of Illinois, 1987.

Trelease, Allen W. *White Terror: The Ku Klux Klan Conspiracy and Southern Reconstruction.* New York: Harper and Row, 1971.

Tuttle, William M., Jr. *Daddy's Gone to War: The Second World War in the Lives of America's Children.* New York: Oxford University Press, 1993.

Varon, Elizabeth R. *We Mean to Be Counted: White Women and Politics in Antebellum Virginia*. Chapel Hill: University of North Carolina Press, 1998.

Walker, Henry. "Power, Sex, and Gender Roles: The Transformation of an Alabama Planter Family during the Civil War." In *Southern Families at War: Loyalty and Conflict in the Civil War South*, edited by Catherine Clinton, 175–91. New York: Oxford University Press, 2000.

Walser, Richard. *Literary North Carolina: A Brief Historical Survey*. Raleigh: State Department of Archives and History, 1970.

Weiner, Marli F. *Mistresses and Slaves: Plantation Women in South Carolina, 1830–80*. Urbana: University of Illinois Press, 1998.

Welter, Barbara. *Dimity Convictions: The American Woman in the Nineteenth Century*. Athens: Ohio University Press, 1976.

Wheeler, Marjorie Spruill. *New Women of the New South: The Leaders of the Woman Suffrage Movement in the Southern States*. New York: Oxford University Press, 1993.

Whites, LeeAnn. *The Civil War as a Crisis in Gender: Augusta, Georgia, 1860–1890*. Athens: University of Georgia Press, 1995.

Wiener, Jonathan M. *Social Origins of the New South: Alabama, 1860–1885*. Baton Rouge: Louisiana State University Press, 1978.

Wiley, Bell Irwin. *Confederate Women*. Westport, Conn.: Greenwood Press, 1975.

Wilson, Charles Reagan. *Baptized in Blood: The Religion of the Lost Cause, 1865–1920*. Athens: University of Georgia Press, 1983.

Winter, William. *Vagrant Memories*. New York: George H. Doran, 1915.

Woodward, C. Vann, ed. *Mary Chesnut's Civil War*. New Haven: Yale University Press, 1981.

———. *The Strange Career of Jim Crow*. 3rd ed., rev. New York: Oxford University Press, 1974.

Wright, Gavin. *Old South, New South: Revolutions in the Southern Economy since the Civil War*. Baton Rouge: Louisiana State University Press, 1979.

Wyatt-Brown, Bertram. *Southern Honor: Ethics and Behavior in the Old South*. New York: Oxford University Press, 1982.

Zuczek, Richard. *In the Great Maelstrom: Conservatism in Post–Civil War South Carolina*. Columbia: University of South Carolina Press, 2002.

Articles

Anderson, George M. "The Civil War Courtship of Richard Mortimer Williams and Rose Anderson of Rockville." *Maryland Historical Magazine* 80 (Summer 1985): 119–38.

Bailey, Candace. "Sarah Cunningham's Music Book: A Manuscript Collection of Music for a Young Girl of Scottish Descent in Savannah, c. 1840." *Early Keyboard Music* 25/26 (2009): forthcoming.

Baker, Paula. "The Domestication of Politics: Women and American Political Society." *American Historical Review* 89 (June 1984): 620–47.

Brown, Alexis Girardin. "The Women Left Behind: Transformation of the Southern Belle, 1840–1880." *Historian* 62 (Summer 2000): 759–79.

Bruhn, Christopher. "Taking the Private Public: Amateur Music-Making and the Musical Audience in 1860s New York." *American Music* 21, no. 3 (Autumn 2003): 260–90.

Censer, Jane Turner. "A Changing World of Work: North Carolina Elite Women, 1865–1895." *North Carolina Historical Review* 73 (January 1996): 28–55.

———. "Reimagining the North-South Reunion: Southern Women Novelists and the Intersectional Romance, 1876–1900." *Southern Cultures*, Summer 1999, 64–91.

Cimbala, Paul A. "Black Musicians from Slavery to Freedom: An Exploration of an African-American Folk Elite and Cultural Continuity in the Nineteenth-Century Rural South." *Journal of Negro History* 80 (1995): 15–29.

Davis, Robert Scott. "Selective Memories of Civil War Atlanta: The Memoir of Sally Clayton." *Georgia Historical Quarterly* 82 (Winter 1998): 735–50.

Demos, John, and Virginia Demos. "Adolescence in Historical Perspective." *Journal of Marriage and Family* 31 (November 1969): 632–38.

Ellis, Katharine. "Female Pianists and Their Male Critics in Nineteenth-Century Paris." *Journal of the American Musicological Society* 50 (1997): 353–85.

Epstein, Dena. "Black Spirituals: Their Emergence into Public Knowledge." *Black Music Research Journal* 10 (1990): 58–64.

Faust, Drew Gilpin. "Altars of Sacrifice: Confederate Women and the Narratives of War." *Journal of American History* 76, no. 4 (March 1990): 1200–28.

———. "Christian Soldiers: The Meaning of Revivalism in the Confederate Army." *Journal of Southern History* 53 (February 1987): 63–90.

Fordney, Chris, ed. "Letters from the Heart." *Civil War Times Illustrated* 34 (September– October 1995): 28, 73–82.

Fox-Genovese, Elizabeth. "Scarlett O'Hara: The Southern Lady as New Woman." *American Quarterly* 33 (1981): 391–412.

Glover, Lorri. "An Education in Southern Masculinity: The Ball Family of South Carolina in the New Republic." *Journal of Southern History* 69 (February 2003): 39–70.

Harwell, Richard Barksdale. "John Hill Hewitt Collection." *South Atlantic Bulletin* 13, no. 4 (1948): 3–5.

Hoole, W. Stanley. "Charleston Theatricals during the Tragic Decade, 1860–1869." *Journal of Southern History* 11, no. 4 (1945): 538–47.

Jabour, Anya. "Grown Girls, Highly Cultivated: Female Education in an Antebellum Southern Family." *Journal of Southern History* 64 (February 1998): 23–64.

Kerber, Linda K. "Separate Spheres, Female Worlds, Woman's Place: The Rhetoric of Women's History." *Journal of American History* 75 (June 1988): 9–39.

Koza, Julia Eklund "Music and the Feminine Sphere: Images of Women as Musicians in 'Godey's Lady's Book,' 1830–1877." *Musical Quarterly* 75 (1991): 103–29.

Mates, Julian. "The First Hundred Years of the American Lyric Theater." *American Music* 1 (1983): 22–38.

McGerr, Michael. "Political Style and Women's Power, 1830–1930." *Journal of American History* 77 (December 1990): 864–85.

Moseley, Caroline. "Irrepressible Conflict: Differences between Northern and Southern Songs of the Civil War." *Journal of Popular Culture* 25 (1991): 45–56.

Nguyen, Julia Huston. "'No Church in this Place': The Religious Lives of Frontier Women in Antebellum Louisiana." Paper presented at the Southern Association of Women Historians 2006 Conference, University of Baltimore County, Maryland, June 2006.

Pease, William H., and Jane H. Pease. "Traditional Belles or Borderline Bluestockings? The Petigru Women." *South Carolina Historical Magazine* 102 (2001): 292–309.

Ping-Robbins, Nancy. "Musical Criticisms and Attitudes about Music in Part of the Antebellum South." *Sonneck Society* 8 (1982): 58.

Radano, Ronald. "Denoting the Difference: The Writing of Slave Spirituals." *Critical Inquiry* 22 (1996): 506–44.

Rau, Albert G. "John Frederick Peter." *Musical Quarterly* 23, no. 2 (1937): 306–13.

Rundell, Walter, Jr., ed. "'If Fortune Should Fail': Civil War Letters of Dr. Samuel D. Sanders." *South Carolina Historical Magazine* 65 (July 1964): 129–44, 218–32.

Schwerdt, Amanda K., and Madeline M. Keaveney. "'They Ain't Whistlin' Dixie': A Narrative Analysis of White, Southern Women's Civil War Diaries and Journals." *Women and Language* 24 (2001): 43–44.

Scott, Anne Firor. "Women's Perspective on the Patriarchy in the 1850s." *Journal of American History* 61 (1974): 52–64.

Smith-Rosenberg, Carroll. "The Female World of Love and Ritual: Relations between Women in Nineteenth-Century America." *Signs* 1 (Autumn 1975): 1–29.

Stowe, Steven M. "The Rhetoric of Authority: The Making of Social Values in Planter Family Correspondence." *Journal of American History* 73 (March 1987): 916–33.

Stowell, David W. "A Family of Women and Children: The Fains of East Tennessee." In *Southern Families at War: Loyalty and Conflict in the Civil War South*, edited by Catherine Clinton, 155–73. New York: Oxford University Press, 2000.

Talbott, John E. "Combat Trauma in the American Civil War." *History Today* 46 (March 1996): 41–47.

Tawa, Nicholas. "Songs of the Early Nineteenth Century, Part I: Early Song Lyrics and Coping with Life." *American Music* 13 (1995): 1–26.

———. "The Ways of Love in Mid-Nineteenth-Century American Song." *Journal of Popular Culture* 10, no. 2 (1976): 337–51.

Taylor, A. Elizabeth. "The Last Phase of the Woman Suffrage Movement in Georgia." *Georgia Historical Quarterly* 43 (1959): 11–28.

Tick, Judith. "Hodges, Faustina Hasse." *Grove Music Online*, edited by Laura Macy. http://www.groveonline.com (accessed 8 September 2006).

Vorachek, Laura. "Reading Music: Representing Female Performance in the Piano Method Book and the Novel." Paper presented at the Conference on Nineteenth-Century Music, University of Durham, England, July 2004.

Wanzer, Sidney Hovey, and Anna Bradford Agle. "Dearest Braddie: Love and War in Maryland, 1860–61." *Maryland Historical Magazine* 88 (Spring 1993): 337–58.

Wiener, Jonathan M. "Female Planters and Planters' Wives in Civil War and Reconstruction Alabama, 1850–1870." *Alabama Review* 30 (April 1977): 135–49.

———. "Planter Persistence and Social Change: Alabama, 1850–1870." *Journal of Interdisciplinary History* 7 (Autumn 1976): 235–60.

Winans, Robert B. "Black Instrumental Music Traditions in the Ex-Slave Narratives." *Black Music Research Journal* 10 (1990): 43–53.

Unpublished Dissertations and Theses

Cooke, Mary. "Southern Women, Southern Voices: Civil War Songs Created by Southern Women." DMA diss., University of North Carolina-Greensboro, 2007.

Hindman, John J. "Concert Life in Ante-bellum Charleston." 2 vols. Master's thesis, University of North Carolina at Chapel Hill, 1971.

Hines, James R. "Musical Activity in Norfolk, Virginia, 1680–1973." Ph.D. diss., University of North Carolina at Chapel Hill, 1974.

Lott, R. Allen. "The American Concert Tours of Leopold de Meyer, Henri Herz, and Sigismond Thalberg." 2 vols. Ph.D. diss., City University of New York, 1986.

Mahan, Katherine Hines. "History of Music in Columbus, Georgia, 1828–1928." Ph.D. diss., Florida State University, 1967.

Nix, Elizabeth Morrow. "An Exuberant Flow of Spirits: Antebellum Adolescent Girls in the Writings of Southern Women." Ph.D. diss., Boston University, 1996.

Pope, Christie Farnham. "Preparation for Pedestals: North Carolina Antebellum Female Seminaries." Ph.D. diss., University of Chicago, 1977.

Pullum-Piñón, Sara Melissa. "Conspicuous Display and Social Mobility: A Comparison of 1850s Boston and Charleston Elites." Ph.D. diss., University of Texas at Austin, 2002.

Smith, Jewel. "Music, Women, and Pianos: The Moravian Young Ladies' Seminary in Antebellum Bethlehem, Pennsylvania (1815–1860)." Ph.D. diss., University of Cincinnati, College-Conservatory of Music, 2003.

Stoutamire, Albert. "A History of Music in Richmond, Virginia, from 1742 to 1865." Ph.D. diss., Florida State University, 1960.

Thomas, Jean Waters. "Music of the Great Sanitary Fairs: Culture and Charity in the American Civil War." Ph.D. diss., University of Pittsburgh, 1989.

Thompson, David B. "Piano Music in the South during the Civil War Period, 1855–1870." D.M.A. thesis, University of South Carolina, 1997.

Williams, Grier Moffat. "A History of Music in Jacksonville, Florida from 1822–1922." Ph.D. diss., Florida State University, 1961.

Index

Page numbers in italics indicate illustrations.

Candace Bailey is an associate professor of musicology at North Carolina Central University, where she teaches music history and ethnomusicology. Some of her previous publications include *Seventeenth-Century British Keyboard Sources*, *The Keyboard Music of John Roberts*, "Blurring the Lines: *Elizabeth Rogers hir virginall booke* in Context" in the journal *Music & Letters*, and *Late-Seventeenth-Century English Keyboard Music*, part of the Recent Researches in Music of the Baroque Era series.